SO-BQY-428

# DIARY

# DIARY

## VOLUME 2

(1957–1961)

## WITOLD GOMBROWICZ

translated by LILLIAN VALLEE

general editor JAN KOTT

**Northwestern University Press**
**Evanston, Illinois**

392971

Northwestern University Press
Evanston, Illinois 60201

Printed in the United States of America

This translation was funded with the assistance of the National Endowment
for the Arts, the National Endowment for the Humanities, and the Wheatland
Foundation.

First published in France under the title *Dziennik 1957–61.* Copyright 1962
by Instytut Literacki. English translation © 1989 by Northwestern University
Press.

All rights reserved. No part of this book may be reproduced in any form or
by any means without the prior written permission of the publisher.

**Library of Congress Cataloging-in-Publication Data**
(Revised for volume 2)

Gombrowicz, Witold.
  Diary.

  Translation of: Dziennik.
  Contents: v. 1. 1953-56—v. 2. 1957-1961.
  1. Gombrowicz, Witold—Diaries. 2. Authors, Polish—
20th century—Diaries.
PG7158.G6692A3413   1988      891.8'58703      87-24882
ISBN 0-8101-0714-7 (v. 1)
ISBN 0-8101-0715-5 (pbk. : v. 1)
ISBN 0-8101-0716-3 (v. 2)
ISBN 0-8101-0717-1 (pbk. v. 2)

# Contents

1957

# I

I have not been completely understood (I am referring to the articles that are appearing in Poland on the subject of *Ferdydurke*) or rather they have extracted from me only what is "timely" and corresponds to their current history and current predicament. I am resigned to this: this partial—I might even say egotistical—interpretation, always from the angle of current need, is inevitable. Before the war, *Ferdydurke* passed for the ravings of a madman, because in a time of jubilant creativity and straining for political power, my book ruined the parade. Today, when the Mug and Fanny have really irked the nation, *Ferdydurke* has been elevated to the rank of satire and criticism. As if I were Voltaire! Now they say it is a wise (hah! even a clear and concise) book, the work of a sober rationalist who judges and metes out punishment with premeditation, a virtually classic and most carefully pondered work!

To go from being crazy to being a rationalist—is this a promotion for an artist? Yet this Ferdydurkean rationalism breaks down at some point, for the critics and the articles usually close with the troubled statement that Gombrowicz has probably "not thought his ideas all the way through" because somehow the work does not want to fit into the "concept" they have so busily deduced. Or perhaps it doesn't fit because the concept is too narrow? I will try to describe our greatest misunderstandings.

*Ferdydurke* is difficult to interpret because it contains a very special view of man. How do they see this man of mine? And how do I see him?

They say—and correctly—that in *Ferdydurke* man is created by people. But they understand this primarily as man's being dependent on a social group, which imposes custom, convention, and style upon him. . . . They even say that this is an altogether banal truth, a cliché and a forcing of open doors.

There is one thing, however, that they have not noticed. Namely, that this process of forming man through people is conceived of much more broadly in *Ferdydurke*. I do not deny that the individual is dependent on his milieu—but for me it is far more important, artistically far more creative, psychologically far more profound, and philosophically far more disturbing that man is also created by an individual man, by another person. In chance encounters. Every minute of the day. By virtue of the fact that I am always "for another," counting on someone else's seeing me, being able to exist in a specific manner only for someone else and by someone else, and existing—as a form—only through another. Therefore, it is not a matter of my milieu's imposing a convention or, speaking in Marxist terms, that man is a product of his social class, but that the depiction of man's encounter with man in all of its fortuitousness, directness, wildness, results in showing how Form, and often the most unpredictable, absurd form, is born of these accidental encounters. Since I do not need form for myself, I need it only so another person can see, feel, and experience me. Can't you see this Form is something far more powerful than a simple social convention? And that it is an uncontrollable element? As long as you understand *Ferdydurke* as a battle with convention, it will trot calmly down the well-beaten path; but if you understand that man creates himself with another man in the sense of the wildest debauchery, *Ferdydurke* will neigh and leap forward as if you had jabbed it with a spur, carrying you off into the realm of the Unpredictable. *Ferdydurke* is more a form-element than a form-convention.

They say further that in *Ferdydurke* (and in my other works) I wage a battle with distortion, with hypocrisy. . . . Undoubtedly. But isn't this also a simplification of my intentions and my concept of man?

Why, my man is created from the outside, that is, he is inauthentic in essence—he is always not-himself, because he is determined by form, which is born between people. His "I," therefore, is marked for him in that "interhumanity." An eternal actor, but a natural one, because his artificiality is inborn, it makes up a feature of his humanity—to be a man means to be an actor—to be a man means to pretend to be a man—to be a man means to "act like" a man while not being one deep inside—to be a man is to recite humanity. In these circumstances, therefore, how is one to understand the struggle with the mug, with the grimace in *Ferdydurke?* Not that man should get rid of his own mug—for beyond it he has no face—here one can only demand that he be conscious of his artificiality and confess it. If I am condemned to deception, the only honesty to which I have access is the admission that honesty is inaccessible to me. If I can never be entirely myself, the only thing that allows me to save my personality from annihilation is my will to authenticity, that stubborn-in-spite-of-everything "I want to be myself," which is nothing more than a tragic and hopeless revolt against deformation. I cannot be myself, yet I want to be myself and I must be myself—this is the antinomy, one of those that do not let themselves be resolved . . . and do not expect me to provide you with medicine for incurable diseases. *Ferdydurke* merely confirms man's inner division—nothing more.

And degradation?

Why have they almost completely ignored the degradation which plays so strongly in my works, which alone lends my form its true flavor?

They have concentrated on the problem of deformation—they have forgotten that *Ferdydurke* is also a book about immaturity . . . man cannot express himself on the outside not only because others warp him—he cannot express himself because, first of all, only that which is already ordered in us and mature lends itself to expression, and all the rest, that is, our immaturity, is silence. Therefore form will always be something compromising—we are degraded by form. And it is not difficult to see how, for example, our entire cultural inheritance, which exists precisely because we have concealed our immaturity, is the work of people pulling themselves up to a certain standard, of people who are wisdom, seriousness, profundity, responsibility only on the outside (and being incapable of revealing their immaturity never mention the other side of the coin)—just as all of our arts, philosophies, moralities, compromise us, for they are above us and more mature than we are; they plunge us into some sort of second childishness. We cannot handle our culture internally—this is a fact which has not been adequately considered, but which nevertheless determines the tone of our "cultural life." Deep inside we are eternal striplings.

Man's degradation via form also happens in other ways, however.

If my form works itself out through contact with others, these people can be superior or inferior to me. In shaping my form through beings found on a lower rung of development, I gain a lower form, more immature than the one due me. I draw your attention, dear critics, to all the places in my art where the Inferior, the Younger, creates the Superior in its own way, because there you have the most intense poetry I can create.

But let us also not forget that man does not like maturity because he prefers his youth. That is why *Ferdydurke* also contains both of these strivings—it is as I have already indicated in this diary, "the image of the battle for one's own maturity by someone enamored of his own immaturity." Here, therefore, the formula becomes degrading once again.

And, finally, will a man who is always beneath value, always compromised (insofar as to be a man means to be "worse," worse than that which he produces), not seek an outlet for his inner life in the appropriate realm, in trash? Bruno Schulz grasped this in his study of *Ferdydurke,* published in the prewar literary monthly *Skamander.* He calls it "the sphere of subcultural, undereducated and rudimentary contents," where human immaturity finds release. "Our immaturity"—he continues—"(and perhaps at bottom our vitality) is tied in a thousand knots, braided with a thousand atavisms to a second-rate suit of forms, to a second-class culture. While under the cover of official forms we honor higher, sublimated values, our real life plays itself out secretly and without higher sanctions in that dirty realm, and the emotional energies located in it are a hundred times more powerful than those the thin layer of officialdom dispenses."

I will add: he who does not extract and does not feel this "degradation" in *Ferdydurke,* in *The Marriage,* and in my other works, has not grasped my most important point.

\* \* \*

They conceive of my work as just one more struggle with society, a critique of society. Let us see if my man does not explode this concept.

These, in brief, are his characteristics:

(1) Man created by form, in the profoundest, most universal sense.
(2) Man as the creator, the indefatigable producer of form.
(3) Man degraded by form (always being an "under-" or an "im-"—undereducated, immature).
(4) Man in love with immaturity.
(5) Man created by Inferiority and Youngerness.
(6) Man subject to the "interhuman" as a superior, creative force, our only accessible divinity.
(7) Man "for" man, knowing no higher instance.
(8) Man animated, elevated, magnified by other people.

These features of my man are the ones that occur to me right now. Do you want to reduce all of this to one single revolt against the social forms of being?

\* \* \*

Occasionally they have rather strange grievances. They demand—or at least some of them do—that I "solve" this world—that I take care of its tragic contradictions, change it into a "constructive" little world. This is a bit childish. I most certainly will not untie the Gordian knots of life. My morality? It depends, first of all, on my expressing protest in the name of my humanity—on the irony and sarcasm that express my rebellion. Second, it depends on the belief that everything that helps us decipher our true nature and predicament in the world is our triumph over nature.

In my opinion, only a literature that cannot be taken seriously attempts to solve the problems of existence. Serious literature poses them. One man will not solve the problems of existence—they solve themselves, if they solve themselves at all, in humanity.

Serious literature does not exist to make life easy but to complicate it.

\* \* \*

I must combat the pettiness of the reader. His is a pusillanimous reading of my texts. It seems that they are afraid of getting the entire meaning, not because it would terrify them but only because they are not accustomed to a complete contents. They try violently to change me into one more specimen of a conventional literature, yet they themselves claim that my writing defies all conventions.

I don't say this about all the reviews that have appeared. It does happen that a critic will allow himself a little boldness and panache now and then only to follow them with an immediate and hurried withdrawal into the land of platitudes.

*Trans-Atlantic?* What will happen to *Trans-Atlantic,* which should be appearing in Poland any day now? Everything I write is equally basic and universal. Try as I might, I cannot reduce my subject, which will always be man and the world. But *Trans-Atlantic* also concerns Poland, and that little word "Poland" is all it takes to have all the local complexes echo in response.

# Sunday

Sometimes, when reading these articles, I forget that I am, after all, an artist. I begin to believe that I am the author of a multivolumed philosophical work. . . . There is constant talk about my "concepts," almost never about my art.

No, I would not accuse most of my commentators of a lack of intelligence. After having read Janusz Kowalewski's silly article about the *Diary* in the émigré press, I realized that this level of discussion would be impossible in Poland. And when I compare these critiques of *Ferdydurke* with those from before the war, I see that the atmosphere

. . . of the times . . . is quite different. I reproach them, as I have said, for their timidity, for their conceptual narrowness, which, however, is understandable considering that they write more for the masses than the aristocratic critics of the West do. Still, I note a flaw in the very function, attitude, and arrangement of this criticism. Columns full of diligent analyses that can be neither exhaustive nor clarifying because they are too short, columns that must weary the reader because they are too long . . . what purpose do they serve? Who needs them? And so devoid of artistry! The dreariness of Polish life pulsates from this forced, tiring, straightforward thinking that wants to understand, to realize, to explain to others but does not know how to thrill—it lacks imaginativeness, *Schwung,* charm, radiance, poetry, playfulness. This criticism is like a finger put to a quivering string—it kills the vibrations. There is something wrong in their approach to art—and in the long run it can have a negative influence on the artistic temperament of the nation.

This is probably tied to the Polish "beauty crisis."

On the whole the criticism is very much *comme il faut,* it has very good manners—how much more unpretentious and sensible, less aggressive and unceremonious than before. . . . With the exception of Mr. Kisiel in *Tygodnik Powszechny.* That he refers to me as that "guy" and can't even get the title of my novel *Trans-Atlantic* right does not bother me, but everything in that little piece is shallow, nonsensical, swimming in a soup concocted of nonchalance, a dismal journalistic arrogance that endows columnists with some sort of euphoria when it comes to babbling just any old thing. He proclaims that *Ferdydurke* and my *Diary* are "nothing more than endless variations on the topic 'Poland and I.' " And he reproaches me with having "messianic and polonocentric illusions." I have read many untruths about myself, but something so utterly wrong from A to Z, neither here nor there, so "concretely invented" as my Argentine friends from the group Concreto Invencion say . . . ha, Mr. Kisiel, I cannot reciprocate other than by pinning to your chest, my dearest buddy, the Order of the Fellowship of Jokers Gab-Gab and Blahblahblah.

# Thursday

In the dining car it is five in the afternoon, we are approaching Tandil, which is reminiscent of Salzburg from here—the slender tower of the church rising from the hills. Streams of spring light pour into space, the sun trembles in the air, color after color rises from the meadows until the last dispersion in the peripheries of the heavens. Lost in dreams. It is warm. . . . The train stops in a field. I see before me, through the window, grass, rails, a scrap of paper.

Exhausting! I have seen it all a thousand times before. A thousand times the train has stopped and I have seen: the rails, a scrap of paper. The entire landscape summed itself up: rails, scrap of paper. Riveted to the paper, I don't take my eyes from it, I wait until the train moves and the paper moves—left behind. I have done this a thousand times before. I, paper, and rails. Rails, I, and the paper. The paper, rails, and I.

## Sunday

Sandauer is defending himself in Poland—he is under siege. . . . I watch this from America. I am taken aback because Adolf Rudnicki and I were once close friends—we made our debut together and that united us. On the other hand, there is the distance, the chilling distance of years and kilometers. I watch Poland as if through a telescope and can see only the most general contours of their existence, and this invites ruthlessness.

From this distance only what is not petty remains. Why then has this local hullabaloo over Sandauer's running Rudnicki into the ground in a way that seemed too cruel to Rudnicki's admirers—why has this literary tempest reached me across the Atlantic undiminished, while their most successful books remain barely perceptible? I have just read Sandauer's reply, "Three Times . . . No!" in *Życie Literackie.* I will not enter into the specifics of the dispute, I don't know how right Sandauer is in regard to Rudnicki, completely, somewhat, or not at all, but the tone of the reply thrilled me—a tone that I have not encountered thus far in the literary press, a tone that is categorical. Is it possible that a real dialogue about art is finally taking place in Poland? This wonderful article is like breaking open a window in a room that has not been aired for years. It is a fist striking at a fiction. At a conventional literature. At a conventional life.

This I like! Indeed I believe that the chief goal of Polish postwar existence is getting at reality. For many years they have lived in a perfectly artificial system, locked in it as if it were a glass ball. Yet the weakening of the system is certainly not synonymous with a return of a genuine play of powers and values—for, after all (Sandauer is right here), a certain arrangement has survived from that time, an arrangement made between people and groups interested only in hanging onto their present positions, and this "mutual courtesy" perpetuates paralysis and mystification. Were pride and self-interest the only things keeping this arrangement intact? What about goodness? What about decency? Various feelings and sympathies? Just so as not to hurt anyone? Who knows if softness is not what lends an arrangement the toughness and resistance of a wall, the weight of a cliff.

That is why criticism, devastating criticism, is essential. With the aim of smashing the arrangement, jolting people out of their places and forcing them to become what they really are. Sandauer is a critic who has a profound understanding of the unprecedented, vital, and crucial role of the critic in this "new start" of Polish literary life. He has grasped its purifying and invigorating potential.

To be a pale moon shining with borrowed light, to be second-rate, conventional, vapid, cheaply provincial and inflated—or to sail out onto the broadest waters in fearless confrontation with the world, to earn the right to the fullest existence possible? This is the dilemma of Polish art, barely wheezing after its last serious illness and handicapped by its tradition of nonconsummation. . . . For me, from my vantage point in the West, the matter is as clear as day. Nothing stupider could happen to us than to continue to nurture a timidity that does not allow us to bare ourselves. Poland and Poles must be stripped bare—at least in art. Sandauer was accused of speaking about Polish writing with an excessive openness and honesty in Paris. How do you want a decent man to speak to the world? Dishonestly?

# Tuesday

As a supplement to the polemic with critics:

First. —Let them get rid of the notion that I am an enemy of "interhumanity" (forms that become established between people). I have to rebel because this deforms me—but I know that this is unavoidable. This is how it should be.

For example. The fact that, according to me, "people mutually force themselves to admire art" (although no one is so directly enchanted by it) certainly does not undermine the value of art. Except that it works differently than we suppose.

Second. —There exist two orders: the human and the inhuman. The world is an absurdity and a monstrosity to our indestructible need for meaning, justice, love. A simple thought. A sure one . . .

Don't make a cheap demon out of me. I will be on the side of human order (and even on God's side even though I am not a believer) to the end of my days and in dying as well.

# II

## Saturday

The history of my becoming is the history of my constant adjustment to my literary works—which always surprised me by being born in an unpredictable way, as if not of me. . . . To a certain degree my books are a result of my life—but my life was formed in greater measure from them and with them. How was it with *Trans-Atlantic?* Once when returning from Caballito at night, I began to amuse myself by composing reminiscences from my first days in Buenos Aires on the model of some sort of Grand Guignol, and, at the same time, by dint of the past, I felt anachronistic, draped in an antique style, entangled in some sort of almost ancient scleroticism—and this cheered me up so much that I immediately commenced writing something that was to have been an antiquated memoir from that time. How unsettling is that opening phase, when one has to extract the first shape of a work, so awkward and unenriched by all the small inspirations that the pen encounters only much later. Only obstinance allows one to tear through that repulsive fog-ridden beginning. But naturally—and as always—the commenced work began to slip away from me and began writing itself: what I had conceived as a chronicle of my first undertakings after landing had transformed itself somehow—God knows how, probably by way of those thousands of submissions made to form—into a strange novel about Poles, with a "puto," a duel, and even a sleigh chase. . . . After a little more than a year, I noticed that I was the author of *Trans-Atlantic*. But what was this *Trans-Atlantic?* A queer and whimsical thing drawn out of thin air, woven of tens of thousands of excitements, a fantastic work. Poland? Poland had slid under my crazy quill accidentally, only because I was writing about Poles—and perhaps because I thought of it as an anachronism; it lent itself to my little theater, to that old-fashioned scenery.

Yes. But now the work is supposed to go among people—Polish people—and the Polish reader will begin to pound, as on a drum, on the flimsy, imagined transatlantic Polishness—until it emits the rumbling sound of the war drum.

Here is an account of the course of events.

I am on the lookout for some sort of publisher; after all, I have to do something with this text. Somehow I get the address of Paweł Zdziechowski in Paris. Through him the contact with Giedroyć. Fragments of *Trans-Atlantic* are supposed to appear in *Kultura*. (I don't take this much to heart, I am still on the peripheries of the emigration, practically a foreigner.)

But letters arrive from writers I know and to whom I have sent the typescript. "God Almighty, do you realize what you have written?!" Or: "This whole thing is impossible for 'fellow Poles in exile' to bear. Too cruel. Such things must be written if one can, but—unfortunately— publishing them must be put off until later, when the models have died, the scenery has fallen down, and the times have changed. . . . Of course one doesn't have to put it off, but then woe! Woe to the author!"

What's this? So—I begin to understand—there's going to be a scandal. Just as with *Ferdydurke* in its time. Even more dangerous because I am lost in the world, alone, without support. I ask Wittlin to be the midwife for this difficult birth.

I write an introduction to the fragments that *Kultura* is supposed to print: "I assume that the book you have in your hands will seem quite jarring—as if some lay or even heretical spirit had torn into your piety. . . ." The preface is in some ways a new provocation because I do not intend to win anyone's indulgence—I want to pay for disregard with disregard, of which I have known plenty from my countrymen and which constantly threatens me. Yet at the same time, I attempt to relieve the tension by explaining my blasphemous sneering—which not only accentuates the Polish problem in *Trans-Atlantic,* but forces me even further into seriousness.

The fragments appear in *Kultura.* Immediately afterward Wittlin pours the clear oil of his prose onto the raging waters. An eloquent, courageous, and calm article, worth its weight in gold to me (but again, in defending the work, he has to extract and fill in the contours of the Polish problem and so other aspects of the work grow pale).

Polemics. W. A. Zbyszewski pricks me in *Wiadomości* with his journalist's pen, in his way, that is, affecting impudence and utter shallowness. Should I reply? While editing a short reply to Zbyszewski's two bits, my thesis formulates itself clearly for the first time: to overcome our current Polishness. The thesis drops into a vacuum. No one even twitches. Only Mieroszewski, alert as always, comments in *Kultura:* "Crazy thoughts stalk the minds of our contemporary Polish writers. These are extraordinary views."

I reply to Straszewicz. Here for the first time I find a certain tone— of sovereign individualism—that I will continue to deploy. Remember that at that time my voice was not yet tempered for such polemics and articles. I used only an "artistic" style, borrowed from my books.

*Trans-Atlantic* appears in book form, with Wittlin's preface and my own. Outrage. Letters. Reactions pro and con. Now my role is clearly delineated. My second entry into my native literature in twelve years takes place under the sign of rebellion against the homeland.

\*   \*   \*

I outline this chronology because from it one can see how the nation—let us assume that the emigration is a nation—shapes the work and a writer for itself. A writer and a work are something changing and elusive—only the reader preserves them in some sort of definite and commanding sense. In setting out to construct my rickety transatlantic I had no clue that I would sail it to the shores of my homeland as a mutineer and pirate. And if my raving, almost somnolent blasphemies had not been extracted and waved about, they would not have become my flag and I would not have discovered that my ship was a war frigate, whose assignment was to fight for a new Poland. I—that is, who? I— a child. For the captain of the ship was neither a responsible thinker nor an exquisite politician; merely a child who noticed, somewhat un-settlingly, that he was riding into seriousness on a thing begun in jest.

But now this tempest in a teacup forced me to find objective and serious reasons, to secure myself in seriousness—and then slowly I realized that I was in possession of a dynamic idea, capable of trans-forming our national sense of self and giving it new vigor. The idea was certainly nothing that could *épater* the modern intellectual—especially after Hegel—and was no discovery of America; it was a rather natural consequence of our thinking today, which turns with such passion to-ward movement and becoming, casting off the static, defined world. But as an instrument to plow through the Polish consciousness of the home-land, radically refreshing our spirit, as a crucial juncture, one of those creative antitheses of development, a new point of departure . . . yes, this could be exploited! No, no, nothing new, even for the least enlight-ened of Poles—this thought had rattled around in many minds, every second it let one know it was there like a pike in a pond, one could discover it in many innuendos—but to make it a rallying cry, goal, and program? Elevate it to the rank of chief thought about the nation?

What was the point? This is how I saw it. I walk up to a Pole and say to him: —You have spent your whole life falling to your knees before It. Now try something just the opposite. Rise up. Think not just that you must serve It—but that It is also supposed to serve you, your development. Therefore get rid of the excessive love and honor that shackle you, try to liberate yourself from the nation. To which that Pole would answer furiously: —You've gone crazy! What would I be worth if I did that? To which I say: —You must (because today it is unavoidable) decide what is the highest value to you: Poland or yourself. We must finally know what your ultimate reason for being is. Choose what is more basic to you: being a man in the world or a Pole? If you give first place to your humanity, you must recognize that Poland can be useful only insofar as it works in favor of your humanity—but if it hinders or deforms you, it must be overcome. Decide then! But he would answer passionately: —Not true, and you will not deceive me with your sophistry, for I, being a Pole, can attain humanity only in my nation. Can a dog be only an animal? No, a dog is an animal, but as a dog, a concrete dog, a bulldog or pointer. And a goose? A horse? Don't take away my concreteness, for it is my life. I then say, taking him by the arm: —Are you deluding yourself into believing that you can attain the concrete, that is, reality, by not expressing all your feelings? Admit, that It limits, inhibits you. . . . He: —Silence! I can't listen to this! But I: —You want to exist genuinely yet you are afraid of your own thoughts? . . .

The eternal dialogue, the classic invitation to revolt . . . Perhaps I would have undertaken this denationalizing reluctantly. . . . Why, I have already said: I am not an admirer of cosmopolitanism—neither the scientific, dry, theoretical, and abstract cosmopolitanism with its cerebral schema of ideally universal systems—nor that which is born, in murky heads, of a sentimental anarchy, of a mawkish dream of "freedom." I have trusted neither one nor the other. On the contrary, my perception of man as a being creating himself in connection with other, concrete people pushed me in the direction of all kinds of closely bound associations. Yet the point is that now, in this phase of my dialectics, I did not feel at all that I was striking at Polishness; on the contrary, I had the impression that I was rousing and enlivening it. How could that be? After all, didn't I want to liberate them from their Polishness? Yes, indeed . . . but this challenge really had a strange feature, thanks to which a Pole became more of a Pole the less he was devoted to Poland. Sophistry? Let us try to be more precise.

A Pole is a Pole by nature. Whereby the more a Pole is himself, the more will he be a Pole. If Poland does not allow him to think and feel freely, it means that Poland does not allow him to be himself fully, that is, to be a Pole fully. . . .

Does this still seem like sophistry? In that case let us look for examples in history. Germans in Hitler's day stoked adoration of the nation to a white heat, yet this kind of German was almost a fabrication, completely deprived of his Goethe tradition, bah, of his normal German humanity. Because of this, Germany became more powerful while the individual German became weaker because he had to surrender a part of his individual strength and resilience to the nation and, what is more, to become less typical, less real as a German. Let us take France next. Is, for example, a Frenchman who sees nothing but France more of a Frenchman? Or less of one? But to really be a Frenchman means exactly that: to see something beyond France.

A simple law. Collective strength is the sum of concessions each person extracts from himself . . . that is how the power of an army, state, or church is created. The power of a nation. But this happens at the expense of the individual.

And what if a nation is so geographically and historically situated that it cannot attain power? What then? That spontaneous and natural Polishness, contained in each of us, suffers a great loss because we have surrendered full honesty and freedom of the spirit in exchange for a collective power—which we have not gained because it is unattainable. And what then? We immolate ourselves but nothing but smoke remains of the sacrifice.

Thus my desire to "overcome Poland" was synonymous with the desire to strengthen our individual Polishness. I simply wanted the Pole to stop being the product "of" an exclusively collective life and "for" a collective life. I wanted to complete him. To legitimize his other pole— the pole of individual life—and stretch him between the two. I wanted to have him between Poland and his own existence—in a perspective more dialectical and full of antinomies, conscious of his internal contradictions and capable of exploiting them for his own development.

\*   \*   \*

I strove for a Pole who could take pride in saying: I belong to an inferior nation. With pride. For, as you will easily see, such a statement degrades me in my role as a member of the collectivity, but at the same time it raises me above the collectivity: I did not allow myself to be cheated; I am capable of judging my own position in the world; I know how to take stock of my situation; I am therefore a man of full value. (Parenthetically speaking, only then would you be able to love Poland *without reservations* —because it could no longer rob you of value.)

I went even further in this demand than had been accepted—even the French, English, or Americans, who have infinitely more freedom in this area than we, could not manage so extreme a formulation. After all, they didn't need it! They belonged to powerful, dominant nations that not only did not ruin their personal lives but even enhanced them. With us things were different, we could not allow our cultural past, our collective level, our convulsive history, our national poverty, to delineate our limits. No, it had not been my intention at all just to relax our patriotism to the English or French level. To Poles I proposed a stance toward the nation that was even more radical—without precedent— something that would immediately set us apart from the bulk of nations, would make us a nation with an exclusively different style. —Madness!—you will say.—A pipe dream! —Really? —I will ask.—And why are we the most fervent patriots in the world? Isn't it exactly because there is material in us to be the coldest antipatriots? In us the stoked love of homeland has reached its maximum, our dependence on it has become the worst imaginable—therefore, it is from us, not from anyone else, that the salutary antithesis will spring, the creative opposition that will be a step forward.

I didn't consider myself a dreamer in this—on the contrary, I was faithful to a realism that had entered my bloodstream much earlier. I had no doubt that Poles—tired and despairing because of the history of their homeland—live with an ambivalent feeling at the bottom of their hearts. Did they adore It? Yes, but they also cursed It. Love It? Yes, but they also hated It. It was holiness and a curse for them, strength and weakness, their pride and humiliation—but Polish style, formed and imposed by the collectivity, with only one side of the coin allowed to be expressed. Our literature, for example, deprived of all real individualism, could manage to express nothing but affirmation of the nation. And that reluctant, hostile, indifferent, or scornful feeling remained unacknowledged and meandered on its own as sin, anarchy. . . . Thus all my efforts boiled down to creating a principle that would allow me to set into motion openly this second pole of feeling, to reach this facet of the Polish soul, to sanction the heresy.

\*   \*   \*

I wielded mighty arguments. Of course, a basic turnabout in our relations with the nation could be achieved only in the name of individual dignity, individual development. And this position was inordinately strong and timely, both as much among the émigrés as in Poland, as in the entire world—for the necessity to defend what was once called the human soul grows stronger under deforming and inhuman collective powers.

Something else also troubled me. Yes, as I have already said, I hated the nation because I couldn't bear it; and I couldn't bear it because of cowardice. But in this case what were my advice and lessons worth if they derived from my basic inability to cope with life? I, a decadent, how could I point the way to healthy individuals?

But this terrible problem, being not just my own torment, had already been mulled over several times. For it is well known that progress and development are not the work of people who are of average health, of those who barely have an inkling . . . but are worked out by deformed persons, exiled from decent "normality." A sick man is better able to grasp the absolute essence of health—because he does not possess it, he longs for it. He who lacks an internal balance can therefore become an expert on matters of balance, and the advice of a deformed man can be useful to a healthy life. Those who because of personal flaws cannot join the herd and who wander the peripheries see the path of the herd more clearly and know the surrounding forest better.

I believed then, and believe to this day, that the embarrassing genesis of my idea should not hurt—that a thought born in the little hell of my insufficiency, softened by childhood, could become objectively important. And healthy. On the condition that (beginning with myself) I do not conceal of what and how it was conceived.

I am not selling a cat in a sack. Feet and cards on the table, if you please—you have me just as I am, I am not praising the merchandise— if my existence can be of some use to you, use it in any way you wish.

\* \* \*

The consequences of such a change in our attitude toward Poland would be rich and profound—it would cause a series of refreshing and electrifying revisions, ensuring us dynamic development for quite a while. For example—a revision of Polish history. I do not claim it would be necessary to liquidate the historical school that analyzes the span of our history from the vantage point of Poland's existence, recognizing as positive that which promotes this existence, and negative that which stands in its way. However, this school should be supplemented by a different one in which history would be considered from the perspective of the development of man in Poland—and then it might turn out that these two developments, of the state and of the individual, do not always go hand in hand and that periods that were the most successful for the nation were perhaps not the happiest for the individual. At any rate, it might be clear that these two developments are not identical. This, however, would not be of primary importance.

The most important thing would be that finally we could get at least one foot out of history . . . and thereby regain our footing, we who are so swiftly borne under by the vortices of our past. For in no longer being forced to love and worship Polishness, we would not need to love our history. Seeing our value not in what we are but in what we are capable of overcoming in ourselves, our current form, we could relate to history as an enemy. I am the result of my history. But this result in no way pleases me. I know, I feel, that I am worthy of something better and I do not intend to give up my rights. I base my value on my dissatisfaction with myself as a historical product. In which case my history becomes the history of my deformity and I turn against it — thus freeing myself from it.

Allow me to dream. This would be a monumental achievement of the spirit — it would be as if we had come out of a river and felt the ground under our feet. I am not saying that this new, cold, perhaps reluctant, perhaps sarcastic or scornful tone in Polish history would become the key to opening up whole regions of our past, blocked until now — and that, for the first time, we could speak directly about the great creators of our national personality. The problem is more serious. It would mean no more or less than our wanting to begin our life from the beginning and our ceasing to be only a consequence of the past. This, in one fell swoop, would allow us to resist the current history that is being perpetrated upon us now. We could extricate ourselves both from the past and from the current moment in one leap and we could judge both — in the name of our ordinary humanity, our ordinary human needs and our universality. Let us not forget that only by opposing history as such can we oppose today's history — *tertium non datur*. Yet let us also not forget that I want to be neither extreme nor dryly theoretical in this matter and that I do not lose sight of the rich variety of life — I do not aim to eradicate an affirming love but only to enrich our possibilities by activating, as I have already said, the other pole of our antinomy, by revealing the other side of the Polish coin.

So much for history. But I have also wished that we could revise our art . . . because it is not mandatory that we be sentenced to adore forever our own artistic works and the forms they have shaped. This forced adoration is parochialism; it leads to upsetting the proportions between us and the world (that is, reality); and it is also prickly with complexes and breeds stupidity, lies, pretentiousness . . . but what is more and most important is that we do not know how to adequately scorn rubbish because it is ours and this renders us defenseless against it; we have to adjust ourselves to our expression even when it doesn't know how to express us. I have already tried to talk about literature in this diary, not as a source of national pride but often as something of a national calamity—and this, in my opinion, is not bad, this tone is worthy of commendation because it is the only way to avoid having literature cut us down to its size, so that we might realize ourselves as something better than what we have produced.

These are only two examples to indicate the far-reaching practical consequences of ideas. Of course—there has never been a lack of various "self-criticisms;" so many times have we settled accounts with our "national flaws." This was temporary, stopgap self-criticism, however, that clung spasmodically to Polishness, while somewhere in its depths it confirmed Polishness as an absolute value. What I speak of would be more conscious, more categorical, more basic—a position from which we could reach for world citizenship.

*   *   *

Communicating by means of art is an amusing misunderstanding. A prose work mixed with poetry is not a mathematical model and is different in each head. Much, much depends on the head. Not long ago I read the following in the Polish press about *Trans-Atlantic:* "Here Gombrowicz's intention is unusually accurate and appropriate: to depict through the distortions of the grotesque and parodic, and to accomplish a vicious satire of the *sanacja*\* regime. . . ."

Thus establishing my intentions, the author laments that subsequently, everything disintegrates. *Ecce* head!—like a melon born from the soil of their social pressure. . . . But I am certain that more than one will follow in his footsteps. For today people demand, not a gratuitous, but a utilitarian art, harnessed to the grindstone, industrious as a blind horse. And for many, *Trans-Atlantic* will fall apart right after the first few pages, after the scene of the talk with the Minister, "ah, such a clever satire on ministers, bureaucracy, all as it should be, but then later nothing but fantasies, complexes. . . ."

*Trans-Atlantic* does not fall apart. Its construction is my success; it is a gradual sinking into a deeper and deeper phantasmagoria, the growth of my own autonomous reality; the whole point is that the work is nothing but itself. It is not a satire. It is not a "settling of accounts with the national conscience." It is not philosophy. It is not a philosophy of history. What is it then? A story I told. In which, among other things, Poland appears. But it is not Poland that is the subject; the subject, as

---

\*Political movement of supporters of Piłsudski after his death.

always, is I, I alone, these are my adventures, not Poland's. Except that I just happen to be a Pole.

This in itself is a satire inasmuch as my existence as a Pole in this world is a satire.

This is not the fruit of an early pondering of the Polish question—I was writing about myself—myself in Buenos Aires—only later did I begin to think about Poland—and now I draw these thoughts, like so much explosive contraband that I carried unknowingly, from the hull of my bottomless ocean liner.

One way or another, it was this ship that took me back to Poland.

I returned, but no longer as a wild man. For I had, at one time during my youth in Poland, been completely wild in relation to it, incapable of handling it with style, incapable even of speaking about it—it served only to torment me. Later, in America, I found myself beyond Poland, adrift. Today things are different: I return with specific demands, I know what I must exact from my fellow Poles and I know what I can give them in return. Thus have I become a citizen.

1958

# III

## Tuesday

The New Year, approaching from the east with a speed equal to the rotation of the earth, caught and overtook me in La Cabania at Duś's house, while I sat on a couch holding a glass of champagne. Duś sat in an armchair under a lamp. Marisa next to the radio. Andrea on the arm of another chair. No one else.

Scattered chessmen in front of Duś.

A dramatic moment. What will happen? What will the future, having arrived, give birth to? "If only I didn't have nightmares . . ." Perhaps we'll get through it without catastrophe. The coming of the new year is the rushing, the terrible rushing of time, humanity, the world, everything is racing like mad into the future and the magnitude of this astronomical race takes one's breath away. I sped along with everyone else, my destiny rolled from one year into the next with a boom, and, at this very minute, this second, something has happened even though nothing has happened. The year has begun.

My growing sensitivity to the calendar. Dates. Anniversaries. Periods. With what diligence I now surrender myself to this tallying of dates. Yes, yes . . . why didn't I write down something every single day from the moment I learned to write? Today I would have many volumes filled with notes, and I would know what I did twenty-seven years ago at this exact hour. What for? Life escapes through dates, just as water runs through one's fingers. But at least something would have remained . . . some trace. . . .

My concluding history begins to give me an almost sensual delight. I immerse myself in it as in a strange river that strives for *clarification*. Slowly everything is filling out. Everything is concluding. I am beginning to decipher myself, though still with difficulty, as if I were looking through hazy glasses. How strange: finally, finally I begin to see my own face making its way out of Time, accompanied by the foretaste of irrevocable finality. Pathos.

# Wednesday

I was walking along a eucalyptus-lined avenue when a cow sauntered out from behind a tree.

I stopped and we looked each other in the eye.

Her cowness shocked my humanness to such a degree—the moment our eyes met was so tense—I stopped dead in my tracks and lost my bearings *as a man,* that is, as a member of the human species. The strange feeling that I was apparently discovering for the first time was the shame of a man come face-to-face with an animal. I allowed her to look and see me—this made us equal—and resulted in my also becoming an animal—but a strange even forbidden one, I would say. I continued my walk, but I felt uncomfortable . . . in nature, surrounding me on all sides, as if it were . . . watching me.

# Thursday

Today, after breakfast, a discussion—Verena, Duś, Jacek, and I—provoked by my contention that a man on a horse is a weird and ridiculous thing, an affront to aesthetics. In this equine Acropolis, my thesis struck like a blasphemous thunderbolt.

I explained that an animal is not born to carry another animal on its back. A man on a horse is as weird as a rat riding a rooster, a chicken riding a camel, a monkey riding a cow, or a dog riding a buffalo. A man on a horse is a scandal, an upsetting of the natural order of things, violent artificiality, dissonance, ugliness. They called on works of sculptors celebrating the equestrian. I laughed in their faces. Statues! Why art has always paid homage to convention—it was almost like fashion! Custom decides everything. For centuries we have looked at equestrian statues just as we have looked at men on horseback, but if we rubbed our eyes and looked afresh, we would scowl in distaste—because a horse's back is no more a place for man than the back of a cow.

We discussed this during a morning stroll while sixty thoroughbred mares in the pastures fixed their soft, warm eyes upon us. And I attacked horseback riding. A delight? A pleasant and beautiful amusement? Ha, ha, ha! Jumping up and down on a beast, rising and falling with legs spread apart, bouncing a butt off the inevitable back, astride an unwieldy and stupid beast, difficult to mount, just as difficult to dismount, and almost impossible to steer? "Race" on it with the speed of a bicycle? Or repeat again and again the same one-hundred-thousandth jump over an obstacle, on an animal that does not lend itself at all to jumping? Struggle with this desperate equine ungainliness, which can never really be overcome? Why, these so-called delights are pure atavism! There was a time when the horse was indeed useful, he determined the superiority of a man, a man governed others from a horse, a horse was wealth, power, the pride of its rider. The cult of horseback riding and the adoration of a quadruped, which is an anachronism, have survived those antediluvian times. You automatically imitate the admiration of your grandfathers and bruise your seats to honor the myth!

The monstrousness of my blasphemy echoed wildly from one end of the horizon to the other. The master and slave of sixty purebred mares eyed me wanly.

## Thursday

Cows.

When I pass a herd of cows, they turn their heads toward me and their eyes do not leave me until I pass. Just like at the Russoviches' in Corrientes. But then I paid no attention, whereas now, after the matter of "the cow who saw me," these looks seem like seeing to me. Grass and herbs! Trees and fields! The green nature of the world! I immerse myself in this expanse as if I were pushing off from shore and a presence consisting of a billion beings overwhelms me. O pulsating, living matter! Resplendent sunsets; today two white-and-coffee-brown islands— mountains and towers of glowing stalactites—rose before me in a crown of rubies. The islands melted together creating a bay of mystic azure so utterly without blemish that I almost believed in God—and then dark, creeping billows gathered right over the horizon—just one luminous point, a single beating heart of light, remained among the deep brown bellies of clouds crowding the horizon. Hosanna! I don't really want to write about this; after all, so many sunsets have been described in literature, and especially in ours.

I mean to say something else. The cow. How am I supposed to act toward a cow?

Nature. How am I supposed to behave toward nature?

So I head down the road, surrounded by pampa—and I feel that I am a foreigner in all of this nature, I, in my human skin . . . a stranger. Disturbingly different. A separate creature. And I see that Polish descriptions of nature, like all others, are worthless to me in this sudden opposition between nature and my humanity. An opposition clamoring for a resolution.

Polish descriptions of nature. So much art has been invested in them with what hopeless results. How long have we been smelling the flowers, basking in sunsets, immersing our faces in clumps of spring-green foliage, inhaling early mornings and singing hymns in honor of the Creator: who thought up these wonders? But this humble and profound prostrating of ourselves, kneeling, sniffing and smelling, has merely removed us from the most unrelenting human truth—namely, that man is not natural, he is antinatural.

If the nation to which I belong had felt at one time that it differed in its essence from a horse, it was only because the Church lectured it about the immortal human soul. But who created that soul? God. And who created the horse? God. Thus man and horse merge in the harmony of that beginning. The contrast between them is reconcilable.

I am getting to the end of the eucalyptus-lined road. It is getting dark. The question: am I, deprived of God, closer to or farther from nature as a result of this? Answer: I am farther away. And even this opposition between me and nature becomes, without Him, impossible to mend—here there is no appeal to a higher tribunal.

But even if I were to believe in God, the Catholic view of nature would be impossible for me, in contradiction to my entire consciousness, at odds with my sensibility—and this because of the problem of pain. Catholicism has treated all of creation, except for man, with disdain. It is difficult to imagine a more Olympian indifference to "their" pain—"theirs," the pain of plants or animals. Man's pain has a free will and, therefore, is punishment for sins, and his future life will make just amends for the injustices of this world. But the horse? Worm? They have been forgotten. Their suffering is deprived of justice—a naked fact gaping with the absolute of despair. I am bypassing the complex dialectic of the holy doctors. I speak of the average Catholic, who, walking in the light of a justice that endows him with everything he deserves, is deaf to the immeasurable abyss of that—unjustified—suffering. Let them suffer! This does not concern him. Why, they have no souls. Let them suffer, therefore, senselessly. Yes, it would be difficult to find a teaching that concerns itself less with the world beyond man (the ahuman world); this is a doctrine proudly human, cruelly aristocratic—and how can we be surprised that it has led us into a state of blissful unconsciousness and holy innocence regarding nature, which surfaces in our idyllic descriptions of dawn or dusk.

# Friday

I am pushed toward these lower strata, toward a confrontation with horse, beetle, plant, by my striving for "contact with inferiority." If I try to make superior consciousness dependent on the lower consciousness in the human world—if I want to bind maturity to immaturity— shouldn't I descend even lower on the ladder of the species? To embrace the entire downward scale?

But—I am reluctant . . . I admit—this bores me. I do not feel like thinking about this. And I don't like, I practically can't stand—to travel in thought beyond the human kingdom. Is it because the kingdoms surrounding us are too enormous? A reluctance to stray too far from one's own home?

To understand nature, to look at it, examine it—that's one thing. But if I attempt to get close to it as if it were something that is equal to me because of the life common to all of us—when I want to be on friendly terms with animals or plants—I am overwhelmed by an obstinate lethargy, I lose animation, I return all the more quickly to my human house and I lock the door.

Let us write this down, because who knows if this is not one of the most important characteristics of my humanity: some sort of resistance appears in me and takes the form of boredom, fatigue, whenever I want to grasp and recognize that lower life.

# Friday

Today "I became a fly killer," which simply means that I killed flies with my wire swatter.

Who knows where the flies come from (the windows in my room have screens). I liquidate them this way almost every day. Today I killed about forty. Of course, I don't kill all of them right away—some of them, seriously mangled, fall to the floor, and every so often I find such a fly, left to face its death alone. I immediately finish it off. But it does occasionally happen that one escapes into a crack in the floor, and becomes inaccessible to me with its pain.

In my youth I tortured animals. I remember how in Małoszyce I amused myself with the country boys. We chopped up frogs with whips. Today I am afraid—this is the right word—of the suffering of a fly. And this fear, in turn, terrifies me, as if some awful weakness toward life were contained in it. I am in fact afraid of this, that I cannot bear the pain of a fly. With age, I underwent a general evolution, whose tragic and malignant character I do not want to hide; on the contrary, I would like to emphasize it as strongly as I can. And I claim that it is characteristic not just of me, but of my entire generation.

I will note its salient points:

(1) *The devaluation of death.* — Death, be it human or animal, becomes less and less important to me. It is becoming more and more difficult for me to understand people who consider taking someone's life the greatest punishment. I do not understand revenge, which is pleased to shoot someone suddenly in the back of the head — as if that person felt something. I have become almost completely indifferent to death (I am not talking about my own).

(2) *The enthronement of pain.* — Pain becomes the starting point of existence, the basic experience from which everything begins, to which everything is reduced. Existentialists with their "life for death" do not satisfy me, I would pit life only against pain.

(3) *Pain as pain, pain in itself.* — This is the most important of all. Only this shift in feeling is really horrifying and awful and enormous. It relies on my caring less and less about *who suffers*. . . . I think that currently two schools of thought exist on this point. For people of the old school, the pain of someone in the family is, aside from their own, the worst: the pain of a dignitary is more important than the pain of a peasant; the pain of a peasant is more important than the pain of a boy; the pain of a boy is more important than the pain of a dog. They exist in a limited circle of pain. But for people of the more recent school, pain is pain wherever it appears, equally horrifying in man as in a fly; in us the experience of pure suffering has become informed, our hell has become universal. Some consider me insensitive because it is difficult for me to hide that the pain of those nearest to me is not the pain nearest to me. And my whole nature is attuned to discovering that — lower — suffering.

God-fearing families — as I recall from bygone days — sat in their country manors at supper, speaking decently, innocently . . . while flypaper dangled right over the table, and on the flypaper flies in predicaments worse than those of the damned in medieval paintings. This did not disturb anyone because in the sentence "the pain of a fly" the accent fell on "fly" not "pain." Today it is enough to spray a room with insecticide for clouds of tiny beings to begin to writhe—and no one pays any attention.

Yes. But how am I to reconcile my discovery of universal suffering with what I jotted down yesterday—with my reluctance to recognize the ahuman, inferior, world? This is one of the strangest rifts within me. I am overcome by inferior suffering and my entire being is attuned to uncovering it. Yet an icy boredom, almost drowsiness, overtakes me when I want to equate myself with these creatures in existence and try to acknowledge their full right to exist. This is a tedious and sluggish desire—is it tedious and sluggish because it exceeds my strength? To what, therefore, has the evolution, contained in the three points above, led me, me and many more like me? We are even more muddled—and even more uncertain in relation to nature than people of bygone times, who, one has to admit, exhibited more style in these matters than we do.

[Deleted here is a passage of Duś's doggerel.]

## Wednesday

Mail. A clipping from a newspaper in Poland—I learn about the program "Witold Gombrowicz's Books" on Radio Warsaw. And about Artur Sandauer's talk, in which he said, among other things: "Today it is difficult to imagine how a writer who is the pride of the Polish nation, whose 'unrealistic' books surpass all other realistic—holy God, forgive us—masterpieces, was sentenced by our cultural bureaucrats to so many years of exile."

My independence, self-sufficiency, or even frivolous impudence, my taking potshots at everyone, universal provocation and exclusive reliance on myself—all of this was a result of my social and geographical situation. I was forced not to pay attention to anyone because no one paid any attention to me—I was formed in almost complete isolation—I think that few literati have known such extreme isolation. In prewar Poland I was treated nonchalantly, almost ignored—then I was crushed by the war—then I was put on the censor's index by the Communist regime—and here, in Argentina, I was deprived of even a literary café, of even a group of artist friends in whose bosom every gypsy, innovator, avant-gardist can curl up in the cities of Europe. I became bold because I had absolutely nothing to lose: neither honors, nor earnings, nor friends. I had to find myself anew and rely only on myself, because I could rely on no one else. My form is my solitude.

Well, yes . . . until suddenly . . . I am the "pride of the nation." Can it be? Didn't he get a bit carried away? I realize that my rebirth in Poland can be sudden. Polish publishers jumped at my books. And something has changed in the tone of private letters and articles in the Polish press, I sense forces gathering around me, this growing wave may toss me aloft. Could this be?

But this would completely change the address on the long letter that is my writing. I wrote for my enemies—and now I will write for . . . the nation?

(I am strolling down a eucalyptus-lined avenue and as it turns out— I am furious! *Chimangos* —small hawks—screech and fly directly over my head.)

What if these shoulders should raise me on high?

A sudden sharp turn. Oh, that it not throw me from the saddle. . . .

What will I do there, at the top, with everything that formed itself in degradation? How does one move stylistically from degradation to elevation?

Sandauer . . .

Luckily (unfortunately!) it is more than doubtful that the nation will be so docile as to agree with Sandauer's opinion. I know that for the time being I will still have to win people in Poland to my side—one at a time.

Yet if I were finally able to become "the pride of the nation"?

This tormenting riddle . . .

When such exciting *piropos* fall on you, let your frustration think, for its own health, about the high-flown adjectives bestowed upon your fellow writers. No need to worry. Yet . . . I cannot rid myself of the certainty that my victories are more real than the victories of poets like Tuwim, let's say, or Lechoń.* Insofar as my art is less conventional . . . and more difficult . . . and more original and written against the current. *Ferdydurke,* if it is victorious, is more victorious. . . .

. . . This makes me ridiculous. My delighting in this, my excite-

---

*Julian Tuwim and Jan Lechoń were the most successful and well-known Polish poets in the interwar period.

ment, makes me ridiculous and offends me. I am offended. Pride. Obstinacy. Cold. Distrust. Opposition. "To not allow oneself to be pulled into the nation."

My literature must remain that which it is. Especially that something which does not fit into politics and does not want to serve it. I cultivate just one politics: my own. I am a separate state. Perhaps now, when they approach me with outstretched arms . . . is when the battle really begins. This is an attack from their side—an attempt to conquer and I must defend myself!!

(I am incensed. I know that I am incensed. I know that I know that I am incensed. Because I know that I am incensed, I thrash my arms [no one sees]—I, "pride of the nation"! What strength, at such moments, is my childhood!)

# Friday

The eucalyptus-lined avenue all the way to the end, this time at dusk, under the sign of two disturbing thoughts.

(1) That nature is ceasing to be nature for us in the old sense of the word (when it represented harmony and peace).
(2) That man is ceasing to be man in the old sense of the word (when he felt himself to be a harmonious part of nature).

The twilight hour is incredible . . . there is such an imperceptible and inevitable evaporation of form. . . . It is preceded by a moment of enormous clarity, as if form were resisting, didn't want to give in—the clarity of everything is tragic, persistent, even frenzied. Right after the moment when the object becomes itself most concrete, alone and left to itself, without the play of light and shadow in which it luxuriated until now, a more pervasive weakening, evaporation of matter follows; lines and blots join causing a tiring blur; contours put up no resistance; the outlines, in dying, become difficult, incomprehensible; there is a general retreat, withdrawal, a sinking into growing complexity. . . . Before the actual coming of darkness the shape becomes stronger once more, but not with the power of what we see but with the power of what we know about it—the cry proclaiming its presence is now merely theoretical. . . . After which there is a mixing of everything, blackness pours out of holes, thickens in space, and matter becomes darkness. Nothing. Night.

I groped my way home. I walked hard and stiff straight ahead, drowned in unseeing, absolutely certain that I was a demon, an antihorse, antitree, antinature, a being from elsewhere, a newcomer, foreigner, alien. A phenomenon not of this world. Of another world. The human world.

I returned completely unaware that somewhere, close by, was a terrifying dog, crouching, ready to lunge for the throat, pin to the wall. . . . But enough . . . for now.

# IV

To be with nature or against it? The thought that man is contradictory to nature, something beyond and in opposition to it, will soon cease being an elitist thought. It will reach even the peasants. It will penetrate the entire human race from top to bottom. What then? When the last reserves of "naturalness"—deriving from the lower strata— exhaust themselves?

## Tuesday

Yesterday evening a neighbor, Tadeusz Czerwiński, came to visit and right off began to tell us something, but we were not listening closely and his narrative took shape very slowly. . . . Duś's hounds (we finally understood him to say) had run into Garanio's field and attacked a sow. Garanio had jumped out with a shotgun, killed one of the hounds, and wounded another—the rest escaped. I am giving only the crux of the narration, which was rich in branches, like a tree.

Duś ran out onto the porch with a flashlight, and the golden hounds, as usual, rose at seeing him and surrounded him. But there were only five—Step and one young hound, by Saeta, were missing.

Thirteen-year-old Andrea burst into tears. Duś's rancor—rising like the song of Isolde—prevailed over all else. He would have exchanged his most beloved horses for Step. He had a desperate face— and this was a face that was strangely weakened, like the face of a small child—weakened perhaps by the pettiness of that despair, on account of a mere dog . . . for which he could not demand full recognition from us.

He took a revolver out of a drawer—got on a horse—and a gallop bore him away into the night. We waited, disturbed and helpless in the face of the anger that vanished into the fields, carried off by a horse. Would he kill Garanio for killing the dog? No, it didn't end that badly. Duś, upon arriving at Garanio's *estancia* and seeing Garanio's dogs, wanted to shoot them—but the *estanciero* came running out and began asking his forgiveness, explaining that he had acted in defense of a sow, whom the dogs would have torn to pieces. So the anger left poor Duś and only sorrow for his most faithful dog remained: Why did you do this to me? he asked. I have always been a good neighbor. He left. He began searching for the bodies in the night. He found them. It turned out that Step was still alive. Hidden in the bushes, he was dying. He was brought home on that strange sleigh that one uses here on the ground as one might elsewhere on snow.

Duś, Jacek Dębicki, Miss Jeanne, and I went to the stable—there was the dog, gasping and shaking spasmodically. Council: cut short his agony? His suffering was terrifying—and he was locked in it, inaccessible to us, separate, alone.

The scene that disturbed me: night, the stable, all of us practically in the dark hovering over an unleashed, diabolical pain. We were capable of putting an end to this. . . . It would have been enough to shoot. Would we shoot? We, four human beings "from another world," a higher world, four demons from antinature, four antidogs. The only thing that joined us to this creature was our understanding of its pain—we knew the taste.

Should we put an end to the torment? A vote. But this demands a more detailed narrative.

The first antidog. Miss Jeanne. Handsome, twenty years old, multimillionaire parents, herself shuttled from Paris to Rome, from Rome to London to the States, on ships, airplanes, first-rate schools, luxurious institutes, always different, out of which she has gotten nothing except the five languages she wields like a native. Which language does she think in? Luxurious—and a Communist—because luxurious—from the excess, the surfeit. . . . Sober, energetic, spunky—modern and an atheist. Seeing her bent over the dog, I realized that Communist justice, just like Catholic justice, does not include animals. Within this doctrine humanity ends with man. It forbids the exploitation of one human being by another—but agrees to the exploitation of animals. Which is, let us add, incomprehensible. It is not all well and good. For if religion casts animals into the margin, as soulless, then materialism acknowledges no basic difference between this suffering matter and human matter. . . . How then will Miss Jeanne act toward the suffering dog—if her reasoned morality has nothing to say? What will she do?

She made a female of herself! Strange . . . in a wink, she undressed herself . . . not so much of her communism, but of her humanity. She suddenly changed into a female—she took refuge in her sex . . . what a sudden eruption of gender into the realm of pain, as if gender could cope somehow with the pain. . . . She became a female, that is, love, that is, pity. She bent over the dog with a mother's tenderness. Is it possible that as a female she could do more than as a human being? Or, did she retreat into her sex in order to escape her own humanity?

When she became a woman, however, death seemed worse than pain to her. She began to love the dog cruelly—demanding his life even at the price of his pain. —No, no—she said, trembling.—Don't kill him!

The second antidog from a higher human sphere. Jacek Dębicki. A zealous Catholic. Yet his Catholicism is as useless here as Miss Jeanne's communism. Nor is God a factor. There is no salvation for the dog. And hence my impression that in leaning over the dog, he was leaning away from God—he is now "face-to-face" with the dog and therefore not "face-to-face" with God. An entirely different register of existence. He is "with the dog" as if, giving up his immortal soul, he put himself on its level, identified with it in its suffering. And out of the blue an animal—rebellious and blasphemous—terror of pain mounts in him. But what do I see? I see (because I almost saw this, rather, I "knew" this) that in another register he is not getting rid of even an iota of his Roman Catholic dignity, and the terror changes into pity . . . a legalized . . . civilized . . . well brought up . . . ah, I almost forgot that God, himself ruthless to animals, allows man to pity them—so *he is allowed;* he even has the "approval" of the Church! But the humanity that he rediscovered in himself is not a fraternal socializing with the animal but with his own humanity, that is, with his feeling of the dog's pain from on high—from the distance of that soul—and, what's more, he again possesses an element of nonchalance and cruelty. The decision he makes will be dictated by three considerations: first of all, by his animal compassion, which is almost wild, spontaneous; second, by his more human and spiritualized calculation that the soulless life of a dog is not of great significance; and third (a thought even more spiritual), that one should end this ordeal—which is somewhat embarrassing to God and the soul—as soon as possible.

Kill him—he said.—He won't make it.

The third antidog. Me. For me, there is no higher authority. Even the dog doesn't exist. Only a piece of suffering matter writhing before me. Unbearable. I cannot stand it. Gripped by the suffering in this stable, I demand that an end be put to it. Kill him! Kill him! Stop the machine of pain! Let this not be! There is nothing else one can do, just this! But this we can do!

The fourth antidog: Duś. Agronomist, landowner, a hunter, sportsman, horseman, and lover of hounds. Between him and us—a complete disharmony; he is from a different reality. He is not afraid of pain "as such," as I am. He does not seek universal justice, like this Catholic or that Communist. He disregards abstractions, does not grasp them, does not want to. He exists among creatures of flesh and blood, he is a creature among creatures, a body among bodies. In the depths of his spirit, he does not know what equality is. He is the master. He has come to love this dog; therefore, he would, without scruple, sentence forty million ants and ten thousand whales to suffer . . . if it would bring relief to the dog. For this creature close to him, he is ready for any sacrifice but he does not want to know everything, identify with everything, he wants to remain within the circle of his own limited feeling. He would rather not see what is beyond his gaze. And he has come to love the dog with the love of a master. He loves the dog because it adores him—he loves the canine adoration in the dog. Therefore, the egoism of the master and ruler, the aristocratic feeling born of a ruthless human superiority, all of nature exists for him, it serves him, he, subordinating to himself all inferior beings, is the dispenser of favors. And he seemed to me to be the most "anti" of all of us—in that dark stable, leaning over the dog, the absolute king of creation, proclaiming: everything exists for me.

But perhaps this was most consistent with nature. And if the dog could understand, he would understand him, not us!

With the delicacy of a griefstricken mother, he said: Let us wait. Perhaps he won't die.

It is a fierce love that prolongs agony in order to save the dog—for itself.

This dramatic scene would not have been so tense and urgent if not for the wheezing of the dog, his eyes following our every move.

## Thursday

Necochea. The seaside.

I walk straight ahead along an enormous beach, hardened and brown from the daily tides that flood it. The houses of Necochea disappear behind the cliffs.

Emptiness, sand, undulation—that drowning, soporific thunder. Space—distance—boundlessness. Before me, all the way to Australia, nothing but furrowed water and its gleaming crest, to the south the Falkland and the South Orkney islands—the polar cap. And behind me the "interior": Rio Negro, the pampa. . . . Sea and space thundering in eyes and ears create confusion. I walk and leave Necochea behind— until at last even its memory disappears and only the growing distance persists, eternal, like a secret I take with me.

I stay at the Hotel Shangri-La.

# Sunday

I wander over to the Hotel Quequen, on the other side of the port, but there is no one there from the Argentine high life*—none of the Anchorens, Santa Marinos, etc., I came to know through Duś and Henryk Sobański.

They left because January had come to an end. Their grandparents gathered in this hotel (at that time a first-rate hotel) every year in January, which is why they also arrange a rendezvous in Quequen (now an anachronistic hovel, bereft of comfort). In January this *boliche* squeaks with millions and rings with names.

The local aristocracy, or rather the so-called oligarchy, consists of a few families whose genealogical tree begins with the sudden wealth of a great-grandfather. But these millions are weighty. The influence of money is so strong on people that a few generations of such wealth is enough for the differences between them and, let us say, the Radziwiłłs, to be minimal. They look good and dress all right and have impeccable manners—embedded in an aristocratic calm in their circle. But just in their circle. Unfortunately, I am the one who—when we confront each other—knocks them off balance. An intellectual? Artist? Perhaps an atheist? Anarchist? This embarrasses them, shames them, fills their provincial kindness with trepidation . . . they fear tactlessness.

# Monday

I met him on the beach. He was wonderful! He greeted me magnanimously. He kindly asked how I was. With a majestic finger, he indicated the kiosk where one could get *langostinos*. He smiled with the benevolence of a prince. With regal courtesy, he allowed me to go first along the board leading to the cabin.

All because he was not in pants but in bathing trunks.

# Wednesday

. . . of the Mr. Grubiński** type. Since Mr. Sakowski—although less Latin-Hellenic and daintily Renaissance—is really Grubiński—except not so mortifyingly smooth. Their highest wisdom consists of

---

*"High life" in English in original.
**Grubiński and Sakowski were Polish émigré writers in London.

the following: "All this has already been tried." "There is nothing more banal than originality." "The only things I have not become accustomed to are empty talk, affectation, and pitiful clichés."

A credo typical of eunuchs! What an irony of fate that *Wiadomości,* which in its *Sturm und Drang Periode* ate Grubiński alive every week, today, in old age, has two Grubińskis in its stable. Yet in a way it is a pity that Grydzewski did not delegate a less flimsy mind to discuss the *Diary,* which, for whatever it's worth, contains a portion of my life. I hold nothing against Sakowski—the *Diary* would miss at least one of its (less lofty) destinies if it did not provoke his type of mentality, and his reactions are, in this case, as natural as those of a cat whose tail has been stepped on. I admit that I hurt him badly. I tore into the boudoir of his soul like a barbarian and I smashed his most beloved tomes of poetry; I trampled Tuwim, I dishonored Lechoń, I profaned his dearest saints and sweetest delicacies, even Boy Żeleński. His entire little shrine in ruins! O horrors! This is the source of his aversion to me, in his article, written in the *parlé francé* style.

And that little old man, Kajetan Morawski, was greatly concerned in that same issue of *Wiadomości* that I might be a "futurist." God almighty, why this is *Kurier Warszawski,* * *redivivus!*

And if this were not enough, Janusz Kowalewski jumped on me, too—quarrelsome and inflexible, truculent and thrashing with his little feet. But that was in another newspaper.

# Tuesday

Something happened yesterday . . . something like a continuation of the dog at the *estancia*. . . . And if I said that there is nothing equal somehow to the repugnance of the dilemma that I experienced . . . that I found myself where humanity must retch. . . . I could say this. I could also torment myself with it—it is really up to me.

I was lying in the sun, cleverly concealed in the mountain chain that sand forms when blown by the wind to the edges of the beach. These are mountains of sand, dunes, abundant in ravines, slopes, valleys, a curving and shifting labyrinth, overgrown here and there with brush that vibrates under the unceasing toil of the wind. I was shielded by a substantial *Jungfrau,* nobly cubic, proud—when one of those hurricanes that endlessly lash this scorched Sahara kicked up about ten

---

*Respectable, conservative newspaper in interwar Poland.

centimeters from my nose. Some sort of beetles—I don't know what to call them—bustled along this desert for reasons unknown. And one of them, within my reach, lay upside down. The wind had overturned it. The sun beat on its belly, which certainly must have been unpleasant considering that this belly was usually left in the shade—there he lay, thrashing his little legs—and it was obvious that nothing was left to it except a monotonous and desperate thrashing of its legs—and it was growing weak, perhaps it had been there for hours; it was dying.

I, a giant, inaccessible to him in my enormity, an enormity that made me invisible to it—I watched that thrashing of legs . . . and extending my hand, extricated him from his agony. He moved ahead, returned to life in a split second.

I had barely done this when I noticed a little farther away, an identical beetle in an identical predicament. And he, too, was thrashing his little legs. I didn't want to move. . . . But—why did you save that little guy and not this one? . . . Why that one . . . when this one? . . . You make one happy and the other should suffer? I took a stick, extended my hand—and saved him.

I had barely done this when I saw, somewhat farther, an identical beetle in an identical predicament. Thrashing his little legs. And the sun was beating down on his belly.

Was I supposed to change my siesta into an ambulance for beetles in their death throes? But I had become too friendly with these beetles, in their strangely helpless thrashing . . . and you will probably understand that once I had started this rescuing, I had no right to stop at some arbitrary point. It would have been an awful thing to do to this third beetle—to stop exactly at the threshold of his defeat . . . too cruel and somehow impossible to do. . . . Bah! if there had been some sort of boundary between him and the ones I rescued, something that could have authorized me to stop—but there was absolutely nothing, only another ten centimeters of sand, always the same bit of sand, "a little farther away," it is true, but only "a little." And he waved his little legs in the same way! Looking around, however, I noticed "just a little" farther, another four beetles, thrashing and being scorched by the sun—there was no helping it, I got up and rescued them all. Off they went.

Then what should my eyes behold but the gleaming-hot-sandy plane of a neighboring slope and on it five or six little thrashing dots: beetles. I rushed to their rescue. I saved them. And by this time I was so wrapped up in their suffering, I was so absorbed by it, that, seeing new beetles all along the plains, ravines, and canyons, an endless rash of tortured dots, I began to walk the sands as if I were demented, rescuing, rescuing, rescuing! But I knew this could not last forever—for it was not just this beach, but the entire coast, as far as the eye could see; it was sown with them so there had to come a moment when I would say "Enough!" The first unrescued beetle would have to happen, too. Which one should it be? Which one? Which one? Each time I said "this one"— I saved it, unable to bear that awful, almost vile arbitrariness—because why this one, why *this* one? Until I finally broke down, suddenly, easily, I suspended my empathy, stopped, thought indifferently, "Well, time to go back," and left. But the beetle, the beetle I stopped with, remained behind thrashing its little legs (all of this was a matter of complete indifference to me by now, as if I had grown disgusted with the game— but I knew that this indifference was imposed upon me by the circumstances and I carried it within me like a foreign object).

# Thursday

The café on the *rambli,* * where at this evening hour there is dancing; a samba is underway, discreetly elegant, beating from the windows along with the light onto the immobility of rustling waters . . . all the way to the pole, to Australia. Sumampa. Such exotic names crouch behind me in the interior, still full of the language of Indians so recently exterminated.

Waiters. Young people dancing with abandon. *Refrescos* and *helados* . . .

. . . And what if I said that the business with the bugs had been humiliating? And "dishonorable"? But most of all, "basely helpless?" I could describe it this way. It all depends on me. Here at the dance I can surrender myself to disgrace, or ask for one more helping of ice cream and dismiss it as a silly incident with bugs.

Yes, I am the master of my terrors, my fears. Which *should be* appalling to me? I must first nod to the devil—then he will show himself. Perhaps I beckon too often . . . and what's more, I cultivate a certain category of fear, which I know belongs to the past—these are still fears in embryo, which will become troublesome only to the generation now maturing.

Numbers! The numbers! I had to abdicate from justice, from morality, from humanity—because I could not cope with the numbers. There were too many of them. I'm sorry! But this is the same as saying that morality is impossible. Nothing more or less. Because morality

*Pier.

must be the same in relation to all, otherwise it is unjust, and therefore immoral. But that number, that enormity of numbers, concentrated itself on the one bug I didn't rescue—on the one I stopped at. Why him and not a different one? Why must that one pay for the fact that there are millions?

My pity, ending at precisely that moment—no one knows exactly why at that bug, the same as all the rest. There is something unbearable, impossible to swallow, in this infinity suddenly made concrete—why that one?—why that one? . . . The more I think about it, the stranger I begin to feel; I have the impression that I dispense only a partial morality . . . a fragmentary . . . arbitrary . . . and unjust . . . morality, which (I don't know if this is clear) is of its very nature not continuous but *granular.*

## Saturday

Painting . . . I don't know. Maybe I exaggerate this phobia.

I will not deny that in spite of everything, there is something in a painting, even if it is a faithful copy of nature, that disarms and attracts. What is it? A painted landscape undoubtedly says something else to us than does the same landscape in nature; its effect on our soul is different. But not because a painting is more beautiful than nature, no, a painting will always be incompetent beauty, beauty spoiled by the clumsy hand of man. It is possible, though, that this is the reason behind the attraction. The picture shows us the beauty that was felt, seen by someone like the painter. The picture not only says: "this landscape is beautiful," but also: "I saw this and was struck by it and that is why I painted it."

If we consider that the contemplation of an object, whatever it may be (landscape, apple, house, man), fills us with the despair of loneliness—because then you find yourself alone with the Thing and the Thing crushes you—perhaps this fear of the thing, as such, would explain the paradoxical phenomenon that an imperfectly painted trunk is closer to us than a natural trunk in all of its perfection. A painted tree trunk is a trunk filtered through man.

## Sunday

Today again, at tea, there was a discussion about painting at Atilio's (what else could they possibly talk about?). The catch is, though, that one cannot talk about painting. These conversations, therefore, remind one of dialogues between mutes — they smack their lips, flail their arms, bare their teeth. . . . "What do you mean, you don't understand that blot?" . . . "In this is something . . . something . . . something like, you know, well . . ." "Lovely, lovely, by golly . . . dog damn it!" . . . "Brilliant, on my word!"

Why do they talk if they are only supposed to paint? After all, the language of the best works on the subject of the plastic arts is not much richer. And that mute blather continues among people . . . it goes on. . . .

I don't like these . . .

I met an Austrian at Pocz Oddone's. An architect. He clamors for urban planning and rationally aesthetic, functional interiors, etc. I told him that people had more important concerns than aesthetics. I also said that an excessively subtle sense of beauty could get us into deep trouble! To explain to an average member of the middle class that his mirrored dresser, commode, and little curtains are frippery would make life altogether repugnant to him. We, in our poverty, could use a more universal skill — the discovery of beauty in everything, even in frippery.

He didn't understand me. Conceited. European. Didactic. Educated. Modern. Architect.

# V

## Wednesday

The weather wheels into dirty inclemency, the clouds, not certain whether they will rain or not, creep out of the sky; occasionally the sun shoots out, illuminating the beach, where gold, blue, and white dance before my eyes. On the sand: games, jokes, capers—but bitterly, terribly paid for because these people have to undress! Incredible cynicism! Their play is an act of desperate shamelessness, yes, they dared to do this . . . they undressed . . . they removed their shoes, socks, stockings, underpants, ties, shirts, blouses, jackets . . . and heigh-ho! . . . fraternizing with nature, they frolic in their birthday suits! But this nudist is not naked, he is undressed! What impudence! Yes, yes, the wife of that pharmacist, look at her, she digs into the sand with her feet, her heel, denuded, rises, crawls out—and the head of the sales department cuts capers, kicks a balloon, wheezes, cries out! Ha, wholeheartedly! Naked! But in an undressed, stripped nakedness! And an undressed boss! The pharmacist's wife without underpants! And the toes strangely complement the fingers! And the whole beach roars with the mad provocation of carnal repugnance. God, allow me to vomit up the human body! A dog appeared. An unblemished dog who passed with canine elegance—distinguished. . . .

I watched this from a little hill, and with me was Atilio, a sophisticated expert on Mexican art. He said: Lovely little scene. There is a little Turner in this, isn't there?

Oh sure—a lovely scene, made up of horrors.

## Thursday

Piniera claims that every crazy aesthete who has respect for himself in Havana must have an "antiquity"—a clock from the epoch of Louis XIV, or a medallion—which he wouldn't part with, bestowing on it the enthusiasm he would have had for cathedrals, museums, and all the old things of Europe in general if fate had allowed him a pilgrimage to Europe. As it turns out, Atilio, who is Mexican, also has his antiquity. Yesterday he removed a silver cup from a splendid leather case and showed it to me with reverence.

—Authentic!

Well, perhaps. . . . This was a furiously Renaissance cup of imposing proportions, full of some sort of sculpted scenes in every millimeter—a thicket of incredible figures, ornaments—to unravel this, to penetrate the many years of the artist's work, one would have to devote hours to methodical analysis. I doubt that any one of its possessors had ever taken the time to do this—it was unlikely that the cup had ever really been "examined" by anyone, ever. As for me, I limited myself to the pronouncement, from a bird's-eye view, that the work seemed good . . . afterward I remembered my mother's old china, parading in rows on shelves and also full of fine points never uncovered by anyone. It was enough that the porcelain was authentic. . . .

After caressing the cup lasciviously (whereby he also embraced the effort of past centuries) and casting a synthetic look at it (for all the world like the one we used to cast at our porcelains), Atilio put it back in the case. And he took a stack of art books out of his suitcase. —I always take these books with me, he said.—I wouldn't be able to live without them! These were books about the cathedral at Chartres, about Picasso, Michelangelo, Etruscan vases, Giotto's frescoes, and the Greek temples. —Ah!—exclaimed Atilio, turning the pages.—Ah, have a look at these, Mr. Gombrowicz, here . . . here . . . And here!? Really? I glanced, then he glanced, but this was more like bathing in an ocean . . . knots of form washed over us, like waves; we were drowned and lost in it. Chartres knocked me over like a mountain of water. How many months, years, would it take to know a cathedral that was, from top to bottom, all the way to the arches in the nave, rock that had been worked over, tormented, saturated with passion, humanized—as if entire swarms of workers had thrown themselves on the rock, like waves. How could one onlooker absorb the effort of so many artists? And Giotto and Picasso and Michelangelo were already waiting in ambush, as we flipped through the illustrations of the cathedral. —Ha!—Atilio tossed— Ha! Splendid!— We were drowning. We were drowning in this like in a store with too many luxuries; like children hunting butterflies, we kept grabbing at this line, that spot, pale testimony to what was eluding us. . . .

We did not see much . . . instead we conducted an inventory . . . like a miser who passes pieces of gold from hand to hand, we sated ourselves on these riches, practically without looking . . . trusting that someone must exist, after all, who *has* examined these things. Take this Giotto fresco. I cannot devote too much time to it, but I trust, I trust, that *someone else* has, has examined it. . . . Here, however, I was surprised by a deadly thought: what if that someone else did not exist? And what if *each person* shifts this burden of examining onto another person and what if this delight is passed from hand to hand, pushing it into nothingness? Atilio shrugged his shoulders:

—Pshaw! You say this to me, Mr. Gombrowicz. Why, I've invested half my life in art. . . .

He lied. Apparently he never did anything except casually leaf through this oversized book of plastic arts. He merely leafed through it . . . occasionally glancing here and there . . . pecking at it like a chicken. . . . But how could anyone prove he was lying?

# Friday

Senora Mercedes H. de A. has come all the way from Buenos Aires expressly to see Atilio's cup (Atilio is not returning to Buenos Aires, he is going to Chile)—this lady is skinny, hermetic, voiceless, and she took the cup into her hand, looked at it, put it down and whispered: Ah-h-h. —I would never have forgiven myself if I had allowed you to leave Argentina without my having seen the cup!— After a brief pause, she whispered: —I would also like to know what you think about Pettoruti, about his last color? Atilio grimaced: —I preferred him from five years ago. —We agree then!—she cried out almost inaudibly, pleased. She got into her car and drove off.

As I watched the enormous car carry off Madame Mercedes, I thought of that Polish girl, the blonde, a young painter whom I met when she showed up here from Poland via Paris, a few years ago. She had no car. She spent a few months in Argentina, running from exhibit to exhibit. From painter to painter. Industrious. No, that one would not waste a single minute. Focused. Panting with the desire to enrich her painter's estate. Like a pointer sniffing out "values." Never speaking of anything else. Copying, sketching, writing down, planted firmly in the problems of the plastic arts and constantly, without a moment's respite, educating herself sincerely, modestly, diligently. There is nothing more irritating than her greedy and pious, her poltroonish industry.

At least Mercedes . . . I don't know which is worse: that exhausting, proletarian avidity, vehement in its "self-education," or the pluto-aristocratic gesture of the rich lady who, having driven four hundred kilometers to see a cup, barely devotes one careless glance to it—but why should she have looked at it; it was enough that she, Mercedes, paid it a visit! Art objects are exasperating because they are so material, and yet they are also the church and the drawing room, art and jewelry. . . . At the hotel I found Jerzy Rohde's diary—he is the secretary to the Argentine embassy in Paris and a writer—entitled *Five Years of Paris*. "Cuantas expresiones del arte, hijas del supremo buen gusto!" (How many works of art are born of the most distinguished taste!) This blissful exclamation point graced his enraptured lips at the sight of Gobelins, Clodion's bronzes, Roettier's silver, Fragonard's paintings, and other miracles of the ennobled French Jew Monsieur de Comondo at his Parisian residence, a copy of the Petit Trianon. Mr. Rohde admires both works and *duquesas* but the *duquesas* a little more. (*Loli Lariviere—la encantandora—me lleva al salón de la duquesa de La Rochefoucauld* . . . ) I have studied about fifty pages and am beginning seriously to wonder whether our attraction to old Fragonard and to the old Duchess de La Rochefoucauld does not spring from the same source— from the intoxicating word "aristocracy."

# Saturday

Not long ago at a banquet in honor of Racquel Forner (in my opinion, a mannered and bad Argentinean painter) and her husband, the sculptor Bigatti (because having snagged some award or other, they were leaving for the States), I saw them, painters, an entire body of them, talking, lashing each other with discourse, having a holiday. I observed this from the sidelines, from another table in the same restaurant. "One can only wonder," as people say. It is indeed strange to see how a mechanism of degradation becomes one of elevation in such circumstances. Each of these painters secretly scorned his colleagues because, well, an Argentinean brush is nothing compared with a Parisian brush—yet here, at the banquet, all together, affirming mutual honors, they became quite a lion, altogether in one heap they became a paean to their own honor; and their table rang with praise, their table seemed momentous, even appealing, because of the number of persons participating in the act of self-elevation.

That it did not last long is another matter. Shortly, their peacock tail closed up and a more workmanlike atmosphere got the upper hand.

The conversation focused itself on exhibits, awards, the sale of paintings—they were like owners of companies, worrying about their little factory, prudent and a little embittered, full of ill-feeling toward society, which is ignorant, does not want to buy. . . . They are usually anarchists . . . sometimes Communists, but in fact they are inextricably bound up with the bourgeoisie. Only a bourgeois could afford what appeals to them—beautiful interiors, Renaissance cups, valuable antiques, the refinement—all this is a denial of mass production, that is, proletarian production. And no matter what is said and done, their valuable objects exist only for someone to possess, to materially possess, so they become someone's property—possessing in this art means a lot and it cannot take place without private capital.

## Sunday

I spoke about England with Mrs. Kropka Czerwińska.

Now I am at the beach, among bodies, and I write, lying on my stomach. I wonder . . . I wonder if my rebellion against the plastic arts did not begin with my portraits. . . . I posed for artists a few times and I was always troubled by it because of that stranger's eyes moving all over my form, because of my being sacrificed to those alert eyes, intent, almost excessively observant . . . and he there, behind the easel, making of me whatever he liked. A highly abnormal situation in which one should expect a great deal—in a creative-artistic sense. . . . But even during the sitting I had the impression that the painter's advantage over me was illusory—simply because he was unable to master my form, and the technical difficulties connected with re-creating my nose, ears, cheeks on the canvas make a diligent craftsman out of him rather than the lord and ruler of my body. And as the work progressed, the combination of lines and blots re-creating a form became more and more complex—the more he transferred me to the canvas, the more I lorded it over him, the more difficult it became for him to change something in this arrangement, "to do something" with me, to remake me. I assume that if a cliff or tree could feel something, they would experience exactly these kinds of triumphantly ironic feelings toward the painter attacking them with his paintbrush, feelings, I would say, of triumphant powerlessness, which resulted from the painter's surrender to form in order to grasp it—and at the very moment that he grasps form and transfers it to the canvas, he will no longer be able to manage it because this very same "thing" rules the painting and rivets us with its relentless thingness. It seemed to me as well that the humiliating physicality of the process, that oily re-creation of the nose, ears, eyes, hair, that melancholy sensuality, surrendering to nature, deprives the painter of the *capacity to create,* and in each case the margin earmarked for creativity becomes, in proportion to my becoming concrete in the painting, more and more narrow and insignificant. And then the portrait was ready. It was shown to me. Disenchantment!

What happened?! He turned me into a thing! He painted me exactly as if I were a rock, ha! and now I see that he paints human beings the same way he does other objects. And so what if his eyes missed me! . . . He painted me as if it were not I but my shoe that was important!

# Tuesday

I met a band of misshapen nudists—sensually bearded or at least hairy—near Quequen; they were helping the fishermen draw in their nets. I felt myself recoil. I can't stand their bohemianism in glasses and a beard, their slovenly but urban corporeality, that artistic "simplicity" combined with refinement. . . . But I went up to them, greeted them and said (as always when they get in my way): I don't believe in painting (*no credo en la pintura*)!

They answered by exploding with laughter.

I said: Let us imagine that one of you had painted this fisherman. What do you think, would I be able to judge the art of a painting if I were deprived of a sense of color, of form, and if my taste were not adequately informed? In other words, if I could not look freshly, with a painter's eye?

They: Of course not! In that case you wouldn't get anything out of the painting!

I: Really? But if I am able to do all that, why would I need a painting?

They: What do you mean?

I: Well, yes! If I am capable of seeing, I prefer to look at the living face of a fisherman. Instead of one painting, I'll have ten, because that face is always different, I see it from a different angle, in a different light. If I can extract the painting value from a living face, why would I need the immobile one in your painting? And if I am unable to do that, your picture will tell me nothing interesting.

Should I cast off the dazzling whirl of form, light, color that is the world for your lifeless kingdom where nothing moves! Don't you see how I want to get at you? . . . I simply want to say that your brush is incapable of rendering the plasticity of the world. For the world is form in motion. Even when the form is still, the light and air change. But you, on your canvases, condemn nature to paralysis by taking the life from its form: by subtracting movement.

They: What? What? Painting does not express movement? Absurd! Movement in a painting, even though it is suspended, frozen, is still movement—it is movement even more precisely for that reason!

I: Ha, ha, ha, ha, ha!

Lies! Ah, how I love these typical lies about art, always ready to prove its weaknesses are its strength!

Yes, just between us . . . No one is listening . . . Yes, privately . . . Admit that if you could bring this divine quickening movement to your palette, you would be in paradise.

Why not confess that a paintbrush is a clumsy instrument? . . . It's as if you took to painting explosions of cosmic light with a toothbrush.

No art is so poor in its means of expression—except perhaps sculpture. Painting is one great resignation from what cannot be painted. It is a cry: I would like to do more, but I cannot. This cry is oppressive.

Would you like to hear a short tale about your bankruptcy?

Formerly painters strove for the most faithful rendering of nature. But why re-create something that already is? And besides, isn't this condemning oneself to work that is eternally slipshod? Nature paints better. No Titian can paint the fisherman's face with equal excellence— error is impossible, every shadow, every spot is exactly as physics dictates.

Not being able, therefore, to match nature, one begins to rescue oneself by way of the "spirit." More and more human spirit is crammed into a painting. At this point, however, the sensuality of painting, antispiritual in its very essence, crawls out. What should one do with the spirit when one deals almost exclusively with matter? Pump it into a painting as sublime content—as anecdote? . . . But this spirit would then be somewhat comic, an afterthought!

Then it became more and more clear that the painter was not supposed to express external nature or the spirit but his view of nature . . . that is, himself, without transgressing the limits of his own physical sphere . . . to express himself with purely a painter's means, contour, color. . . . Thus began the deformation of the object. But how is one to express himself in a painting deprived of movement? For existence is movement, it takes place in time. How can I pass myself on, or my existence, operating only with combinations of immobile shapes? Life is movement. If I cannot render movement, I cannot render life. Notice that I am thinking of real movement, not the suggestion of movement that a painter gives us in sketching, for example, a jumping horse.

Compare, in this regard, line and color with the word. The word unfolds in time, like a procession of ants, and each one brings something new and unexpected; he who expresses himself in words is born anew each second; scarcely has one sentence been completed than the next one supplements it, completes it, and behold in the movement of words the endless play of my existence expresses itself—when I express myself in words, I am like a tree in the wind, rustling, quivering. And the painter is chucked out in one shot, all in space, immobile on the canvas—like a clod. We take in the entire picture at a glance. And so what if we notice a certain play of elements in the painting, if the play does not develop or unfold? Painting can undoubtedly communicate the vision of the painter, his spiritual adventure with the world, but only in the cross-section of one moment—and for me to be able to penetrate his personality, I would have to have a thousand such visions; only they, all together, would be capable of introducing me to his inner movement, his life, his time.

What deception to claim that van Gogh or Cézanne communicated their personalities! To paint apples a little differently from natural ones— and to want to rival the airborne becoming of poetry and music with these apples . . . A man expressed by an apple! An unmoving apple! If I, a writer and poet, were told that I should communicate via apples, I would sit down and cry in humiliation. But if we are talking about art and its masters, we are visited by a certain indulgence . . . sympathy, and even adoration, lead us to overlook some trifling and some not-so-trifling inaccuracies, just so we do not upset the status quo . . . how ready we are then to swear that it was apples or sunflowers that led us to Cézanne or van Gogh, but we forget that if they became our close acquaintances it was because biographies filled in the enormous gap left by the sunflowers and the apples. If the word had not conveyed their lives to us, there's not much we could do with their self-portraits.

Painting, then, even though it was already deforming, continued to suffer chronic insatiety—those martyrs of the paintbrush (that clumsy instrument) felt that they could not express themselves on a larger scale by imitating existing forms in nature, even if they underwent an extreme transformation. What were they to do? How were they to liberate themselves from the Thing; the Thing to which they were chained like dogs? Wouldn't it be possible—to destroy the Thing, take it apart and create one's own language out of this—an autonomous language? That is how abstract art began. But so what if it does not move either or, strictly speaking, is congealed movement. In music pure form is attainable, because music is a becoming—after the pianissimo of the violin comes a stroke of percussion, here form renews itself every minute—but an abstract painting is like one chord . . . it is as if a musician invited someone to a concert and then offered him just one chord. Abstraction has taken away from painting the imitation of life that it had when it was imitation of nature—and did not give it another vitality in exchange.

To hell with your painting! I have had enough of it! Enough of this mania!

They: Listen, mister! You are insensitive! Ignorant! You understand nothing! You don't get it!

I: Look at these three matches I put down on the sand.

Imagine that in a certain group of people there arises a stubborn rivalry on the subject of how to arrange these three matches so that they would be more revealing artistically. If I make a triangle of them, for example, they will be more interesting than if I place them side by side. But one can devise even more interesting arrangements.

Let us imagine that the great effort of many fine "matchists" became invested in this; that some turned out to be more, others less, ingenious; that hierarchies arose; that schools and styles emerged; that there arose an expertise on the subject. . . . But, I ask you, why would this be absurd? Why, even with just those three matches man could express something—about himself, about the world. By concentrating all of our attention on these three matchsticks, we could uncover the mystery of the cosmos in them—they are a part of it and one knows that the universe is reflected in a drop of water—nevertheless they are no more and no less than a Thing in all its majesty—for in their behavior the laws of nature express themselves—for in looking at these matches with the appropriate concentration we perform a solemn act, we confront consciousness with Matter.

All of this—under the condition that we begin to *look closely* at them. The question remains—is it worth it, is it worth it, is it worth it? We could use trees rather than matches or animals or anything else just as successfully and with even better results for this initiation.

And I don't deny that if we begin to look with such concentration at Cézanne, Cézanne will become a revelation. The question remains— is it worth it, is it worth it, is it worth it? Why not seek these revelations elsewhere?

In my opinion, you err in thinking that the paintings themselves are something of a revelation and that is why people look at them. In my opinion, just the opposite has happened. Paintings have become revelations because people have begun to search for revelations in them— that is why the offensive poverty of this art has burst into profundity and riches.

Why then has mankind begun to look closely at paintings?

You will find answers to this in the mechanisms of human cohabitation, in its historical development. Painting, in spite of everything, is pretty, right? It serves to ornament. Hence a market for paintings has arisen, just as it has for jewelry. People began to pay because—to paraphrase Pascal—if a Titian hangs on my wall it means that I am somebody, because I am rich. This pretty object—a painting—has thereby inflamed the possessive instinct in kings, dukes, bishops, all the way to the bourgeoisie, and the need has created a whole scale of values. There are many reasons for this; people, just like individuals, have their games and manias. . . . Who, for example, could have foreseen that a certain type of stone, such as a diamond or ruby (whose artistic effect is minimal), would arouse such powerful desires in man? And what about postage stamps?

Of course, a painting is not a postage stamp. It is, however, art, although quite limited in its means of expression. Combine the artistic charge of a painting with other powers, not having much in common with art, and you will understand why it has been raised so high by our feelings, almost to the level of holiness.

The only question is—is painting worth keeping at these heights?

Today this is what happens to you: *first* the complicated herd instinct, which creates itself historically, throws you on your knees before a painting—and *only then* do you try to force yourselves to explain that if you reeled with admiration, it was because the work was worthy of it.

Is it worth surrendering oneself to such intricate games with one's own feelings?

Stop becoming enraptured—that's a lot simpler.

\* \* \*

(Everything I have reproached them with is quite arbitrary. And does not exhaust the subject. One could attack them from a different angle—from ten different angles—their Achilles' heels number in the dozens.

But my purpose is not to explain but to revolt. I wish to protest! I believe that others will follow me. Providence, allow me to endure a few more years in the opposition—it will find its own.

To derail enthusiasm, which moves along a well-worn track!

My war with painting, like my war with poetry, is primarily a struggle with the milieu—painters, poets—with the group, with the profession. . . . Never before has the law borne itself out more truly than it does here: the conditions of production create the Spirit in its own image—nothing better illustrates Marx's thesis than the awful artistic mystification, which they, Marxists, do not dare touch. Painters, poets, their zealots and acolytes, are a typical example of an accommodating consciousness—they not only believe, they want to believe. My reproach is that their faith comes to them too easily, even too eagerly—maniacs, exploiting for their artificial passion a certain artificial state of things, created by historical circumstance. And not a single one wants to sober up. Each one does his utmost to drown in his mania. And they want to drown me in it, too. I will defend myself!)

# Saturday

I showed them the matches. Too bad that I neglected to show them a cigarette.

Doesn't a cigarette provide us with great pleasure? Almost as great as eating? Who, though, would dare compare bread to cigarettes? Bread is a genuine necessity but a cigarette became a value only when an artificial need was born, created by habit.

Therefore, don't be so proud that today's humanity inhales with such pleasure the fragrant incense rising from art exhibits. I do not doubt man's inborn need for beauty. But I ask whether in certain types of art (such as a poem or painting) the producer does not fabricate his recipient as well.

This pressure, this forcing of paintings onto people—this is something to think about!

# Friday

From my letter to Artur Sandauer in connection with Mr. Kisiel's article in Poland's *Tygodnik Powszechny,* whose title was: "Sandauer and Gombrowicz, or the Conspiracy of the Absent."

*In reading the passage from your essay that was cited and attacked by him, I thought how incapable he is of reading us, neither you, nor me, how he understands nothing of our work. I am completely unfamiliar with your essay except for the passage included by Kisiel—I haven't the least idea what you wrote, but, in spite of this, allow me, my dear Sandauer, to say how your words should be interpreted from my vantage point.*

*Here they are as cited by Kisiel:*

"Something has arisen which is a complete novelty in Polish literature: self-irony, self-denigration. In laughing at himself and sneering at the gamut of Polish issues, Gombrowicz rids himself of that self-importance and solemnity that for many long years has been a feature of our culture; thus he seems to present the perspective of creating a more authentic, more national, culture. . . ."

*It was this that roused Kisiel—and he explains triumphantly in his article that your "novum" is really* nihil novi*, that our literature, beginning with the bards,* *has been full of this "self-irony and self-denigration." "This has been a basic tradition and convention of Polish literature for the past 150 years," he writes.*

*But he writes this because he does not understand what you are trying to say. Kisiel maintains that in* The Wedding *Wyspiański denigrates himself and practices self-irony. In fact—nothing could be further from the truth.* The Wedding *does, perhaps, compromise the Polish nation, but he himself, Wyspiański, is the highest judge here; and it is he who casts thunderbolts and tears at his robes.* The Wedding *does not, therefore, compromise Wyspiański, just as the thunderbolts, curses, and sneers aimed at the nation beginning with Słowacki and Norwid, Bobrzyński or Brzozowski and ending with Nowaczyński, have nothing to do with self-denigration.*

*In writing "self-denigrating" didn't you have in mind that in* Ferdydurke *I accepted a posture that was quite unexpected, proclaiming my own immaturity and accusing other authors of hiding theirs? Wouldn't this constitute a certain "novum" in our writing? And even in all writing? And here one can speak about "self-denigration," under the condition, of course, that this confession of immaturity will not serve merely as a polemical stratagem or humorous effect. What sort of dialogue would have erupted between Wyspiański and myself if we could have met for coffee at a café? He: —I grieve over the shortcomings of the Polish nation because I am more mature than the Polish nation. I: —I don't bemoan the Polish nation at all; I bewail only my own immaturity and the nation concerns me only as one of the components of my immaturity. I, therefore, lock horns with the nation, just as I lock horns with every other phenomenon that obstructs or negates the possibility of maturity; which does not mean that I am more mature than my fellow Poles, no, I am simply more aware of my immaturity and this allows me a little distance; but I also confess that this immaturity*

---

*Polish Romantic poets, chiefly Adam Mickiewicz and Juliusz Słowacki.

*fascinates, beguiles, and fills me with delight. For I am at one and the same time a mature Immaturity and an immature Maturity. . . .*

*Let us forget about the last sentence, perhaps it is too difficult for persons unaccustomed to this kind of thinking. . . . But one can see from the above that my "criticism" of the nation has nothing in common with traditional criticism in our literature; that it is based on a different self-image, different vision, different theory. And that it is not really criticism, but a battle for my psychological existence and a battle for the form that delineates this existence —a battle in which I, an individual, grapple with the milieu not in the name of a higher, objective, purpose, but in the name of my own purpose.*

*And now, if you go on to write that I am "sneering at the gamut of Polish issues" —how am I to understand this? Certainly not in the way that Kisiel understood it, that I am sneering at what is clumsy about them, but instead that I condemn them as a whole, with their good and bad sides, because they are "off the subject," because they are concerned with the existence and development of the nation and not with the existence and development of the people who make up the nation. Because these Polish issues revolve around the collectivity, while I insist on the problem of the individual. Because they are issues above our station and stature, the work of an artificial maturity that makes one person more of a patriot than he really is in the presence of others —which has nothing to do with our authentic psychic life. And it would be good if Kisiel finally understood that the course of my revolutionary and rare thesis is this simple truth: an individual is something more fundamental than a nation. The individual takes precedence over the nation.*

*But, Mr. Sandauer, how should one interpret your words that here is "the perspective of creating a more authentic, more national, culture"? Is it not because the Pole has more reasons than a Frenchman or an Englishman not to identify himself with his national form (something which Kisiel does not grasp); and that this greater distance from form could ensure us an altogether original contribution to European culture? Imagine the shock —if the proud "I am a Frenchman" of a Frenchman and the "I am an Englishman" of the Englishman met with the Polish, unexpected "I am not wholly a Pole, I am above being a Pole. . . ."*

*Have I explained your intentions well? I repeat, I am not familiar with your lecture, I do not know the context of these words and whether you used them in a narrower sense —but I intentionally applied the broadest, deepest meaning to them to show that these few lines could be interpreted in whatever way the soul desired: superficially, like Kisiel, or a little more profoundly. It is possible to drown these two sentences in our immortal banality —load them with all the platitudes, slogans, schemas, perversions,*

*and mannerisms of Polish national thought—or one can find fresher con-
tents. Except that, in the second case, one must have some concept of the
ideas forming the skeleton beneath the living flesh of my books . . . . one
must know something about form and immaturity. . . . But is it worth
demanding so awesome an intellectual effort from Kisiel, who, being a
Sarmatian,\* is not a philosopher and whose highest philosophical efforts
express maxims like: "Poor souls, these egocentrics. Can an egocentric be
a prophet? Maybe, but a false one." Just as for that other connoisseur, Mr.
Sakowski of London's* Wiadomości, *at whose mercy I live here, in emigration, my* Diary *is rife with nonsense, which he, Sakowski, cannot
comprehend for all the world and is forced to attribute to a strange pose or
to a stupid craving for originality, so for Kisiel my treatment of Poland is
yesterday's reheated leftover—a peculiar thing in an author to whom he
otherwise attributes a sizable dose of innovation. The conclusions of these
two gentlemen sound so strange because their expertise has blinded them
to what every intelligent reader notices—that my views make up an organic
whole, that my attitude to art or to the nation, or to other similar matters,
is simply the branching of a tree whose root is my concept of form. Yes—
but Poles don't like to get down to the roots, Mr. Sakowski or Kisiel are
instead "social" beings, far from boring themselves or others with thinking
that is too rigorous. After all, what's the Catholic Church for? The Church
will, once again, absolve Kisiel of the disagreeable task of rigorous thinking.*

*One more little word. I smiled when I read the following passage in
Kisiel's article:*

"That which is universal and creative in Gombrowicz ensures him
a place in the history of literature without regard for the anachronisms
of the thirties. On the other hand, Gombrowicz is not suited to be a
leader of intellectual life in Poland today: his judgments about this life
are as dogmatic as they are naive and outdated. Sandauer has elevated
him to the role of leader, and a few young people are inclining in his
direction. . . ."

*Now what's this? Is Kisiel letting the cat out of the bag?
Let him relax . . . his fears are groundless. . . .
I really believe that from here, from America, I see Poland a lot better
than Kisiel, who is embedded in it, like a potato in a sack of potatoes
. . . whose dialectics smell a bit musty, who thinks in clichés culled from
Polish literature; who, furthermore, is unbalanced, provincially unbal-*

---

\*Term often applied to Polish country squires to designate their provincial, undered-
ucated, but extremely self-satisfied posture.

*anced, chafing from a sense of Polish inferiority only to elevate himself a moment later with that Polish "nevertheless" megalomania ("the conflict of two ideas, animating millions of people in Europe and directing general attention to Poland"). Yes, I definitely see this better from here, from the world, and more soberly, and I think about it much more freely. But — never fear —I am not thinking of being a "leader" of any sort. I —a leader? Why, I don't even aspire to the title of "Polish writer." I simply want to be Gombrowicz, nothing more.*

# VI

## Wednesday, Tandil

I arrived in Tandil a few days ago and took a room at the Hotel Continental. Tandil is a city—surrounded by low hills bristling with rock, like fortresses—of seventy thousand inhabitants and I have come because it is spring and to get rid of the last microbes of an Asian flu.

Yesterday I rented, for a reasonable rate, a lovely apartment somewhat on the outskirts of town, in the foothills, where there is a great stone gate and a park joins a mountain forest of conifers and eucalyptus.

Through the window, opened wide onto the dazzling sun of the morning, I see Tandil in the hollow, as if on a platter—this little house floats in a gentle cascade of palm and orange trees, pines, eucalyptus, wisteria, multitudes of trimmed shrubs and the strangest cacti tumbling toward the city while in the background a high wall of dark pines climbs almost vertically toward the peak, on which stands a confectionery castle. There is nothing more floral or springlike, more blossoming or radiant. And the mountains surrounding the city—dry as pepper dust, bare, rocky, and jutting out in enormous boulders—have the appearance of pedestals, prehistoric bastions, platforms, and ruins. An amphitheater.

Before me Tandil: three hundred meters away yet as clear as if it were in the palm of my hand. It is by no means a health resort with hotels and tourists but an ordinary provincial city. Brushing my teeth in the sun and inhaling the fragrance of blossoms, I considered ways of "penetrating" the city I was warned against: "You will be bored to death in Tandil."

I ate a marvelous breakfast in a small café suspended over gardens—ah, nothing much, coffee and two eggs but awash in blossoming!—after which I entered the city and its squares, the rectangles of blinding white houses with flat roofs, sharp angles, drying laundry, and under a wall—a motorcycle and a large, flat square exploding with greenery. One walks in the hot sun and the cool air of spring. People. Faces. One and the same face, walking in pursuit of something, running some errand or other, preoccupied, unhurried, kind, calm. . . . "You will be bored to death in Tandil!"

I looked at the sign on one of the buildings: *"Nueva Era,* Daily."
I walked in. I introduced myself to the editor but didn't feel like chatting,
I was somewhat drowsy, dreamy-eyed, and because of all this I answered
him badly. I said I was *un escritor extranjero* and asked if anyone intelligent lived in Tandil, someone worth getting to know.

—What?—retorted the editor, offended.—We do not lack intelligent people. Our cultural life is rich, there are seventy painters alone!
Writers? Well, we have Cortes; he is a big name, he publishes in the
press of the capital. . . .

We called Cortes and arranged a meeting for the next day. I spent
the rest of the day wandering the streets of Tandil. A corner. On the
corner stands the plump, behatted owner of something or other next to
two soldiers, farther down a woman in her seventh month and a wagon
with delicacies—whose vendor sleeps blissfully on a bench, covered
with a newspaper. And a loudspeaker sings: "You have imprisoned me
in your dark eyes. . . ." I sing to myself: "You will be bored to death
in Tandil." A weather-beaten gentleman in boots and a cap.

# Thursday

From here, from the mountain, Tandil looks surrounded by prehistory—shattered mountains of rock. I ate a delightful breakfast in the
sun, trees, flowers.

But I feel uncertain, alien, this unknown life is bothering me. . . .
I go to the "Centro Popular," where I had agreed to meet Cortes. This
is a sizable library of about twenty thousand volumes—deep within is
a small room in which some sort of arts and culture committee is meeting. As I walk in, the session is adjourning and Cortes introduces me
to those gathered. After five minutes of conversation, I get the picture:
Cortes, a Communist-idealist, dreamer, upstanding, full of good intentions, well-wishing, decent—that fifteen year old is not a girl but the
wife (in her twenties) of that young man over there, also an idealist
made sublime by Marx. The secretary, on the other hand, is a Catholic,
and a third man, who looks like Rembrandt, is a militant Catholic. They
are united by faith.

They have never heard of me. What did I expect—this is a backwater. But I become cautious. I know immediately what tactics to use
in these circumstances and I do not make the mistake of introducing
myself; on the contrary, I act as if I were well known and I merely give
them a hint of my Europe through my tone, my form—this manner of
speaking must be piquant, careless, unceremonious, with a dash of

intellectual chic. Paris. This grabbed them. They say: Ah, you've been to Paris! I, casually: — Well, yes, it's a city just like Tandil, houses, streets, a café on the street corner, all cities are the same. . . . They like this. That I did not pride myself on Paris but instead denigrated it resulted in their seeing the Parisian in me; I see that Cortes is almost won over and the ladies are interested but still a little suspicious.

Nevertheless . . . they demonstrate a lack of attention — some sort of absentmindedness — as if they were consumed by something else — and suddenly I begin to understand that even if Camus and Sartre themselves were to show up in Tandil, these people would be incapable of overcoming their stubborn inattentiveness, their thinking about something local, about something Tandilian. But what's this? Suddenly they become animated: they begin to talk, interrupting one another. About what? About their affairs, about the fact that almost no one came to the last lecture, that they have to force people to come, that Fulano does come but that he immediately falls asleep, that the doctor's wife has taken offense. . . . They talk as if they were talking to me, but it is really among themselves that they lament, groan, certain of my writer's approval, that I, as a writer, will share in full their bitter sorrow over their "grass-roots work," all of that Tandilian *Żeromszczyzna.* * Br-r-r- . . . "You will be bored to death in Tandil." Suddenly Tandil crashes over my brain, that rancid, unleavened, coarse content of a modest, limited life, behind which they, as behind a cow, boring and eternal, are made concrete for all time.

— Let the people be! — I say.

— But . . .

— Where did you get the idea that everyone has to be intelligent and enlightened?

— What?!

— Leave the yokels alone!

The word "yokel" (*bruto*) fell and what was worse, "populace" (*vulgo*) — at which I became aristocratic. It was as if I had declared war. I had torn away the mask of convention.

Now they became cautious.

— You deny the necessity for universal enlightenment?

— Of course.

— But . . .

— Away with teaching!

---

*After Stefan Żeromski, Polish novelist of the Modernist period whose works often featured characters sacrificing their personal lives for the public good; here used pejoratively.

This was too much. Cortes picked up his pen, looked at its tip under the light, and blew. — We don't understand one another — he said, as if he were worried. And a young man in the shadows muttered malevolently:

— You're probably a fascist, eh?

# Friday

I had indeed said too much. It was unnecessary. Nevertheless, I feel better . . . that aggressiveness strengthened me.

And what if they brand me a fascist? . . . That's all I need! I have to talk to Cortes — patch things up.

# Saturday

What's going on?

Often a soul forms itself murkily, bluntly . . . from just any old series of haphazard incidents. The encounter with them in the library, well, it was nothing but it acted like a catalyst. Now the roles are clearly distributed. I am an aristocrat. I have been revealed to them as an aristocrat. I am an aristocrat in Tandil . . . which at the same stroke came to embody common provincialism.

One should understand, however, that this was the mere outline . . . the mere outline of some sort of theater against the background of a million other events filling my day, events, which I cannot enumerate, events, in which the outline of drama dissolves like sugar in tea — so much so that the shape is lost and only the taste remains. . . .

I write this after another conversation with Cortes which instead of patching things up, aggravated the whole situation. I was irritated. I was irritated by the angelic sweetness of a Communist priest.

I will not repeat the entire conversation. I told him that the idea of equality contradicts the entire structure of the human species. The thing that is most splendid in people, the thing that establishes their brilliance when compared with other species, is exactly that man is not equal to man — while an ant is equal to another ant. *These are the two great modern lies:* the lie of the Church, that all have the same soul; the lie of democracy, that everyone has an equal right to development. You think that these ideas are a triumph of the spirit? Not at all, they derive from the body, this view is founded chiefly on our all having the same body.

I do not deny (I continued) that the optical impression is not to be doubted: we are all more or less the same height and we have the same organs. . . . But the soul, this specific characteristic of our species, intrudes onto the uniformity of this picture, and it causes our species to be so individuated, so precipitous and vertiginous, that between man and man arise differences a hundred times greater than in all of the animal world. Between Pascal and Napoleon and a little village peasant there is a chasm greater than between a horse and a worm. What's more, a peasant differs less from a horse than from Valéry or Saint Anselm. An illiterate and a professor are only superficially the same people. A director is someone different from a worker. Are you telling me that you don't know that—intuitively speaking, in the margin of theory—our myths about equality, solidarity, and fraternity are incompatible with the real situation?

I admit that I doubt whether in these conditions one can speak of the "human" species—isn't this a concept that is simply too physical?

Cortes looked at me with the eye of a wounded intellectual. I knew what he was thinking: fascism! and I was going crazy with delight proclaiming this Declaration of Inequality, because for me intelligence was changing into harshness, into blood!

# Tuesday

—*Tilos*—*pinos*—*platanos*—*naranjos*—*palmeras*—*glicinas*—*mimbres* —*alamos*—*cipres*—breakfast on the veranda of the café in this bouquet; in the distance, ancient amphitheaters and bastions, great piles of rubble, circuses gleaming with sun.

I loaf and wander about Tandil. Their monotonous bustle—the deadening pedestrianism of these comings and goings—their antlike thrift, their equine patience, bovine languor, when I . . . when I . . . I cannot get to anyone because they are drowned in their own world and their isolation is unfathomable, each chases after his own, theirs is the solitude of animals, horses, frogs, fish. They are defined by their routine tasks, nothing else. The whole city is one great big hustle and bustle. What should I do?! *A la recherche du temps perdu*—I find this book in the library, I take Proust home and I read: I read in order to immerse myself in an element that is more familiar to me, to be with my brother, Proust!

# Wednesday

Is he really a member of the family? Yes — we are both from the same distinguished family. We should embrace one another. A subtle work, sharp as a blade, vibrating, thin and hard — what a delightful counterpoint to this clumsy, heavy, massive, Tandil existence. We are both of the aristocracy — both refined! But no! To hell with him, he irritates me, disgusts me, I see too much of my own caricature in him.

He has always irritated me. I could never reconcile myself to the panegyric attached to him. This monster . . . refinement due to suffocation, eternally stuffed into bedclothes, overheated and sticky, enfeebled and muffled, drowned in medicinal compounds, condemned to all the dirt of the body, walled up in his cork-lined room . . . my ordinary, Polish provinciality is revolted by his French decadence. One could admire and even adore the energy inspired from on high that decreed that this life — swaddled in the folds of a maternal skirt, coddled; limited to bed, books, paintings, drawing-room conversations, snobberies — should give birth to a work that is hard and cruel, touching on the most concealed nerves of reality. One might see the redeeming secret of the aristocracy in this transformation of softness into hardness, delicacy into acuity. One might even risk the statement that his sickness is transformed into health. Which is in keeping with the very essence of art. In art it is not a healthy person who creates a healthy work or a strong person who creates a strong work but quite the contrary: the sick man is better able to grasp the very essence of health, strength. . . .

Noble health.
No one knows
How you taste
Until you waste away.*

It is not odd, therefore, for him, a sick person, to have a keener sense of health; for a person confined to the four walls of a room to attain the most distant horizons, and for artificiality to lead him to splendid authenticity.

But . . . What a shame! His compensation is incomplete. It is like an underdone steak — on these pages I uncovered entire pieces of this half-cooked meat, wretched, sick meat. . . .

---

*Fragment from a *fraszka,* or short occasional poem, by Polish Renaissance poet Jan Kochanowski.

The flaws of Proust's book are enormous and innumerable—a gold mine of defects. His duel with Time, based on an exaggerated, naive faith in the power of art—this is the professional mysticism of a crazed aesthete and artist. His psychological analyses could drag out into infinity, for they are only an embroidering on observations—they are not exploratory, they lack a fundamental revelation of the world, they have not come from a single penetrating look, they have not come from a vision, they are only the minutely detailed work of the (uninspired) intellect. His rich statements constantly rub up against mannerisms; it is almost impossible to determine when their sumptuous beauty tumbles into artificial effort. His brand of metaphor betrays his weakness: it is not, in most cases, a metaphor that reduces secondary phenomena to a more elementary form, but the reverse—it will always tend to translate the great, elementary world into his own secondary reality, into the language of his "sphere," to explain nature through a painting, not painting through—nature. There is perversion in all this—an intentional lack of loyalty to life. As for the world that he has brought to life in his romance, there is nothing narrower—his people are all of one mold, this is one family in which the same inherited traits appear in various combinations—Charlus, Norpois, Madame de Guermantes, are cut from the same cloth, they all say basically the same thing. Monotony of plot characterizes a work with poor innovation and imagination, but appealingly diligent in cultivating detail. There is nothing that unmasks the "unbaked side" of Proust more than his intelligence—which can be wonderful—but how often it also stumbles, who knows how and where, into helplessness, naïveté—these are the remnants of an unconquered naïveté, overrefinement, which has not been digested into knowledge but which has remained just that: overrefinement.

Why do we admire him? We admire him, first of all, because he dared to be delicate and because he did not hesitate to show himself as he was—sometimes in tails, sometimes in a bathrobe, accompanied by a bottle of medicine, a little bit of homosexual-hysterical lipstick, phobias, neuroses, weaknesses, snobbery, all the misery of a refined Frenchman. We admire him because beyond that strange, tainted Proust we discover the nakedness of his humanity, the truth of his sufferings, and the power of his honesty. Too bad! If we look a little closer, again, beyond the nakedness, we uncover Proust in a bathrobe, in tails, or in a nightshirt together with all the accessories—the bed, medicines, bibelots. This is a game of hide-and-seek. No one knows what the ultimate is here: nakedness or costume, drawing room or life, illness or health, hysteria or power. That is why Proust is a little of everything, profundity and shallowness, originality and banality, incisiveness and simplicity

. . . cynical and naive, elegant and unsavory, graceful and clumsy, amusing and boring, light and heavy. . . .

Heavy! This cousin of mine crushes me. Because I do belong to the same family after all—I, the refined . . . I am from the same milieu. Except without Paris. I did not have Paris. And coarse Tandil is trying its hardest to get at my delicate skin, unprotected by Parisian balm!

# Thursday

Cortes suggested a young poet to me whose name was Juan Angel Magarinios, son of the owner of the Hotel Residencial. I asked him to invite a few other poets to the café.

At five o'clock, three boys showed up who hadn't the slightest idea who I was and asked how I had found myself in Argentina. The fourth, a slight sixteen year old, upon hearing my name, smiled and said: — Ferdydurke!

They call him "Dipi." So I now have two readers in Tandil (the other is the eighteen-year-old son of the museum director, Ferreir).

They all write. —So I now have what I wanted: readers and a table of artists in the café, colleagues. What a shame that not one of my colleagues is over twenty!

# Friday

Cox is also a pal of mine. This thin, tall, seventeen-year-old bean pole who has something of the bellhop about him—a familiar manner and easy knowledge about everything, the most perfect disregard I have ever encountered, an awful worldliness, as if he had come to Tandil straight out of New York (yet he has never even set foot in Buenos Aires). Nothing appeals to him—his is a complete inability to feel any kind of hierarchy, a cynicism arising from his skill at maintaining polite appearances. This is wisdom born of a lower sphere—the wisdom of a street urchin, newsboy, elevator or errand boy, for whom the "higher stratum" is worth as much as one can make off of it. Churchill, along with Picasso, Rockefeller, Stalin, Einstein, are nothing but big game peeled down to the last tip if they run into them in a hotel lobby. . . . This boy's relationship to History calms me and even brings me relief, it provides me with an equality that is more real than one composed of slogans and theories. I relax.

# Saturday

Life that is limited. Local life. One lives with whatever the new day brings. No one looks around, everyone looks at his feet, at his own path. Work. Family. Activity. To survive, somehow. . . . A concrete existence.

This exhausts and attracts at the same time . . . oh, so these are the limitations I have craved! I am tired of the cosmos. I confirm a crisis of "universalism" in myself. I assume that many other people today also suffer from it. The diagnosis is as follows: century after century we expanded our horizons; our vision finally encompassed the entire planet; we demand morality "for all," rights "for all," everything "for everybody"—and then it turns out that we are unequal to the task! Catastrophe! Disillusion! Bankruptcy! Why I have already made insects equal to people in my desire for universal justice, the only one possible! But the blow dealt my soul by the first unrescued insect casts me into impotence . . . and now panequality, universal justice, universal love, all that is universal, are liquidating themselves in me—not because I want this to happen—but because I cannot help it—after all, I am not Atlas lifting the whole world onto his shoulders!

I, who not long ago was still angry at Catholics and Communists for their aristocratic egotism toward animals, here with Cortes suddenly deny even people equality! How one thing contradicts another in me!

Do I become the "reaction" then? To that entire process striving for universality? I am so dialectic, so very prepared for the themes the epoch has stuffed me with, for the bankruptcy of socialism, democracy, scientism, that out of sheer impatience I look for unavoidable reaction, I myself am almost reaction!

Narrow myself! Limit myself! To live only with what is mine! I want to be concrete and private! I am sick of ideas that tell me to concern myself with China—I have not seen China, I don't know China, I haven't been there! Enough appeals to see my brother in a man who is not my brother! I want to lock myself within my circle of vision and not reach further than I can see. I want to topple the accursed "universality" that shackles me more than the most confining prison and escape into the freedom of the limited!

I record this desire, today, in Tandil.

# VII

## Wednesday

In Tandil I am the most illustrious of men! No one equals me here!
There are seventy thousand of them—seventy thousand inferiors. . . .
I carry my head like a torch. . . .

## Thursday

I am growing in Poland. I am also growing elsewhere. In Poland
*The Marriage* and *Trans-Atlantic* are being born and a volume encompassing all of my stories, called *Bakakaj* (in memory of the street
Bacacay, where I lived in Buenos Aires). The French translation of
*Ferdydurke* is almost finished. Negotiations concerning the French and
Spanish edition of the *Diary*. *Ivona* is supposed to be staged in Cracow
and Warsaw. Correspondence in the matter of staging *The Marriage*. An
avalanche of articles and commentary in the Polish press. Ha, it's finally
gotten off the ground, now they will fuel one another—the process of
my growing is assured for many years to come! Gloria! Gloria!
Sh . . . ! Sh . . . !
    Tandil!

## Friday

I ate a very nice breakfast. . . . "You will be bored to death in
Tandil. . . ." Out of despair I went to Filefotto's lecture on Beethoven's
symphonies. Filefotto, potato nose on a face like a bun, with a smile of
indulgent irony, says: —There are those who think that the master's
deafness provoked his talent. Nonsense, ladies and gentlemen, how
absurd! Deafness does not cause talent. His talent was a result of the
French Revolution, it opened Beethoven's eyes to social inequality!

I see Beethoven in the little puff-pastry hands of Filefotto; I see how, using Beethoven like a baton, he shatters Inequality. Ah, Beethoven in the hands of Filefotto!

At the same time, in the deeper strata of my being there is something like contentment, like a liberating joy at the thought that an inferior can use a superior.

# Saturday

Yesterday, while I was writing, the door opened and in walked Ada, short, small, teeny-tiny—shriveled to microscopic proportions by her pale fear. She had just had an operation. She can barely stand on her feet. In Buenos Aires I tried to talk her into coming here for a "nachkur" as soon as she was able to move. So here she is. Henry, her husband, will appear in a few days, and until then Ada will wallow in anxiety. "Whatever made me come here? What am I doing here?!" We went for coffee to a café. "God, what a café!" "Ada, get ahold of yourself. . . ." "I can't get ahold of myself. Why am I here?" "It would be nice if you could get ahold of yourself. . . ." "I can't get ahold of myself because I'm not all here yet. What kind of coffee is this supposed to be?" "Why, it's the same kind of coffee as everywhere else. . . ." "What do you mean, the same. . . ." "What kind of horse is that supposed to be?" "A horse like every other, quite ordinary, as you can see." "This horse is not ordinary *because I have not started living here yet!*"

# Wednesday

I didn't know what to do. I remembered that N.N., the owner of the bazaar, had invited me for supper, and I went . . . to try my luck, maybe it'll work out. . . . But at the sight of me a call to arms was sounded, the guards were doubled, the cannon were wheeled out.

I had the impression that I was attacking a bulwark. The man of the house was behind a breastwork of congeniality. The lady of the house and her aunt, Raquel, an old woman, manning the earthworks of holy Catholic principles, were ready to fire in the event that I blurted out some heresy (one never knows with these intellectuals!). The daughter, decked in an armor of token smiles, offered a salad. The son, an engineer, in a soft shirt, plump, neat, little moustache, ring, watch, comfort-loving—a masterpiece of self-sufficiency.

# Friday

Yes . . . The bourgeoisie is distrustful. And the proletariat? I don't understand it! I can't understand it! Ah, for at least a half hour I tried to "understand" the worker, standing on one corner, staring at the one opposite. How and what does he think about? What sort of thoughts does he have, how do they form themselves? It can't be done. There is some accursed gap — some sort of hole in him, through which I cannot pass. Why can I understand children, young working-class people so well, without difficulty — but an adult peasant or worker is locked in by a strange emptiness, awful vacuum? . . .

# Sunday

Look at them, *en familias,* circling the square on their Sunday walk. They're going in circles! It is impossible to believe they walk in circles. This reminds one of the elementary movement of planets and goes back a million years into primal existence. Until space itself seems to bend, Einstein-style, for even while moving forward they are constantly returning. The disarray of this procession! Upstanding, calm, bourgeois faces sparkling with Italian and Spanish eyes, teeth peering out from friendly lips — and this is how that decent petite bourgeoisie promenades with its wives and children.

Soldiers!

A column vibrating with the rhythmic stomping of jackboots marches in from Rodriguez Street. It intrudes onto the square, like a blow. Cataclysm. The promenade is interrupted, everyone runs to admire the soldiers! It is as if the square suddenly came to life . . . but what a disgrace! Ha, ha, ha, allow me to laugh — ha, ha, ha, ha! An invasion of pinioned legs, and bodies, inserted into uniforms, slave bodies, welded together by the command to move. Ha, ha, ha, ha, gentlemen humanists, democrats, socialists! Why, the entire social order, all systems, authority, law, state and government, institutions, everything is based on these slaves, barely grown children, taken by the ear, forced to pledge blind obedience (O priceless hypocrisy of this mandatory-voluntary pledge) and trained to kill and to allow themselves to be killed. The general gives orders to the major. The major gives orders to the lieutenant. After which the hard palms of the pledged and trained field hands grab rifles and begin to fire away.

But all systems, socialist or capitalist, are founded on enslavement, and, to top it off, on the enslavement of the young, my dear gentlemen rationalists, humanists, ha, ha, ha, my dear gentleman democrats!

# Tuesday

Much of what happens to me in Tandil is indistinct . . . dark . . . like that encounter with Ricardon. I met him in a café, a quiet, middle-aged man. He said: —Gombrowicz? Ah, I don't know your books, but I have read about you. Mallea (an Argentinean writer) mentioned you in *Leoplan* (a weekly).

—Yes, that's true. But that was fifteen years ago.

—Yes, about fifteen or so.

—But it was just one sentence—as far as I can remember—he mentioned me only in one sentence. . . .

—Yes, exactly, one sentence. Your name fixed itself in my memory.

—But it is impossible, that you should remember such an insignificant remark after fifteen years especially since it concerns an author you have never read!

—N-n-n-o, why not? It just fixed itself in my . . .

??????? Darkness. A wall. I understand nothing. I ask no more because I know that I will learn nothing. I grow faint. . . .

# Wednesday

Much of what happens to me in Tandil is so . . . inexplicable, as if the person I was talking to and I were just missing each other. The vapor of what is left unsaid rises between them and me. The riddles are multiplying. I am a hundred times more of a foreigner and I carry my foreignness within me. The mistakes are multiplying. My contacts with them are cautious and trite. I have lost my agility—I know that I am clumsy—and I almost conceal myself. They also hide themselves behind themselves.

The curtain, the smoke is thickening. . . . Timidity is growing. . . . A double darkness, made of my and their shame, is rising. Shame because when they find out that I am a writer, they shrink back into their shells like snails. Shame—I am ashamed, because I am alone against thousands.

Half-light, curtain, darkness, smoke, timidity—as in a church, as before the altar of a growing mystery . . .

# Thursday

Our greatest holiness is contained in our most ordinary common-ness. The only time I am not ashamed of this word is when I use it in regard to something trivial, something that is its opposite.

# Friday

I am not the first to seek the Divine in what I cannot bear . . . because I cannot bear it. . . .

On one of the hills, at one end of avenida Espania, rises an enormous cross, which dominates the city—and because of this becomes a kind of liturgy grown lazy, loitering in jeering, shameless Mediocrity, content with itself and laughing with its hand over its mouth . . . something like parody and trash . . . a lower, giggling mystery play—but not less holy (in its own way) than its higher version.

# Saturday

The slender trunks of the eucalyptus forest growing out of a hillside plowed up by boulders are stonelike—the mountain, forest, leaves, everything is ossified, and a solemn stony silence visits this slender and clean, dry, and translucent immobility, brightened by pools of sun. Cortes and I walk along the path. Groups sculpted in marble present the story of Golgotha, the entire hillside is devoted to Golgotha and is called Calvario. Christ falling under the weight of the cross—Christ flogged—Christ and Veronica . . . the whole grove is full of that tormented body. On the forehead of one of the Christs is written—in the hand of one of Cortes's disciples: *Viva Marx!* Cortes, of course, is not concerned with the figures of Christ's Passion—he is a materialist—and he lectures to me zealously on a different holiness, namely, that of the Communists' war with the world for the world, that man has no choice but to conquer the world and "humanize" it . . . if he does not want to remain its comic and repulsive clown, its repugnant tumor forever. . . . Yes, he says, I agree with you, man is antinature, he has his own separate nature; he is, by his very nature, in the opposition; furthermore, we cannot avoid a showdown with the world; either we will introduce our own human order, or we will become the pathology and absurdity of being for all eternity. Even if this battle is hopeless, it alone is capable of realizing our humanity together with its dignity and beauty—the rest can lead only to humiliation. . . . This credo soars and reaches the peak where the enormous Christ on the cross presides; I, from here, from below, see through the tapering eucalyptus the arms and legs nailed to wood; I note in passing that this God and this atheist are saying exactly the same thing. . . .

We are practically at the cross. I steal a glance at the body tormented by its liver, like Prometheus (this is what torture on the cross consists of, agonizing pains to the liver). Reluctantly I recall the complete rigidity of the crucifix wood, which is *incapable* of yielding to the writhing flesh for even a millimeter and *cannot be* horrified at the suffering, even if it exceeds all limits and becomes something *impossible*— this little game between the absolute indifference of the torturing wood and the limitless pressure of the body, this mutual, eternal missing of the wood and the body, shows me, almost in a flash, the wretchedness of our predicament—the world breaks into the body and the cross. In the meantime, next to me, the atheistic apostle, Cortes, does not cease voicing the necessity of a different struggle for salvation. "The Proletariat!" I look askance at Cortes's body, thin, meager, nervous, bespectacled, hideous and bleary-eyed, undoubtedly with an aching liver, tormented by ugliness, so painful, so awfully repulsive—and I see that he, too, is crucified.

I am caught as if in the crossfire between two agonies, one of which is divine, the other godless. But both shout: struggle with the world, rescue it—then man again takes on *everything,* unable to find himself a place, rebellious, and the cosmic, all-embracing, universal Idea explodes with force. . . . Before me, below, the city, from which one can hear car horns and the sound of immediate life, limited and shortsighted. Ah, to escape from this high place down to that one below! I lack oxygen here at the top between Cortes and the cross. This is tragic, that Cortes has brought me here to repeat with other, godless lips the same absolute, extreme, universal religion, this mathematics of Universal Justice, Universal Purity!

Suddenly I notice that someone has written on Christ's left leg: "Delia y Quique, verano 1957."

The eruption of this scribble in . . . no, let us say rather the intrusion of these fresh, ordinary, and untired bodies . . . this breeze, this wave of a human life that was relatively content . . . this breath of a miraculously holy naïveté in existence . . . Darkness. Mist. Veil. Smoke. What religion is this?

# Sunday

What religion is this whose incense assailed me through Delia and Quique, when I found myself on Golgotha, between Christ and Cortes?

I said to Cortes: —Why do you, atheists, deify ideas? Why don't you deify people?

The divinity of the general is obvious. Isn't his finger basically the same as the finger of the most miserable of soldiers? Yet one crook of the general's finger sends tens of thousands of people to their deaths— they will go and die without even asking about the meaning of the sacrifice. What more valuable thing than one's own life can man offer the Highest God? If a man dies at the command of another man, this means that one man can be God to another man. He who is ready to stop living at the command of his leader—why should he recoil from falling to his knees before him!

And the divinity of the Chairman? And the divinity of Directors or Professors? And the divinity of a Landowner or Artist? Service—slavery—a humble submission—the losing of oneself in another man—succumbing entirely to the Higher—this penetrates human kind to the viscera. Ha, you atheists-democrats would like to have people lined up evenly, like rows of vegetables, and subjugated to the Idea. But this horizontal image of humanity is disturbed by another, vertical image . . . and these two images mutually destroy themselves, they do not *submit* to a common law, there is no one theory for them. Is this reason, though, to exclude from consciousness the vertical image of humanity and to be content with just the horizontal? I really don't understand you, atheists. You are not sensible. . . . Why do you close your eyes to this sacrament, if it takes place perfectly without God, and even the absence of God is its *conditio sine qua non?* I, of course, do not see why modern metaphysical anxiety could not express itself in the adoration of man, if God is lacking.

In order for this to happen, all you would have to do is turn your attention to a certain property of mankind, its unceasing need for form. It is like a wave, made up of a million tiny particles, which takes on a specific form every minute. Why, even in a small group of freely conversing people, you will notice their need to attune themselves to this or that form, which creates itself accidentally and independently of their will by dint only of their mutual adjustment to one another . . . it is as if all together they assigned to each person his place, his "voice" in the orchestra. "People" are something that must organize itself every minute—nevertheless, this organization, this collective shape, creates itself as the by-product of a thousand impulses and is, in addition, unforeseen and does not allow itself to be ruled by those who make it up. We are like tones from which a melody issues—like words forming themselves into sentences—but we are not in control of what we express, this expression of ours strikes us like a thunderbolt, like a creative force, it arises from us unrefined. Wherever form arises, however, there will also be Superiority and Inferiority—and that is why among people the process of elevating one person at the cost of others takes place—and the thrust upward, even if it elevates just one person, even if it is the most absurd and unjust, will be an absolute condition of form; it will also mean the creation of a higher sphere within humanity, dividing it into levels; from the bosom of the common people will come a more noble kingdom, which, for the inferior, will be both a horrible burden and a magnificent elevation. Why do you refuse to honor the accidental world of—if not gods, then demigods—that issues from us? Who forbids you to see in this a Deity arising from the people themselves, not descending from the heavens? Doesn't this phenomenon possess divine attributes, which are a result of interhuman power, that is, superior and creative, in relation to each of us separately? Don't you see that here Superiority is created in a way that is not controllable? Why has your reason, atheists, surrendered itself with such passion to abstractions, theories, ideas, justifications, without having noticed that here, right under its very nose, concretely, humanity reels off Gods and new revelations like a firework? Would this seem unjust, immoral, to you—perhaps unjustified spiritually? But you forget that if your spirit were able to conceive it, it would not be a Superior force or even a Creative force.

If only in the end I, I personally, could have ditched, eluded, the Idea—to live permanently in this other church made of people. If I could have forced myself to acknowledge this deity—and not concern myself anymore with absolutes and just feel above me, not high, barely a yard above my head, the play of creative forces, born of us as the only attainable Olympus—and to worship this. *The Marriage* contains this liturgy and I was not joking when I wrote in the introduction: here the human spirit adores the interhuman spirit. Still, I have never been capable of prostrating myself—and between the interhuman God and me grotesqueness was always born instead of prayer. . . . Too bad! —I say this sincerely. —Too bad! For only He—this demigod born of people, "superior" to me but only by an inch, something like a first initiation, such an imperfect God in a word, in proportion to my limitations—could extricate me from this accursed universalism which I cannot handle and restore a salutary concreteness. Ah, to find one's limits! To limit oneself! To have a limited God!

I write this bitterly . . . because I do not believe that this leap into limitation will ever happen to me. The cosmos will continue to devour me. Therefore, I am writing this not altogether seriously, pooh, as rhetoric . . . but I feel the presence of human natures different from my own around me, I feel this otherness surrounding me, containing solutions inaccessible to me . . . therefore, I leave all this to that otherness to do with it what it wants.

# Tuesday

I saw him again! Him! That boor! I saw him while having a nice little breakfast in the café suspended over the gardens. O holy proletariat! He (a fruit vendor who came in a wagon) was mostly dumpy and butt-heavy—but he was also stubby-fingered and chubby-cheeked and a stocky, ruddy, greedy gut straight from a good snooze in his bedclothes with a hot chick and right from the outhouse. I say "right from the outhouse" because his butt was stronger than his mug; he was all butt. The whole was characterized by an incredible striving for boorishness, his liking and relishing of it, stubborn persistence in it, diligent and active transformation of the whole world into boorishness. Plus, the guy was in love with himself!

What was I to do with him? I drank coffee with Bianchotti, to whom I said nothing. . . . What was I to do? If only inferiority were always young! Young! Youth is its salvation, its natural and sanctifying ingredient . . . no, beguiling inferiority is not a problem for me . . . but to find myself eye to eye with, not a boy but a peasant—and to have to bear him in his double ugliness of an aging boor.

Double? Quadruple ugliness—because I, who look at him with all of my bourgeois refinements, complete his repulsiveness, I match it, like a negative; we are two monkeys, one coming out of the other. . . . Two aging monkeys. Brrr . . . Do you know what the worst meeting of all is? To meet a lion in a desert? A tiger in a forest? A ghost? The devil himself? What an idyll! It is worse, a hundred times worse, when a pale intellectual comes upon a heavyset boor in the absence of any youth! This meeting will take place in mutual adult-human revulsion, which you would never experience with a lion that devoured you; it will be bathed in physical decay; and that you must bear this man, together with yourself, in this *abschmack,* in the sauce of this idiosyncracy, in the curse of this caricature!

This adult boor torments and exhausts me. . . . I cannot get away from him! That walking abomination!

# Thursday

Hitler, Hitler, Hitler . . . What rock did he crawl out from under? In the flurry of my life, in the chaos of events, I have long since noticed a certain logic in the accumulation of plots. If a certain thought becomes dominating, facts strengthening it from the outside begin to multiply, it then looks as if external reality were beginning to cooperate with the internal one. Not long ago I noted here that I was called—by mistake of course—a fascist! Now, when I accidentally entered an unfamiliar part of Tandil, the *barrio* Rivadavia, chalk graffiti smeared on the walls, scribbled on boulders, caught my eye:

"LOOR Y GLORIA A LOS MARTIRES DE NURENBERG" (Glory to the martyrs of Nuremberg).

A Nazi in Tandil? And such a fanatical one? After so many years? This fanaticism, where does it come from?—in Tandil—why here? . . . This again will be one of those Tandil blind spots, stupors, most certainly some absurdity . . . which I will not even attempt to unravel . . . but (keeping in mind the "fascism" already offered me) it looked as if this drunkard were drinking a toast to me. . . . An allusion? I have known for a long time that many are the allusions to me and many have drunk my health. . . .

Moreover, this Hitler pounces on me, because a boor disgusted me, because I am vomiting up the boor having been vomited up by him.

# Friday

Hitler was pounded into dirt and dust, and to top it off (in fear of his resurrection) he has been characterized *post mortem* as a diabolical mediocrity, a raucous hell-born sergeant-megalomaniac. You have soiled his legend. You did this out of fear. But fear is also a form of homage. I would advocate not being afraid of Hitler *post mortem*—he rose on someone else's fear, oh, that he not rise, again, on yours.

What strikes one about this hero (and why shouldn't I call him a hero?) is his incredible boldness in reaching an extreme, the ultimate, the maximum. He believed that the man who is less afraid wins—that the secret of power is to go one step farther, that one single step farther that others are incapable of taking—that he who terrifies with his audacity is impossible to withstand and is therefore devastating—and he applied this principle as much to people as he did to nations. His tactics were as follows: go one step farther in cruelty, cynicism, deception, cunning, boldness, go that one mad step jolting you out of the normal, that one unbelievable, impossible, completely unacceptable step . . . to stand your ground when others, horrified, call: I pass! That is why he thrust the German people and Europe into cruelty—he desired the cruelest life as the ultimate gauge of the capacity to live.

He would not be a hero if he were not a coward. His supreme violence was that perpetrated upon himself when transforming himself into Might—thereby making weakness in himself impossible—cutting off his own retreat. His supreme resignation was his resignation from the other possibilities of existence. An interesting problem: how did he pop up as the god of the German people? One should assume that he at first "bound himself" to only a few Germans—"bound himself," that is, proposed himself as a leader—and this was achieved by personal distinction, for on this scale, in the company of a few people, personal qualities still have some value. And in this first phase, when the bond was still fairly loose, Hitler must have had to endlessly repeat his arguments; convince, persuade, bandy his idea—for he was dealing with people who were subordinating themselves to him voluntarily. But all of this was still very human and very ordinary; there always existed, for Hitler and his subordinates, the opportunity to back out, each of them could break away, choose something else, bind themselves to others in a different way. Imperceptibly, however, there came into play the action of a practically unnoticeable actor, namely, the number, the growing number of people. As the number grew, the group entered another dimension, almost inaccessible to one man. Too heavy, too massive, it began to live its own life. It is possible that each member trusted the leader only a little; however, that little bit multiplied by increasing numbers became a dangerous blast of faith. And lo and behold, there came a moment when each of them felt, rather uneasily, that he no longer knew what the others would do to him (the others of whom there were so many, whom he did not know) if it occurred to him to say "I pass" and to take to his heels. The minute he realized this, the doors slammed shut. . . .

This, however, was not enough for Hitler. He, fortified by this mass of people, had already grown—but he was not sure in the least about his people or himself. There was no guarantee that his private nature, his ordinary humanity, might not suddenly stir in him—he had not yet completely lost control of his own fate and he could still say "no" to his own greatness. Here then arose the necessity of transferring everything to a sphere higher and no longer accessible to the individual being. In order to do that, Hitler had to act not with his own energy, but with that which the mass supplied him — that is, a power that surpassed his own. That is what happened. With the help of his subordinates and followers and by exploiting the tensions that arose between him and them, by extracting the maximum audacity from them in order to become even more audacious himself and to arouse them to even greater audacity, Hitler drives the whole group to the boiling point, and makes it more fearsome as a group, together exceeding individual capacity. Each, not excluding the leader, is aghast. The group enters an abnormal state. The people who make up the group lose control of themselves. Now no one can back out because they are no longer in a "human" but rather in an "interhuman," or "suprahuman," realm.

Let us note that this is all very similar to theater . . . to playacting. . . . Hitler pretended to be bolder than he was so that others would be forced to join in the game — but the game elicited the reality and created facts. The masses of people, obviously, do not grasp this mystification; they judge Hitler according to his deeds — and lo, a nation of millions of people recoils in fear before the decimating will of the leader. The leader becomes great. Strange, this greatness. This is a magnification to incredible dimensions, infinitely astounding — because the word, deed, smile, anger, exceed the reach of a normal man, resounding like thunder, trampling other existences, the same, after all, basically no less important. . . . But the strangest characteristic of this magnification is that it creates itself from the outside — to Hitler, everything grows in his hands, but he himself is the same as he was, ordinary, with all of his weaknesses; this is a dwarf who reveals himself to be Goliath; this is a common man who is God from the outside; this is the soft human palm striking like a club. And Hitler is now in the claws of that Great Hitler, not because he has not retained his usual, private feelings or thoughts, his private reason, but because they are too small and too weak and can do nothing against the Giant that penetrates him from the outside.

Let us notice, too, that at the moment the process reaches the suprahuman stage, the idea is no longer needed. It is indispensable at the beginning, when one has to convince, unify supporters to themselves — now it is almost superfluous because man, as such, does not have much to say in this new, suprahuman, dimension. People begin to pile up. Pressures are created. A shape arises having its own reason and logic. The idea exists merely for the sake of appearances; it is the facade behind which the possession of man by man takes place, creating itself first, and only later asking about its meaning.

## Saturday

Farewell, Tandil! I am leaving. My suitcase is packed.

I pour my crisis regarding democratic thinking and universal feeling onto paper because not I alone—know this—not I alone, if not today, then in ten years, will be assailed by the desire to have a clearly delineated world and a clearly delineated God. Prophecy: democracy, universality, equality, will not be capable of satisfying you. Your desire for duality will grow stronger and stronger—a desire for a dual world—dual thinking—dual mythology—in the future we will be paying homage to two different systems simultaneously and a magic world will find a place for itself next to a rational one.

# VIII

## Sunday

Sick.
Blah.
I am si—
I don't feel like . . .

## Monday

I throw myself onto the bed—I rest—usually with Andrzej Bob-kowski's *Pen Sketches*. Two thick volumes. A diary. Subtitle: "France 1940–44."

I am a passionate reader of diaries, the cavern of someone else's life draws me in, even if it is embroidered or fabricated—but this way or that, it is a broth made of the taste of reality and I like knowing, for example, that on 3 May 1942 Bobkowski was teaching his wife to ride a bike in the Vincennes forest. And I? What was I doing on that day? You will see, or you probably will not see: that in two hundred or a thousand years a new science will arise that determines the connections between various people in time and then it will be plain that what happens to one is not without connection to what has happened to some-one else. . . . And this synchronization of existences will open new perspectives, but enough. . . . Bobkowski's notes concern two of my interests, France and Poland—this is the main reason that I study them. They are written with fervor and passion, although I assume this didn't happen without a little touching up *ex post*. The heat of this criticism results in criticism that immediately arouses criticism of the initial crit-icism . . . , etc.—(the meaning of this statement will become a little clearer in a moment).

Homelands . . . How is one to get at them? This is almost a for-bidden subject. When a man writes about his homeland, his style gets twisted. How does one write about Poland, for example, without falling into that classic "because we are Poles," without making a European of

oneself, without making a face, without denigrating oneself, without
making oneself superior—without claptrap, attacks, without biting,
kicking, or roughing up . . . how does one thrust fingers into one's own
wounds without contorting one's face with pain? How does one tickle
this Achilles' heel without making a clown of oneself? I discover in
Bobkowski's book that in the years 1940–44, the same feelings were
hatching in him that crawled all over me when the outline of *Trans-
Atlantic* was ripening—he also grumbles, rebels, blasphemes. . . . But
in me, perhaps because of the greater geographic distance, or perhaps
as a result of the greater spiritual distance (an artistic work is one thing,
a diary another), this anti-Polish process was frozen, I always wrote
about Poland cold, as one of the obstacles making life difficult for me.
For me, Poland was and is only one of my many troubles; I did not
forget even for a moment about the secondary importance of this topic.
In his diary, Bobkowski, who is younger, is less cold than I am—he
pushes Poland away from himself, but in pushing it away, he cuts his
hands until they bleed. I want to liberate myself!—he shouts—I will
not immolate myself on this altar, I want to live at my own expense
. . . but it is exactly this passionate cry that shows that his umbilical
cord has not been severed—its negation would express itself better in
a quiet, even ordinary voice, one of those indifferent voices that remove
the theme from central importance. The "sketches" would have been
stronger stylistically if Bobkowski's open struggle with the myth of
Poland had been deleted from them.

The confusion in our heads regarding this "universalism," which has
become fashionable for us, is extraordinary. Let us take Mr. Kisiel, for
example. For many of us universalism is equal to not writing about
Poland and practically not writing in Polish. For example, Mr. Michał
K. Pawlikowski. In his review of Józef Mackiewicz's *Contra,* we read:

*"I would not hesitate to call Mr. Mackiewicz the most 'un-Polish' of all
Polish writers. Indeed, the setting and climate of* Road to Nowhere *are a
corner of former Lithuania and—if one does not count the language—so-
called Polishness is not the 'tuning fork' of the novel. The plot of* The
Careerist *would be possible in any country. Finally,* Contra *is a work
whose author a foreign reader would not conclude was Polish."*

After which Mr. Pawlikowski decrees that I am a "very Polish"
writer, and Mackiewicz, because of the above-mentioned traits, is
"universal."

But why, Mr. Pawlikowski? What does the universal humanity of
an author have to do with his subject?

Mackiewicz is—of course—an artist of the Polish borderlands
. . . but this—it is obvious—in no way interferes with his "universal
humanity." Because one has nothing to do with the other.

The most universal French or Italian writers were simultaneously
the most French or Italian writers—because art is (as we have known
long and well) the elevation of a private, particular, local, even paro-
chial concreteness to the heights of the universal . . . to cosmic
proportions . . .

The most worldly of Chopin's melodies are the most Polish melodies—for art is (it is almost ridiculous to have to lecture on this) a
demonstration of the typical, universal, and eternal element in that
which is concrete, individual, and ephemeral.

And it is really ridiculous that Jacek Bocheński blusters (like Kisiel)
that in *Trans-Atlantic* I have "an unhealthy romance and mad obession"
with my Polish heritage. With what am I supposed to have it? My
Chinese heritage?

Let us return, however, to Bobkowski. One could say several things
about how in his diary he is working on a new style for the Liberated
Pole . . . and not without an exhausting pushing and shoving . . . for
Bobkowski, a lively intelligence and talent, sees with horror how, after
crawling out of Poland on his hands and knees, he falls into a new
stereotype, this time an antinational one . . . and he must now find some
sort of antidote for this convention of Polishness *à rebours* . . . and that
this new form again demands to be corrected. In a work of art perhaps
this would be shocking. But in a diary? Here we want to have an author
in person and an author at the boiling point, still imperfect. And let us
look at the date. Who in those years 1940—44 was not at the boiling
point?

But it is not Poland that is the most interesting in Bobkowski's
diary, but France.

France, which in the course of centuries became an international
complex. This begs for psychoanalysis. France turns people into idiots—entire nations are enchanted by France—by mythic France and a
fairy-tale Paris! Everywhere in America I come across this stupefied:
Ah, Paris, ah, Paris! But this altar stands in our backyard too, and
prayers, curtsies, capers, leaps, contortions, also take place back there—
although I will bypass that delightful second-hand Frenchness, that absolutely indefatigable imitation, practiced by all those Messrs. Sakowski, that endless bowing to the myth. No, not only former members
of the Ministry of Foreign Affairs are so culturally disoriented, the
devotion penetrates all the way through the upper social classes, and
Bobkowski, a Polish intellectual living in Paris, was unable to avoid its

spell. But the "historical" weight of his confessions consists of the appearance here of the will to destroy the myth—and just as it attacks Poland, it now throws itself with fury onto France, and the young and stormy arm strikes at its own dream. Here our conversation with France begins from a different position and although the author has not yet discovered his complete sovereignty, the tone becomes infinitely sharper and more to the point, the accent difficult to define, betraying that the romance is over once and for all and that only a settling of accounts remains. The tone and accent are all the more valuable to me in that they are contained in notes concerning everyday and ordinary events.

# Sunday

After returning to Tandil, I found the novel *Conspiracy* sent to me from Poland by the author, Mr. Stefan Kisielewski ("Kisiel") with the conciliatory dedication:

*"To W.G., the 'fellow' who pretended he didn't understand my article about him, his constant critical-enthusiastic reader—Kisiel, Cracow. 18.XII.57."*

I replied:

*"Dear Sir,*

*"Please forgive me for not thanking you sooner for the copy of* Conspiracy *with your dedication, but I have been away from Buenos Aires for about six months.*

*"Great—the dedication is nice—but why do you write such idiotic things about me in the paper? I say 'idiotic' not to offend you, but because you are being beneath yourself when you do so. Your first piece contained nonsense, which I could understand only by ascribing to you a lack of knowledge about the material—that you had forgotten* Ferdydurke *and knew the* Diary *from some fragment or other in* Kultura. *The second article shows more reading, yet you still stand by your thesis, so simplistically childish and incompatible with my person, category, reality.*

*"You think that I can be avant-garde and anachronistic, intelligent and stupid, innovative and conventional—that I can write penetrating books and then surrender myself to such lousy banalities as those you attribute to me? No, this doesn't happen. You conceived of my settling accounts with Polishness shallowly, as if the newspaper were speaking and*

*not art. You did not understand its genesis or its ties with the overall form
of my art and my worldview.*

*"This doesn't hurt me—it even suits me, because the more you reduce
me, the more fiercely will I explode, and the polemic with you will be a
polemic with the shallows and the shoals of contemporary Polish thought
(in its Catholic variety). But I am amazed that you appear in this role as
coryphaeus. This is not for you. You are worthy of a better fate. I write
this in all good will, because I assume that 'personally' we are not enemies.
Please do not be angry with this letter. . . ."*

# Friday

Tyrmand!* Talent! This is like a barefoot Warsaw wench in the eyes
of a teenager, like a fat Warsaw cook in the eyes of a student, like a
drunken wh—— in the eyes of a street urchin! Dirt and tawdriness but
desired and bewitching nevertheless! What sex appeal** this saga has,
300 percent Varsovian, the same that once lurked in the doorways of
the houses on Hoża or Żelazna—except that then it merely lurked, now
it explodes!

A criminal novel, a cheap romance? Why yes, and even worse: a
romance from a back alley, full of ramshackle buildings and gutters. Yet
this gleams, spurts, sounds, sings. . . . A romantic moon rises above
the ruins of the city and brawls reach me from dens, caverns, alleys—
again!—how poetic. Tyrmand is the most perfect continuation of our
romantic poetry, he inherited its panache, he continues its writing but
in keeping with the new—proletarian—history. This is writing at the
level of a street ruffian, pimp, racketeer, etc., but the spirit is the same.
Not to mention . . . the body. That sinful Polish carcass with all of its
little blemishes!

A story, of course, that is lies from A to Z—for the pleasure of the
reader and the author alike. Yet how real and Polish is this lying in the
area of the imagination, sentiment, and temperament. Do you know
what this book is? Vodka, pure and simple. The same vodka that somehow allowed the Poles to bear life before the war, except that then they
drank it out of shot glasses while today they are drinking it straight out
of the bottle. Out of it comes that murky "fantasy" without which the
excess of flops and down-and-outs would be impossible to swallow.

---

*Leopold Tyrmand, Polish émigré writer who lived and died in the United States.
**"Sex appeal" in English in original.

Flipping through Tyrmand's pages is like walking the prewar streets of Krucza or Hoża, maybe even Żelażna, on the trail of our pummeled history. Even then I knew Tyrmand was inevitable! That some sort of moon must rise romantically and explode! Yes, exactly! Exactly this kind of hooligan, ramshackle, beaten up, drunken and bashed-in mooniness. I remember a passage from X's letter that I received not long ago (from the States): "My God, this Poland is the grim dream of a madman! That obscurity, suffocation, uncertainty and boredom. . . ." And further: "This new *Pol'sza*\* makes me laugh because, God is my witness, the Saxon\*\* period has stayed with us the longest and has left the deepest imprint. The nation is ignorant, national democratic, truculent, boorish, lazy, belligerent and half-baked, sanctimonious and 'infantile,' and a Kremlin communism has been attached to this mess. Only now how the dust must fly from those besotted heads!"

# Sunday

I do not have much to say on the subject of the victory of Artur Frondizi, who became the president of Argentina; on the other hand, I wish to note that elections do not cease to amaze me. The day on which the vote of the illiterate means as much as the vote of the professor, the vote of the idiot as much as the vote of the wise man, the vote of the lackey as much as the vote of the potentate, the vote of the cutthroat as much as the vote of a virtuous man is for me the most confused of days. I do not understand how this fantastic act can determine, for the next few years, something as important as the government of the country. On what sort of fairy tale does authority base itself? How can this five-adjective fallacy constitute the basis of social being?

# Monday

I visited M. in the hospital—he has been dying for many months, more and more in fact but, so his doctors say, he will go on dying for a few more weeks. He lay immobile, head on a pillow, eaten by death

---

\*Russian for "Poland," used pejoratively.
\*\*Period when kings from Saxony ruled Poland; judged as the time of greatest decay of state and culture.

piece by piece, each day a little more dead. Was he suffering? Very much?

In the room there were also a few living—I would say, assistants, because they were assisting death . . . with their hapless looks, separated from this martyr by the conviction that there is no help and they must wait until he bites the dust. "Man lives alone and dies alone"— Pascal. Not entirely. Men live in a herd and help each other, only when death strikes does a man see he is alone . . . utterly alone . . . like those expiring animals from which the herd moves away on a winter's night. Why is human death still like the death of an animal? Why are our agonies so isolated and primitive? Why have you been unable to civilize death?

To think that this horrifying thing, this agony, prowls among us as wild as it was in the first days of creation. Nothing has been accomplished in the course of these thousand years, this wild taboo has not been touched! We cultivate television and use electric blankets, but we die wild. A timid injection by a doctor may shorten suffering on the sly with increased doses of morphine. A shameful measure, too small for the enormous universality of dying. I demand Houses of Death where each person would have at his disposal modern means to an easy death. Where one could die easily, not by throwing oneself under a train or by hanging oneself from a hook. Where a weary, destroyed man could surrender to the friendly arms of the specialist, so that he could be assured a death without torture or disgrace.

Why not—I ask—why not? Who prevents you from civilizing death? Religions? Ah, this religion . . . today forbidding suicide, yesterday no less vociferously forbidding anesthesia . . . the day before yesterday allowing barter in slaves, persecuting Copernicus and Galileo . . . this Church thundering condemnation, and then retreating discreetly, quietly . . . what sort of guarantee do you have that in a few decades today's condemnation of suicide will not flag and come to nothing? Until that day we are supposed to die like dogs heaving and shuddering—we are supposed to wait patiently, strewing this slow path with millions of agonizing deaths described in obituaries as "after prolonged and agonizing suffering. . . ." But, no, the bill for these "interpretations" of the holy texts is already too high and too bloody and it is better for the Church to give up scholasticism, which intrudes too arbitrarily into life. If believing Catholics want to die in agony—that's their business. But why don't you, atheists, or people only loosely tied to the Church, have the audacity for something as simple as organizing your death? What inhibits you? You have done what you needed to do to move us easily from place to place when changing apartments; but when it comes to moving to the other world, you want it to happen the old way, you want the ancient method of dying.

What muddled clumsiness! And to think that each of you knows exactly: not a single person close to you will escape dying, unless, of course, that person has the extraordinary luck to have a sudden and unexpected death; each will be gradually destroyed until his face becomes unrecognizable—and, knowing this, knowing this inevitable fate, you will not lift a finger to save yourselves the torment. What are you afraid of? That too many people will escape if you crack the gate a bit? Allow those to die who choose death. Do not force anyone to live with the discomfort of dying—this is too vile!

The blackmail contained in artificially impeding death is a dirty trick, an impingement on the most valuable human freedom. For my greatest freedom is contained in my capacity to pose Hamlet's "to be or not to be?" and to answer it freely. The life to which I have been sentenced can trample and disgrace me with the cruelty of a wild beast, but there is in me one splendid and sovereign arrangement—that I can take my own life. If I choose, I do not have to live. I did not ask to be brought into the world, but at least my right to leave remains . . . and this is the basis of my freedom. And also of my dignity (because to live in dignity means to live voluntarily). But the fundamental human right to death, which ought to be included in the constitution, has succumbed to a gradual and imperceptible confiscation—you have arranged things so that it would be as difficult as possible . . . and as horrifying as possible . . . so that it would be more difficult and more horrifying than things should be at our current level of technology. Not only does this express your blind affirmation of life, which is quite animal—but also your unusually thick hide when it comes to pain you yourself are not yet feeling, and agony that is not yet yours—that stupid nonchalance with which one tolerates dying as long as it is someone else's. All these different little considerations—dogmatic, nationalist, everyday-practical—all this theory, practice, spreads itself like a peacock's tail—as far as possible from death.

# Friday

My springs pulsate in a garden whose gate is guarded by an angel with a flaming sword. I cannot enter. I will never get through. I am condemned to an eternal circling of the place where my truest enchantment is sanctified.

I am not allowed in because . . . these springs bubble with shame like fountains! Yet there is the internal imperative: get as close as you can to the sources of your shame! I have to mobilize all my reason, consciousness, discipline, all the elements of form and style, all the techniques of which I am capable, in order to get closer to the mysterious gate of that garden, behind which my shame bursts into flower. What, in this case, is my maturity if not an auxiliary means, a secondary matter?

Eternally the same thing! Dress up in a splendid coat in order to step into an inn on the docks. To use wisdom, maturity, virtue, in order to get close to something that is *just the opposite!*

# Sunday

I can't stand Balzac. His work, him. Everything in him is exactly what I don't like and don't want to like. I can't stand it! He is too contradictory and somehow repulsively, stupidly contradictory! A wise man—and such a dolt! An artist—and how much bad taste from the most distasteful of epochs there is in him! A fatso—yet a conqueror, Don Juan, seedy womanizer. A distinguished man—yet such petit bourgeois vulgarity and such nouveau riche chutzpah! A realist—but also a lousy, romantic dreamer. . . . Perhaps these antinomies should not disturb me; I know their role in life, in art . . . yes, only that in Balzac even antinomy becomes obese, repulsive, seedy, fat, and worse than coarse.

I can't stand his *Human Comedy*. To think how easily the best soup gets spoiled when one adds a spoonful of old grease or a bit of toothpaste to it. One drop of bad, pretentious, melodramatic Balzac is enough to make these volumes and his entire personality unpalatable. They say that he is a genius, that one must be tolerant because of this. The women who slept with his brilliant obesity know something about this tolerance because in order to sleep with a genius, they must have had to overcome many abominations in themselves. But I am not sure if this calculation is worth it and if it is in harmony with nature. In the realm of personal relations—such are our relations with artists—sometimes the trifle has more meaning than monoliths of monumental service. It is easier to hate someone for picking his nose than to love him for composing a symphony. For the trifle is characteristic and describes the person in his everyday dimension.

# Monday

On 4 February of this year ('58), I finished *Pornografia*. This is what I have called it for the time being. I am not promising that the title will stay. I am in no hurry to publish it. Too many of my books have appeared in print lately.

One of my most persistent needs, during the writing of this quite pornographic—in some places—*Pornografia* was: to pass the world through youth; to translate it into the language of youth, that is, into the language of attraction . . . To soften it with youth . . . To spice it with youth—so it allows itself to be violated.

The intuition that dictated this to me is probably based on the conviction that a Man is helpless against the world . . . by being only power, not beauty . . . and, furthermore, in order for him to be able to possess reality, it must first be put through a being that can be attractive . . . that is, that can surrender itself . . . a lower, weaker being. Here there is a choice—woman or youth. The woman I dismiss because of the child, that is, because her function is too specific. Youth is what is left. And here one comes upon extreme formulas: maturity *for* youth, youth *for* maturity.

What is this? What have I written? Whether or not the accent I put on the Spirit of Youth and its Doings is worth anything . . . and how much will be hard to tell for a while.

# IX

## Sunday, Santiago del Estero

Yesterday, late in the evening, I finally reached Santiago after many hours of the train's clattering and rolling: first through the green lowlands of the Paraná, then across the entire province of Santa Fe, until, finally (after many, many kilometers marked by poles that sped away from the train as it stole by somewhere near that lake—so mysterious to me—of Mar Chiquita in northern Córdoba), a desert expanse overgrown with gnarled trees began that great white blot on the map that stretches over tens of thousands of square kilometers of land and that means there is not a living soul between settlements. The train speeds along. Through the windows of the train car, hermetically sealed because of the all-pervasive sand, there is nothing to look at except those miserable little trees (growing out of the sand) and the sparse grass. Night falls, and sometimes, when I put out the light on the window with my hand, those same trees flit before my eyes. How many more hours remain of this trip and through what sort of surroundings? I don't know, I fell asleep.

And finally: Santiago.

One of the oldest cities in Argentina. Founded by Francisco de Aguirre, supposedly on 23 December 1553. The beginnings of local history are mythical, distant and fantastic, even crazy, almost like a dream. At the beginning of the sixteenth century the Spanish conqueror, his head bursting with legends and blinded by the desire for gold and precious stones, tore his way into the soft Indian tribes (called the Huries, Lules Vilelas, Guaycurues, Sanavirones) living in these lands. These maniacs and rapists, criminals and heroes must have been exceptionally courageous to immerse themselves in an unknown space that did not obstruct the imagination. Fourteen soldiers, their heads muddled with tales of bejeweled cities, detached themselves from Sebastian Cabot's expedition in the Fort of Sancti Spiritus and blundered their way into the environs of Santiago for the first time, whereby they discovered the neighboring province of Tucumán, known today as the "Garden of Argentina." Diego de Rojas also searched after the mythical treasure called "the treasure of the Caesars" in 1542; and he was followed by

Francisco de Mendoza, who marched on the fairy-tale cities, which were supposed to have been called "Trapalanda," "Yungulo," and "Lefal." Afterward came Captain Nicolas de Heredia, Captain Francisco de Villagra, and about ten others. But this rather recent past is prehistory here, these are the murky beginnings that have been blurred in the confused, unsettled, or unknown geography, in the swarming of wandering tribes, in the enormous, absorbing, but indistinct expanse over which the imagination of these conquerors galloped, dark, stubborn, determined . . . and isolated from Spain by that enormous expanse of water. It was as if they were on another planet, free and accompanied only by the horse, which here became an alien and terrifying creature.

The Hotel Savoy, where I was assigned an unsightly room without a window and with doors that opened only onto the corridor—you have to leave a light on during the day. I washed up in my "private bathroom," in which the only fixtures native to a bathroom were a faucet and a shower. The evening meal, however, was quite satisfactory: a wonderful chicken in sauce and a carafe of heavy, red wine.

# Monday

I wanted to add that the day before yesterday, before I went to sleep, something happened to me, something rather indistinct. . . . I really don't know how to take this and I am shaken. . . .

After supper, which I ate in the hotel, I went out onto the square. I sat on a bench, concealed by trees and bushes, great palm fronds over my head, and I was somewhat stunned by the lightness of the apparel worn by this hot, starry night, its laughter, its naked shoulders, while I was still in the damp winter of Buenos Aires and my thick winter jacket still warmed me! Such violent change: there it was harsh and cool, while here it was sensual and, at least so it seemed, carefree and lighthearted. . . . Suddenly, it was as if I had immersed myself in the South (here it is called the "North" because it is in the southern hemisphere).

The square turned round me like a carousel, with a laughing Saturday crowd from which enormous dark eyes and raven hair stared at me . . . scintillating laughter . . . limbs light as a dancer's . . . cheerful voices, free and kind. . . . What's this? What's this? The square is alight with the teeth of distant youth . . . for I am not here, but elsewhere . . . my remoteness (because I still see the crowds on Corrientes and hear the honking of the cars) made them distant, even though they were right before me. But I had not yet arrived. I watched as if I had no right to look, as if I were spying. . . .

Silence rings in my ears. The eerie silence of a distant place—all the sounds are mute like in an old film: I hear nothing. Sound frozen at the threshold of its realization.

In this silence, the parade on the square mutely intensifies itself in a revelation of corporeal splendor, in a stunning play of eyes and lips, hands and legs. The snake stretching itself before me bursts into rainbows of beauties the likes of which I have not seen before in Argentina and, dumbfounded, I ask myself: where does this come from, here in Santiago?

At the same time I discover that *this does not exist,* the taste of its absence is overwhelming. I am felled by the sensation of its nonexistence and desperately lost in unfulfillment.

# Sunday

Beauty! You will rise where you are sown! And you will be as you were sown!

(Do not believe in the beauty of Santiago. It is a lie. I have made it up!)

# Monday

The sunlight is blinding and full of colors, as if filtered through stained glass. It seems to saturate objects with colors. Light and shadow. The aggressive blue of the sky. Trees laden with golden and enormous *pomedos,* blooming red . . . yellow. . . . People walk around without jackets.

I went to Miss Canal Feihoo's place via a street dark with shade on one side and white with light on the other. She is the sister of a writer who lives in Buenos Aires. An older person full of the kind of suspicion (I can see this right away) that mistresses of households have for restaurant meals that "are concocted who knows how" and for globetrotters who are also "concocted who knows how." But she received my request (I asked her to help put me in contact with the local literati) very kindly. *Como no!* she had said very quickly and simply. "There are a few, they even publish a magazine. I will call them immediately. . . . My brother meets with them whenever he visits."

When I returned to my room, I tried to get my impressions from the previous night under control. They were exaggerated! I had been seeing things. . . . It's true that here you see that "loveliness" so common in Argentina, there is a lot of it, maybe even more than anywhere else . . . but there is also some sort of Indian difference, a coloring that I have not seen until now . . . but should this be a revelation, no, this is no revelation. Besides, the perpetual problem of *making contact* with a new city and securing oneself company absorbed me and jarred me out of my ecstasy.

# Tuesday

In the afternoon I have a rendezvous with Santucho (one of the literary figures and the editor of *Dimension*) in the Café Ideal.

It smells of the East. Not a minute goes by without having some insistent little urchin thrust lottery tickets in your face. Then an old man with a million wrinkles does the same: he pushes tickets into your face as if he were a child. An old woman, strangely shriveled into an Indian design, enters and she too pokes tickets into your face. A child grabs you by the leg and wants to shine your shoes, and another with a beautiful Indian head of hair offers you a newspaper. A soft, hot, lithe miracle, a girl-odalisque-houri, holds a blind man by the arm and guides him between the tables. Then someone jabs you in the back: a beggar with a small-boned, triangular face. I would not be surprised if a goat, mule, or donkey pranced into this café.

There are no waiters. You have to serve yourself.

A somewhat humiliating situation developed that nonetheless I can hardly pass over in silence.

I sat with Santucho, who is heavyset and has a passionate, stubborn olive face focused on the past and rooted in the past. He droned on about the Indian essence of these parts. Who are we? We don't know. We do not know ourselves. We are not Europeans. European thought, the European spirit, are something alien that invades us, as the Spaniards once did. It is our misfortune that we have the culture of that "Western world" of yours which we have soaked up like paint, so that today we must use European thinking and a European tongue, for lack of our own Indio-American one, our lost substance. We are barren, because we have to think about ourselves in a European way! . . . I listened to this somewhat suspect line of reasoning but was really watching a *czango* (sitting two stools away from us) who was with a sweet young thing. They were drinking: he, vermouth and she, lemonade.

They sat with their backs to me and I could only guess at how they looked from certain clues, such as the arrangement and immobile play of their limbs, that difficult to describe inner freedom of nimble bodies. And I don't know why (was this some distant reflex from *Pornografia,* which I had finished writing not long ago, or a result of my excitement in this city?), it is enough to say that I had a vision of their invisible faces as beautiful, absolutely beautiful and probably elegant and artistic, like movie stars . . . suddenly something happened as if there, between the two of them, they embodied the highest intensity of local beauty, here in Santiago . . . and this seemed all the more likely because, indeed, the very outline of this pair, as I saw it from where I was sitting, was as lively as it was sumptuous.

Finally I could not stand it any longer. Excusing myself before Santucho (who was carrying on about European imperialism), I left the table on the pretext of getting a drink of water but really to stare into the face of the secret that was tormenting me. To look into their faces: I was sure the secret would reveal itself like an apparition from Mount Olympus. In its own sublime elegance! Divinely weightless like a young colt! O what disillusionment! The *czango* was poking at his teeth with a toothpick and was saying something to his girl, who was eating the nuts that went with his vermouth. There was nothing more, nothing, the scene was so barren that I almost tripped, as if my adoration had been knocked out from under me!

# Wednesday

Scads of children and dogs!

I have never seen so many and such gentle dogs! If a dog barks here, it is merely in jest.

The children are all darkly unkempt and skipping around . . . never have I seen children who are so "picture perfect" . . . and delightful! Two little boys walk in front of me with their arms around each other's necks and tell one another secrets. But *how* they do it! One of them points something out with his finger to a gawking band of children. Another solemnly sings to a stick which he has poked through a candy wrapper.

Yesterday I saw the following in the park: a four-year-old toddler challenged a little girl to a boxing match. She hadn't the slightest idea what that meant but, being taller and heavier, she gave it to him for all she was worth. A little group of two and three year olds in long shirts grabbed one another by the hands and began to jump up and down, shouting in her honor: No-na! No-na! No-na!

# Thursday

A strange repetition of the scene from the day before yesterday
with Santucho in the café, although this time with a slight variation.
The restaurant is in the Hotel Plaza. I am sitting at the table of
Dr. P.M., a Santiago lawyer, who represents the estates of wisdom
contained in his library. With us was his *barra,* or group of café cronies:
one doctor and a few business men. . . . I, armed with the best intentions, give myself up to a conversation about politics when . . . uh oh!
I am once again distracted by another little couple straight out of a fairy
tale . . . and there they are, sinking into one another, like one lake
spilling over into another! Again, *belleza!* But I must hold up my end of
the conversation at the table, I must contribute to this soup simmering
with the platitudes (spiced with hatred toward the U.S and with a panic-
stricken fear of the "temptations of imperialism") of South American
nationalists: yes, unfortunately, I must say something to this guy even
though I am watching and listening to the beauty taking place not far
from me — I, a slave, in love with death and passionate, I, an artist. . . .
And again I ask myself how can it be that such marvels sit in this
restaurant just a step away from . . . well, from this garrulous Argentina. . . . "We have always demanded morality in international relations. . . ." "Yankee and British imperialism tries to . . ." "We are no
longer a colony! . . ." "All of this is pronounced by my adversary (and
not just today); I, on the other hand, cannot understand, cannot understand, cannot understand. . . . "Why does the United States grant loans
to Europe but not to us? . . ."

"The history of Argentina shows that we valued dignity above all
else! . . ."

Oh, if only someone could yank the platitudes out of this otherwise
appealing people! This bourgeoisie, sipping wine here in the evening
and maté during the day, is so whiny! If I were to tell them that compared with other nations they live snug as bugs on their splendid *estan-
cias* as big as half of Europe, and if I were to add that not only are they
not hurting but that Argentina is the *estanciero* of nations, an "oligarch"
proudly sprawled over his splendid territories . . . I would grievously
offend them! Better not. . . . So this is exactly what I tell them to their
faces! What do I care!

There, there at the table is the Argentina that has beguiled me —
it is quiet but has the sound of great art — no, no, not this one, which
is garrulous, indolent, and overpoliticized. Why am I not sitting over
there with them? My place is over there! Next to the girl who is like

a tremulous black and white bouquet, next to the young man who looks like Rudolph Valentino! . . . *Belleza!*

But . . . what is happening! Nothing. Nothing, to the extent that even now I do not know how and what it was that reached me from them . . . maybe a word caught midway . . . an accent . . . flashing eyes. . . . Enough so that suddenly I was informed.

That whole *belleza* was just like everything else! Like the table, chair, waiter, plate, tablecloth, like our discussion, it was in no way different — it was the same — the same world, made of the same material.

## Thursday

Beauty? In Santiago? Where in the devil from?

## Thursday

What could possibly happen to you if a train takes you to a small town that is remote . . . off the beaten track . . . unknown . . . colorful?

What could possibly happen to you in a small town that put up no resistance . . . that was too congenial . . . or too timid . . . too naive?

What could possibly happen to you in a place where nothing opposes you and nothing is capable of becoming your limits?

## Saturday

First I write down the facts.

I was sitting on a bench, in a park, and next to me sat a *czango* (apparently from the Escuela Industrial) and his older companion. "If you had gone out wh——ing," the *czango* explained to his companion, "you would have had to scrape up at least fifty. So I should get at least that much!"

How am I to understand this? I am convinced that here, in Santiago, everything can be understood in two ways: as extreme innocence or extreme license. I would not be surprised to learn that the words I overheard were quite innocent, like a joke in a pupil's conversation. But something a little more perverse is not out of the question. Nor is this archperversity excluded: that those words, having the meaning that I attributed to them, were, nevertheless, innocent . . . and even in that case the greatest scandal would depend on the most perfect innocence.

That fifteen-year-old *czango* was obviously from a "good home." His eyes shone with health, kindness, and gaiety. He had not said that wantonly but with the absolute conviction of a person defending a just law. And, after all, he was laughing . . . that local laughter, certainly not excessive but rather engaging.

A thin, iridescent, colorful, laughing face.

Am I allowing myself to be fooled by the appearances of a non-existent depravity? It is difficult to get at anything . . . here everything becomes a jungle in which I lose my way. . . .

That girl, barely grown, is going around with a soldier from the eighteenth infantry regiment? . . .

Another *czangito,* who made my acquaintance in five minutes, told me how his father had died not long ago. If he told me this (as it appeared) to entertain and amuse me with an interesting tale, than this would show that he is a decent and hospitable boy . . . but it would also prove that he is a monster. . . .

A monster?

That transparent, colorful, and blinding sunlight everywhere: in the spaces between trees, in the luminous cascades and streams between the walls and crowns of trees. The goodness of that Santiago. Its equanimity. Its sedate smile. Eight children and three dogs around a palm tree. Ladies are out doing the shopping. Trees covered with violet or red blossoms peek from around walls, and a *motoneta* comes skimming down the middle of the road. The kind glances of Indian eyes. Swarms of bicycles. The sun sets. The streets close with distant landscapes of dark verdure.

On the bench a *niña* is sitting, her figure straight out of a painting, fetlock, smooth wave, gleaming hair . . . but, in addition to this, she is beautifully and strangely elongated . . . where did she get this, from what mixture of races . . . her beau lies on a bench with his head in her lap, looking at the sky. He has a white windbreaker on and an almost triangular face, young and beautiful, without sin. And even if they succumbed to a crime on this bench, it would take place in some other dimension. Is the tone too high, too high-pitched for me to hear? Silence.

# Sunday

This imperceptible madness, this innocent sin, those dark, languid eyes. . . . I am attracted by madness, I go to meet it, I! At my age! Catastrophe! For what reason other than age am I attracted to madness

. . . expecting that it will revive me, as I was, in all of my creative sensuality!

I would receive sin which was and is inspiration with open arms because art is begotten of sin!

Except that . . . there is no sin here. . . . What I would give to catch this little town in the act! Nothing. There's just the sun. And the dogs.

That accursed body of theirs . . .

# Monday

That accursed, easy body of theirs!

Is this the heritage of those naked tribes who bent their backs so easily under the whip? When I complained to Santucho that here the body "does not sing," and that nothing here wants to rise, he answered:

—That's the Indian's revenge.

—What revenge?

—Oh yes. Surely you can see how much of the Indian there is in all of us. Those tribes of Huries and Lules that were settled here were degraded by the Spanish and reduced to the role of slave, servant. . . . The Indian had to defend himself against the advantage of his master. He lived consumed by the thought not to submit to that superiority. How did he defend himself? By making fun of superiority, by sneering at his master, he nurtured a talent for poking fun at everything that aspired to superiority and rule. He demanded equality, mediocrity. In every flight, in every spark, he saw the desire to dominate. . . . And now you have the result. Now everything here is so ORDINARY. . . .

This thickset, stubborn Santiago cacique is wrong, however. Everything here happens without sin, but also without jeering, sneering, malice, or irony. The jokes are friendly and one senses goodness in the very tone of the language. It's just that . . . it will remain the secret of South America that decency, goodness, and the commonplace are becoming very aggressive and even dangerous! I came to the conclusion that when that goodness accidentally hits me from the side with its laughter, or when those boundless, inscrutable, and gentle eyes of a slave impale me, I begin to have the vague feeling that I am meeting a masked threat.

# Tuesday

Donkeys . . . goats . . . often remind me of Italy or the southern Pyrenees, the South in general.

This is where the thought comes from that, in my settling of accounts with this South America, there are more of the Nordic's fears than anything else. It is this shock, from the collision of North and South, that bothered me so much in Europe. Where the metaphysics of the North tumbles head over heels into the corporeal concreteness of the South.

No, this is not true, not true . . . and it is time to disclose the monstrous sensuality of the North. I, for example . . . would I want to be metaphysics? . . . Wouldn't I agree to be the body?

Oh! I am mortally in love with the body! The body is almost my only touchstone. No spirit can redeem corporeal ugliness, and a man physically unattractive will always hail from a race of monsters even though he may be Socrates himself! . . . Ah! how badly I need that consecration of the body! I divide humanity into the physically attractive and the physically repugnant, and the line between them is so distinct that it never ceases to amaze me. And even though I can love someone ugly (Socrates), I would never be capable of *being in love,* that is, of drawing myself into the magic circle, without a pair of divinely corporeal, attractive . . . enfolding . . . arms.

Do you want another confession from me, a Nordic? My metaphysics exists to become flesh . . . constantly . . . without respite. . . . It is like an avalanche with a natural tendency to head for the bottom . . . the Spirit? I will say that my greatest pride as an artist is not at all in inhabiting the kingdom of the Spirit, but in the fact that I have not broken relations with the flesh. I take more pride in the fact that I am sensual than in the fact that I am knowledgeable about the Spirit. My passion, my sinfulness and darkness, are more valuable to me than my light. More? Should I keep confessing these things? I will tell you, therefore, that the greatest artistic achievement of my life is not the few books I have written, but only and simply that I have not turned my back on "illicit love." Ah! because to be an artist means to be mortally, incurably, passionately, but also wildly in love and without wedlock. . . .

"And the word became flesh" . . . who could possibly exhaust the radical contents of these words?

# Tuesday

Is the body of an Indian more of a body? Is their slave body more of a body? Is slavery closer to love out of wedlock?

Questions that you, Santiago, drown in the twitter of birds.

# Thursday

Why did I come to Santiago?

To avoid the damp winter in Buenos Aires because of the poor state of my bronchial passages?

Or perhaps . . .

*Witold Gombrowicz chose Santiago del Estero to avoid the damp winter in Buenos Aires. It turned out shortly thereafter, however, that all this talk about his health was a pretext and that the real, hidden motive of his journey was different. Gombrowicz, checkmated by approaching old age, sought violent rescue and knew that if he did not* establish some link *with youth within the next few years, nothing could save him. In addition, it was an urgent matter of life or death to find some sort of new, unknown connection with the freshness of that new life . . . a mad idea, because it was dictated by a perilous situation that offered no other way out. And at first, it seemed to our traveler that, who knows, perhaps the most fantastic dream could come true, that is how docile and kind Santiago seemed . . . that is how easy . . . soon, however, that easiness would bare its teeth . . . white as they might be!*

# X

## Friday, Santiago

*(Witold Gombrowicz, having arrived in Santiago, succumbed to a wave of belated eroticism, the same as before, years ago. . . . But this time the wave was strengthened by the miasma of this city of Indian blood, easy beauty, and hot sun. And this wave, all the more scandalous because of its belatedness, bore him away again into the vortex of foolishness and shame! But his mastery of these types of situations (which have become his specialty, because an artist must act on the borderline between shame and foolishness) shone once again . . . when, to be exact, instead of giving himself up passively to this madness like any ordinary drunk, he took this madness in hand and took to ordering it, thereby changing intoxication into drama. This, however, happened with the help of the pronouncement that he, Gombrowicz, he, Doctor Faustus, had come to Santiago with the aim of concluding a great discovery, that he had finally decided to find a way of linking old age to youth, so that a generation that was nearing its end could, in its twilight, draw new substance from youth, and experience the beginning once again . . . and, who knows, friends, if it is not within our power to find this mysterious key, which would allow our dying to experience, in its farewell, a taste of new life, to link ourselves to birth! Imagine! If, at first glance, salvation seems possible, it can be contained only in this!*

*This is a pronouncement that is probably somewhat false . . . because, just between you and me, he did not come to Santiago for this reason. Nor could this Faustian swagger seem like the real thing for even five minutes of his mortally-stripped-of-all-illusions sobriety. Yet he has raised this lying to the high heavens without hesitation and unfurled it above his head like a banner on the basis of the following calculation: that, first of all, this lying stops being a lie because of its naive and disarming obviousness, and that, second, even though it is false, it contains something so real and harmonious with nature that it is more difficult to resist this mystification than to resist many other obvious truths. That is why, once again, he threw himself into a mad and aging attack with the shout: "Onward toward youth! To youth! To get at it, experience it, and destroy that barrier of age!")*

# Saturday

. . . the naked back under the whip, black head of curly hair hunched into the shoulders, eyes glancing sideways, ears alert to the swish of the strap . . . This is the poison that is killing me in Santiago. They have this in their blood! In their look. In their smile.

Spears, swords, spurs, armor, the plumed helmets of the white, bearded conquerors invading the naked defenselessness of those Huries, Lules, Vilelas three or four hundred years ago . . . And a hundred years ago? In his memoirs, General Paz describes how in the 1840s, the governor ordered that two Indians have their throats cut daily. . . . These were Indians ("whose eyes I often saw," writes the general) chosen from the heaps of rotting prisoners in the dungeon and then led out to be slaughtered . . . sadism and masochism still play in that colored air and dance in the streets. Their stench poisons me. Such is the perversity of Santiago!

Mix a little slave with the most common of cities . . . but . . . I could be wrong.

# Sunday

Tandil! Ah, Tandil! That obsession! Santiago is like Tandil: the same four-cornered square, similar streets, and the same café, the same church, the same bank, it's just that they are situated differently. Where in Tandil there was a Banco de la Provincia, here there is a Hotel Palace. I walk almost automatically to the bank and I bang my nose into: a hotel. As if I were in a Tandil that is not Tandil but something maliciously tangled, a trap. . . .

Oh Tandil, with your cold, oceanic wind and your stone amphitheaters! . . .

*(The author of* Pornografia *is becoming obsessed with Tandil as an escape from the importunate and tempting horrors of Santiago.)*

My friends, the minors from Tandil! Yesterday a letter came from Dipi and it is difficult to express how easy it is to breathe after that letter . . . here in Santiago! . . . I include it in order to give you a sense of the tone of my relationship with them, one of the tones of it . . . and because what is written there, that Gize (otherwise known as "Quilombo") *te adora* (adores you), is very important to me. This Dipi (alias

"Asno") is sixteen years old and the author of an unpublished novel, a play (which a theater in La Plata is producing), and a few stories:

"Cadaver!

"I was in La Plata and spoke with the director of my play. I have not told you anything about it. It is a farce as they claim, apparently well constructed from a theatrical point of view. In my opinion, it is too simple to be literature. As theater it can be pleasant, but at the present time, I feel that it is of doubtful value . . . it would flatter me to have it put on, but I am not satisfied with it.

"Your epileptico-elliptic letter twisted all our necks into corkscrews. Quilombo has sworn revenge.

"Gize is turning things out, possessed as he is by *Ferdydurke*. If this comes out brilliantly, well, all the better! But I fear that you will turn him into a Gombrowicz. You know that Quilombo is feverishly passionate and that he adores you. He has succumbed completely to your ha! ha! 'genius.' Do not be taken aback by the quotation marks; I acknowledge your genius but then you know my cynicism, my characteristic doubting, negating, poking fun . . . I make fun of you, too (while imagining your sniggers at my expense), but it's as if I were laughing at myself. Do you remember how we understood each other in this, surprisingly, when you were visited by momentary weakness and were walking so pained because of Gize's arrest? Don't try to squirm your way out of this, don't deny it! As for Gize, he moves in Polish, thinks in Polish, and practically speaks Polish. He is really very 'artistic'— perhaps even more than you think. He wants to divide time here into 'pre-Witold' and 'post-Witold' epochs. Well, this is a slight exaggeration, though I admit I have gained a great deal from this Witold epoch. Your sober, elemental, violent, and somewhat deceitful (now don't get upset!) criticism has taught me a lot.

"Write. I would like to know how you are doing. I am brutally curious. But I am also becoming more reasonable in my childhood, from which I prefer not to abdicate as of yet. That is why I want to know what is happening with your expiring life. It is common sense that makes me ask, even though this may appear strange . . . the point is that my common sense submits me to convention and compels me to ask what is new with you . . . because, frankly speaking, you yourself will understand this, I don't really care, because I respect you but I do not adore you. I am far from adoration *à la* Gize. I see that this passage has turned out to be quite abstruse. It's because I am tired. Are all those women still in love with you? Maybe you could pass one on to me, as I am suffering from a lack of women in spite of Fuchi, Puchi, and Tuchi.

"It is sad that a GREAT WRITER writes 'holla' instead of 'olla.' It is a great shame and dishonor; after which you ought to KEEP YOUR MOUTH SHUT FOREVER! We were rolling on the floor with laughter, we and dozens of other people who read your letter. *Ciao!*

Your,

Donkey"

This donkey is named Jorge Di Paola. I christened him the donkey in an attack of sarcasm and from then on he became *asno* to his friends, who were really tickled by this name.

I don't know if I have done the right thing by including this letter. . . .

*(Why did he include it? Was it only to show that he was popular in Tandil? But there is clearly the more sophisticated intention of elevating himself, setting himself apart, which could be formulated as follows: Peek-a-boo! Do you older folks now see how much more intimate my relations with young people are than with you! And how much more important to me a letter like this is, in which there is nothing out of the ordinary, than your most sophisticated epistolary feats. . . .*

*Once again, therefore, Gombrowicz appears to us as someone who will in no way occupy his rightful place in society and who is always plotting with other elements, groups, and phases of development.)*

# Wednesday

I have read this letter many times. And I doubt that it will be understood that this and a few other letters from Tandil have become an escape and haven from Santiago. "You know that Quilombo adores you." Those words sounded like a prelude to hope for me, this was youth showing itself in another, less cruel, role . . . and even in a friendly role. . . . Therefore, I said to myself, "adoration" is not impossible between him and me?

Quilombo, alias Gize, also called Colimba (this in folk dialect means time served in the army as well as "recruit"). Our meeting was the result of casual circumstances that were, nevertheless, deeply and movingly artistic. At first, a weakening. When I got to know him in Tandil, in the Café Rex, I was somewhat weakened by an imminent angina attack and my sensitivity was tremulously, painfully tense. Second, there was his stuttering. That is: he stuttered. . . . I did not know at the beginning what made him so likable, it was only on the second day that I understood that, as a result of his stuttering, he must make a special effort to speak which, together with his Spanish face, alive like an adventure film, bestowed a special amiability upon him.

The angina attack, along with a fever reaching 40° C, kept me bedridden. I lived alone in a small house close to Calvario, on the outskirts of town, and I remember no more desperate days than those that accompanied my recuperation. There was no help from any quarter. I knew that nothing would save me. The days were rainy and windy. Through the window I could see the mountain peak torn to shreds by clouds, or perhaps it was the clouds that were torn to shreds by the mountain peak. And one day was especially terrifying: it came after a whole night's downpour, almost unlike day at all, changed into water, cold, fog, winds, and a white damp darkness. I could see just one dripping tree enveloped in fog, blurred and indistinct, and only that tree, dripping and monotonous. . . . That day my neurasthenic despair reached such a pitch that if I had had the means for an easy death at hand, who knows if I would not have liquidated myself. I knew that the illness was beyond me, but I also knew that my health was worse than my illness. I had reached a state in which health is no less repugnant, and perhaps even more repugnant because it confirms an existence already infected with death and therefore condemned.

Then suddenly I heard a fist pounding on the kitchen door, and Colimba walked in, dripping wet! He got through the water that had been pouring from the sky and, what's worse, he sloshed through the street, forded his way through the slurping and sticky mud until he finally got here, fighting the wind, rain, and cold, and he was cheerful! Witold, *che, como estas?!* His face was rich with adventure, like a film, swinging acrobatically from seriousness to jest, from groan to joy, from poetry to rambunctiousness, from compassion to anger, his face immediately filled the whole room and I probably never had a stronger sense *that the potential of someone's joy is not inaccessible, that one can gain access to someone's joy, if it is young.* That youth is something that it is possible to possess (Please don't make stupid jokes out of this!). It is as if some sort of Wave Mechanics completed and enlarged my feeling of well-being. I felt that I was not just a concrete individual, destined for destruction, but a wave . . . a current, stretched out between the rising and setting generations. Sometimes my hopelessness is visited by a spark of conviction, a completely palpable certainty that *salvation is not impossible.* This is exactly what I was feeling while Gize prepared my food and opened the bottle he had brought.

Even though neither he nor I said a word about it . . . I knew that his coming was the result of his great concern for me, and his adulation. . . . He had come because he was charmed! Enchanted! What's more, I know that his spending his precious little amount of free time with me meant that he was taking it away from his girlfriend, who did not yet completely bore him. . . . How amusing therefore: I, a man of certain age, was a stronger magnet for this young man than a beautiful girl and my charms were stronger than love! What was it in me that could equal a young girl's charms?

The repulsive and sneering comicality of this comparison was the reason I preferred to think about this only with one little corner of my mind, but even that was enough for me to realize that this repulsiveness was the real source of deepest joy. For when an old man looks at a young man, usually it is difficult for him to understand that the young man can have his own tastes and needs, completely independent of what seems the most important and the most characteristic in him to the older man. It seems, for example, to that older person that only the young can appeal to the young, only the handsome to the handsome . . . until, suddenly, it turns out that youth likes old age instead . . . or likes some special category of ugliness . . . that, in a word, it takes a liking to something completely unpredictable and even irreconcilable with its essence (such as the older man sees it). So that, at first, it irritates and offends us, as if it were a betrayal and, what is more, some sort of corruption and warping of an ideal. But not long afterward we are overcome by a wild joy and we begin to understand that not all is lost in such a case! So, therefore, we both push away this realization in revulsion and receive it with joy as a miracle and sign of grace.

In order to gauge accurately one certain, dirty, and repugnant aspect of this joy, one should realize that I acted toward Gize somewhat like an old woman, delighted that his hunger outweighed his revulsion, because, in the end, certain attractive and repulsive forces were at play at the same time. . . . Yet, on the other hand, in order to measure the entire generous splendor of this arrangement in nature one must understand that no one decides about his own attractiveness and that it is exclusively a matter of one's taste. If I, therefore, was attractive to him, then I was and that was that. . . . and I was, too, because I possessed a technique, style, level, horizon, and quality of which he could not even dream at his age because I wrote books that dazzled, because with each accent, face, joke, game, I led him into an unseen and unheard of superiority. What did it matter that I knew my misery? I charmed him! Just one more example from the area of physics in order to make palpable the infernal slipperiness of this conclusion: imagine yourselves endowed with a defect, let us say you have donkey ears. Well, fine, but what if your ears fascinate the princess and what if she falls in love with you because of them? What then? If you cut off the ears, which you don't like, you will stop being attractive to someone whom you like. What should you choose? Isn't it more important that you should appeal to someone who appeals to you rather than appeal to yourself?

And if some possibility of salvation did exist for me in all of this, didn't it depend on this very thing?

I understood it well: my "existence" fascinated him, while his life *in crudo* appealed to me. I adored his freshness and he adored what I had made of myself, what I had become as I developed. The closer I was to death, the more he adored me, because he saw all the more of my already expiring existence. Therefore our understanding would have been possible only if that which is characteristic of youth, that which is hot and impatient, the desire to exist, if that could be exchanged for the hunger for life that is particular to aging. . . . Exchange existence for life? . . . Stop, perhaps there is something to this, perhaps something can be done using this approach, think a minute, don't let this thought get away. . . .

## Thursday

*(So there, in the end, a redemptive thought came to him, an exchange of existence [that is, a formed life, just as man had made it] for that passively natural life, in its young, initial phase.*

*This thought moved him quite perceptibly. Would it be an exaggeration to conceive of all his writing as a search for the elixir of youth? In* Ferdydurke *[written when the author was not yet thirty] he had already been thrilled by the forbidden delight: that man could be created by man . . . by a younger man, right? This in itself was a way of regaining youth. In* The Marriage *he exploits this specific generosity to its core when he exhorts the younger to surrender himself . . . to kill himself for old age. In* Pornografia *he is excited by the fact that youth exists for those older and vice versa.*

*No other world needs youth as much as Gombrowicz's world . . . and one could say that this is a world built by "taking youth into consideration." And if up until now he sought salvation in the violence perpetrated on the younger by the older [The Marriage] or finally in the coordination of these two forms of violence [Pornografia], now we see him in Santiago, overcome by the thought that came to him in Tandil about the possibility of exchanging life for existence, which simply means that two separate categories of human beings exist and that they desire one another. . . . )*

# Thursday

Yes . . . but our rapprochement was, as I said earlier, a coincidence above all else . . . a mere coincidence. . . . If not for the stuttering and the effort to get through the bad weather outside . . . if he had not caught me ill . . .

To this was added the magic of names. "Gize," I like that diminutive, it was good for a pathetic apostrophe, I like to call out, dramatically: "Gize!"

This lent our conversations distinction and luster. On one occasion, my tongue slipped and made "Quilombo" out of "Colimba." "Quilombo" means "bordello" in Spanish, except that it is not as vulgar and can be used jokingly and metaphorically to mean disorder, confusion, a nuthouse. Used as one's name, it becomes very amusing and perversely poetic. *Che, Quilombo, como estas?* I would say with refined politeness and this would establish a distance between us that facilitated intimacy.

I could not get close to him without Form, without the structure of Form. And he (also being an artist with a passion for drawing, but at his age it was not yet clear whether this was genuine talent or mere ability) also demanded Form of me.

How moving was the passage in his letter from Tandil: "Believe me . . . whenever I remember last summer . . . that house, the girls . . . your sad angina when a certain angelic 'Quilombo' took care of you . . . I get sad just reminiscing about it.

"And then your move to Park Mountain and my 'imaginary' as you said, angina . . . and recuperation . . . our talks . . . walks in the sunlight . . . my drawings . . . That was a summer I shall never forget. Never!"

I wrote back: "Ah, my unforgettable Quilombo! You have managed to give these insignificant events the stature of myth and legend. . . . "

# Tuesday

My talk "Contemporary Issues" took place yesterday. I gave this talk out of sheer boredom and to make contact with the intellectuals of Santiago. I did not foresee that this would end demonically.

I tried to characterize current thought by saying, for example, that it is "reduced," that slowly it is becoming accustomed to "dual interpretation," that we feel it as something "acting not only on the outside, but also on the inside, creating the one who thinks." I referred to science, quanta, Heisenberg and wave mechanics. Husserl, and Marcel. My merciful God! I spoke as I always do, as even the finest speakers do, that is, pretending that I was quite at home with this material and that this is my daily bread and butter, when, in reality, any indiscreet questioner could have laid me flat on my back. But I have grown so accustomed to mystification! And I also know that this kind of mystification is not scorned even by the most prominent! I was doing my part, then, and it was coming out pretty well. Suddenly, in the audience, behind the first row of people, I noticed a hand resting on someone's knee. . . .

Another hand, closer by and belonging to someone else, was resting on or was hooked by the fingers to the back of a chair . . . and suddenly it was as if the two palms had grabbed me, until I was terrified, until I began to choke . . . and so again the body in me spoke up. But I looked closer: the hands belonged to students who had come from Tucumán and that calmed me down immediately. I had a vision of Tandil, I knew there was no reason to be afraid, these were well-wishing, friendly hands. I looked around the auditorium once again, all of the hands were friendly and, although corporeal, they were nevertheless at the service of the Spirit, these were hands belonging to intellectuals. . . . This thicket of spiritualized hands did wonders for me. It was probably the first time in my life that I lost that portion of acting, bluster, artifice that had clamped onto my spirit. Suddenly, the seriousness and essence of my work as a teacher outweighed all my dishonesty. I understood the meaning of my assignment; it was something a great deal more important than a professorial lecture, than "cultural work," or an artistic or literary showing off. I was fighting for myself here, trying to draw them out of their flesh and transform them into existence. My fate depended on how much I could win them over and force them to the spirit, for that was the only thing that could save me! I began to speak with such passion that I listened to myself in disbelief, it was so real. . . .

A discussion followed: but their timid and moved voices were only a springboard for my metaphysical one. I was so strong that for the first time in my life I understood what a force I could be if I could believe in myself, the way the saints and the prophets had. Finally one young man rose and expressed his gratitude, and then others came up to me. It was obvious that I was not being thanked for my intellect but for something more important: for fighting the body, corporeality, physicality. . . . I asked for a glass of water. Everyone rushed to fulfill my wish. In a moment a *czango* came in with a carafe on a tray. I went mute, terrified. That *czango* . . .

But the body of that illiterate was so decent . . . it was decency itself . . . this common, calm, freely living, easy-moving, quiet body was sincerity, morality . . . and so much so and so completely that compared to this the meeting sounded like a shrill note, like a high-pitched squeal . . . I don't know. . . . The blessed simplicity of a chest, or perhaps the moving honesty of a neck, and the hands that can barely trace letters, rough and real from physical labor . . . My spirit gave up its ghost. A complete flop. I tasted lipstick on my lips.

In the meantime, the Indian (because he had a lot of this blood in him) poured water for me with the careful movement of a slave, with his hands summoned into being to serve, devoid of pride, but also of meaning. The quieter his hands were, the more terrifying their explosion, because that *czango,* like every servant, was a *quantité négligeable,* "air," and it was exactly because of this, because of his negligibility, that he became a phenomenon from another register, and overwhelming in that margin of his. His unimportance, cast into the periphery, there, became important! I said good-bye and left. I did not want to prolong my being alone with the *czango.* Out on the street it was dark. Santiago's colorful sunset went out and the violent cold of the winter, which appeared right after the disappearance of the sun, forced me to put on my coat. I was still exchanging parting niceties with persons who were seeing me off, when the *czango* . . . walked by, just a few feet away from me.

Was this the same *czango?* Was this him? They were all alike . . . so much so that you could substitute one for another, almost identical one. . . . Therefore, I was inclined to believe that this was a different one, a brother, colleague, companion . . . but did this make any difference? He walked slowly in the direction of the river, Rio Dulce. I followed him. I followed him because it was absurd and unthinkable that I, Gombrowicz, would follow some *czango* just because he was similar to the *czango* who had poured water for me. But once again his perfect unimportance exploded, like a thunderclap, in the margin of everything that passes for important. And I followed him, as if it were my most holy obligation!

I walked on, uneasy. . . . Because I had long given up these walks in the Retiro and along the Leandro Alem (about which I have written before), and now, in Santiago, this situation, the deepest, most essential, and most painful of all of mine, returned again unexpectedly: I was following a village boy. This time, however, there was a new slant to the situation, namely, that it was neither beauty nor youth that was at stake but morality. I walked, led astray by that other honesty, simplicity, purity, which was undermining and destroying my spiritualization.

I walked after his plain back, visible neck, calm hand! And my recent triumph evaporated, poof! it was gone! . . . Yet while I greeted with despair this new march of mine into defeat, I decided, gritting my teeth, that now I would finally find a solution to this problem . . . any solution . . . this could not go on any longer. This had to be done away with. And I believed, I don't know exactly why, maybe because of the intensity with which the body imposed itself on me, that if I was capable of solving the physical shape of the event, if I could find the physical solution to the situation, then that would also lead me to a spiritual solution. At any rate (as long as it lasted), I walked after that *czango* in the dusk, aware that my walking after him was, first of all, the formula of the situation: I and he, I walking after him, I with him . . . we are a problem to solve. . . .

Somehow the problem was growing . . . with that peculiar power with which certain meaningless things swell. This unexpected procession was ringing in my ears, pounding at my temples! Theoretically, I knew why the body before me was so honest, in contrast to the perversity that characterized us intellectuals. The transparency of the body! The honesty of the body! Because the body created a simple and radiant game of needs and values, and for that *czango,* a value was something that satisfied his physical needs, the normal needs of a healthy body, so that he was really the passive playground of natural forces. He was nothing more than nature and that is why he shone before me in the dark: pure, simple, and lucent. Moral like a dog, like a horse! Moral like everyday health! And I? And those like me? Oh, we broke with the logic of the body and were a product of complicated factors, deriving not from nature in general anymore, but from specific human nature, we, a product of humanity, a product of this "second nature" that is the nature of humanity. We were perversity, refinement, and complication, we were the Spirit, oh, unhappy ones! . . . Yet I could not agree to this situation, that I was following him, I, in adoration . . . this would be equal to complete failure. . . . Tearing myself away by force, therefore, I turned into the first street on the left. I broke contact and now I was walking alone. . . . I told myself, shaken up: The hell with it! Don't forget who you are! He is only a meaningless body, one of the many on the compost heap! You are indispensable, singular, original, irreplaceable!

But the fact that, bodily, I was not as honest or as transparent as he carried a weight that was so absolute that I sang hymns of praise to myself in vain. They were spiced with bitterness and a putrid smell rose from me. I felt on that empty street that there was no helping it, I had to murder something. I continued to walk, set on committing murder. I had to reduce him to the level of an animal and remain alone in my humanity. I was not allowed to tolerate my dual humanity any-more, his or mine. Either I had to become a monster or he an animal. There was no other way out. . . . This obvious truth was accompanied by another: that I should not leave him and allow him to be alone, in secret. I decided, therefore, to catch up with him and have it out. What if he had gotten too far away? No, it was almost certain that, having gotten to the park, he would have turned right, walked along the street parallel to mine, but I imagined to myself that I was catching up to him and that I was following him again. . . . No, that would be for naught! Coming upon him from the side, from around the corner, would not be satisfying. . . . I decided to quicken my pace so that I would come out ahead of him, face-to-face, at the next intersection. . . . And that thought dazzled me! Not from behind, not from the side, but face-to-face!

Not from behind.

Not from the side.

But straight at him, head-on, face-to-face! Such was the physical formula for victory. This allowed for the attack. And I needed this war with him, because it made him my enemy, it put him on the outside. I set off almost running, and the running itself, having him in view, changed the situation to my advantage. I turned violently. I slowed my steps. Now I walked along a street with sparse street lamps. One side of the street was formed by the great, black, quiet trees of the park. And then he approached me, still at a substantial distance, dissolved in the lights of the swaying lamps. He was getting closer, and my hostility was expelling him out of me like a rash, there he was in front of me. Kill. I honestly wanted to kill him. And I was killing him in myself with my wanting to kill him. In the certainty that without this murder, *I would never be capable of being moral.* My morality became aggressive and murderous. The distance between us quickly decreased. I, naturally, did not intend to kill him "externally." I merely wanted to murder him in him and I was certain that if I killed him, then even I could believe in God, at any rate I would be on God's side. . . . This was one of those moments in my life in which I understood that morality is wild . . . wild. . . . Then . . . when we came abreast of each other, he greeted me, smiling:

—*Que tal?*

I knew him! He was one of the shoeshine boys that milled around the square. He had polished my shoes a few times. An acquaintance! I had not been ready for this! The murderous encounter fell to pieces. . . . I nodded to him and shouted back, *Adonde vas?* We passed each other and out of this frenzy, nothing remained except the everyday and the ordinary, as the highest tone, as the king of the entire event!

*(Therefore he experienced catastrophe once again. Again that accursed pedestrianism tore through, just when he had his drama organized, and once again everything disintegrated in his hands, as if "the other" simply had not wanted to play . . . and our Faust got bogged down in the everyday. They sure made a fool of him! The drama was taken away from him, the drama that was his only ornament in this battle with the younger set. . . .*

*But from this unconsummated encounter there will remain with him, probably to the very end, the growing conviction that virtue has claws and knows how to murder, that the moral and spiritual world is subject to the universal law of cruelty. In spite of all efforts, the gap between flesh and the spirit grows smaller and smaller, they penetrate each other and harness one another, these worlds. . . .*

*And this is what he had learned in sun-blessed Santiago.)*

# 1959

# XI

## Monday

ONE SOPPING OR MERELY DAMP DOGGIE, YOU CHOOSE.

## Wednesday

Every lawyer, otherwise known as "the patron," basks in the high-flown conviction of his own "cultural well-roundedness" (because, of course, "law educates"), and any old hydraulic engineer considers himself a full-fledged scholar, like Heisenberg. It is almost not worth mentioning that when it comes to the imagination, they haven't the least notion of what it is.

Yesterday. How irritating! For two whole hours I had to bear the conceit of both these species of pseudo-intellectuals-with-diplomas. Incredible stupidity. The attorney with his little lawyer's "look," his world-view, style, form reeking of that pitiful university, just the way a suit reeks of mothballs. . . . His engineership proclaimed the superiority of the hard sciences, because, man, those there philosophical or artistic romances are not for a disciplined mind and "have you gentlemen heard of quanta?" The level was appalling. And each of them was furnished and supplemented by a better half who adored his intellect with real feminine ecstasy. It is a sad fact that each year the universities produce thousands of these jackasses and that sooner or later they find their unfailing she-ass complements.

How is one to prevent the higher institutions of learning from producing such rubbish and from polluting the air in the civilized world? The air around me is getting thick with young cretins of university fabrication, laundered of all natural intelligence. South America, too, is filling the air with a stifling student populace that knows only what is crammed into its head. Stuffed with information, it has lost all sense of the imponderables: character, reason, poetry, and grace. The coarse ugliness of these intellectual workers, specialists in medicine, law, technology, etc., even here in Argentina, is getting annoying. People who are insensitive to art, unfamiliar with life, and formed by abstraction are conceited and ponderous. I like to whip these unaesthetic idiots into a fury or drown them in the chaos of names and theories invented on the spot—oh, they may even beat me up one day! I am amused that these coarse natures sentenced exclusively to science consider all else, anything beyond the sciences, all of the spiritual life of the human tribe, as nothing but the pulling of someone's leg—the consequence of which is that they are in deathly fear of having someone pull their leg.

I take great pleasure in stoking their peasant distrust of the "writer," that jokester *par excellence,* and occasionally I assume a mien or drop an altogether dubious or sometimes even quite comic word. Their simple respect for seriousness is so great that they are struck dumb. Or I attack them with aristocracy and genealogy, a foolproof trick when it comes to driving imbeciles into complete imbecility.

Ah yes . . . the aristocracy . . . ah yes . . . the aristocracy. O aristocracy, perhaps you are something more than a malicious joke. The idol of the people is *utility,* and the idol of the aristocracy is *pleasure.* To be useful and unpleasant—is the goal of every robot and specialist. To be so useful as to be able to be unpleasant—is their dream. The dream of aristocrats is the diametrical opposite: to be so pleasant as to be able to be useless. As for me, I claim and record this as one of the canons of my knowledge of human nature: he who wants to please people has easier access to humanity than he who merely wishes to be a useful servant.

# Thursday

ONE WHITE, TASTY, WELL-FED DOGGIE.

# Friday

I say to my pupils: remember that I am not one of your upstanding, patented and guaranteed professors. One never knows with me. I could lie or say something idiotic at any moment—I could make a fool of someone. With me there are no guarantees. I am a knave—I like having fun—and I don't give a hoot . . . not a hoot, about you and my preaching.

# Saturday

I WILL EXCHANGE ONE MEAN BLACK DOG FOR TWO OLD ONES.

# Saturday

I was walking along a path, across a large meadow in the forests of Santiago; the terrain seemed to be marked for construction, overgrown with sparse grass, white bald hillocks of sand, uninteresting. I was walking along slowly, lost in thought, looking at the ground, the sun had already set. I walked by rubble of scattered bricks and bits and pieces of machines and boxes when all of a sudden the path rose under my feet, not much, just a little, as a result of a light swelling of the ground—and immediately fell. This was enough. I felt that the earth had hit me from below with a wave, I felt her undulation, her unexpected, hidden resilience. Stop! What was this?! Had the path come alive? Had the earth come alive? Stop, stop, for goodness sake, is it possible for objects to come alive . . . but then *you would have to become a lifeless object, irreversibly!* How's that? How's that? Three stones on the path riveted my gaze, one next to the other. . . . Is another interpretation of the cosmos—in which their lifelessness would become life and my life, death—possible? No, away with this thought, this is stretching things a bit, making them too fantastic, but listen, if in addition to the living world and the lifeless world, some sort of third world existed—a third principle—oh! of which we haven't even dreamed, assuring action to an object, transforming an object into a subject? To conceive of these three little stones as *alive* . . . Would an active inertia be possible? Oh stop! What nonsense! . . .

All of this because you are a bright boy. That is why there is no nonsense you can't swallow . . . intelligence and imagination surrender you to stupidity, because nothing is fantastic enough for you . . . and you stand on the path as if led astray by some nonsense, which in a thousand years—in a thousand years, oh, you son of the millennia—is ready to become a thing related to the truth.

# Monday

ONE FAT WET DOG. *A characteristic statement by a high official.* Comrade Minister of Culture and Art said on the radio (December 1958): *"There is something abnormal in today's situation. Let us take a random example: Gombrowicz's book is a literary tidbit reviewed by all of our publications and not just once, but many times, while books for the mass reader are not reviewed at all."*

Then, a moment later, in the same dialogue about "cultural" politics, as they often say on Polish Radio, Comrade Minister again returns to the same obsessive theme:

*"Considering how little available space there is in the press, for example, the fact that Gombrowicz is reviewed twenty-five times and Wanda Meltzer not even once has much to do with the politics of culture."*

I see. This is an obsession all right. And already an indication of a very strict diet. The idyll is over.

Now, there's a fine ballet! What a shame that my colleagues in the West are ignorant of this two-step with their own nations — one step forward, one step back. For ten years you are nothing, for two years prominent, after which a writer, by dint of their cultural ordinances, becomes the author of "literary tidbits," and not at all bad ones at that.

This "at that" disturbs me the most. Perhaps I would prefer them to preserve a wild and absolute silence about me forever, as was the case not too long ago, to burn me at the stake or drown me in the toilet. Art, like faith, is afraid of just one thing: the lukewarm. But they — culturally. With a plan. Oh sure, you can praise a little, lest it look like terror . . . but not too much. This kills "a little bit," like poison in small doses, released slowly.

# Wednesday

DOGS SNAP AT EACH OTHER DURING A HEAT WAVE.

# Thursday

Recalling my numerous fears, I come to the conclusion that my poor resistance or, simply stated, my cowardice — which makes getting into an elevator difficult and appears when I get on a tram, the cowardice which poisons my life — stems from that feature (or perhaps mannerism) of my imagination that causes my suffering to appear most often in some sort of inferior, diminutive aspect. For me, "I am choking" is not the moment when my lungs are bursting but when there begins to be not enough air — but for good. I am ready to compare a back pain when one cannot change position to a broken leg, and the taste of yesterday's tea, a blister on the finger, or darkness to war. Such vision undercuts courage the way pests fell a tree.

What can fear have in common with innocence? Yet for me, maximal horror is something as pure as . . . maximal innocence.
ONE YELLOW DOG, A LITTLE GNAWED ON BUT NEW.

## Thursday

The New Year 1959 in Tandil. From here, from the beautiful villa of the Mauros where I live like a king, spoiled by their hospitality, I watch fireworks bursting over the city, nestled in a dell. And behind me a dark wall of coniferous mountain rears up like a horse and stands mute. From the left and right, large expanses of night, lost among the hills. We drink champagne.

## Thursday

How little I have written this past year! A little of the diary. A little *Operetta,* which I have stopped writing again. Oh well! Infirmity! I am still not in the best of health, although Zellner has been able to put me back on my feet.

What am I supposed to do? Let us make a list—this may interest those who are interested in me. . . . (The blurring of the perspective as a result of my growing fame: I have lost the former, clear distinction between that which is boring in my writing and that which is interesting, because now something boring can be interesting simply because it concerns me; this is how the growing "I" engenders confusion. . . . )

So let us make a list.

Complete this segment of the *Diary.*

Finish the second act of *Operetta,* introducing the plot line "mother slut," and strengthening the parts of Firulet and Charme.

Go over the French translation of the *Diary.* Letter to Suzanne Arlet.

Correspondence. Janusz, Kot, Alicia Giangrande, Giedroyć, *Preuves,* Koszella, etc., Alice de Barcza.

Go over the Heidegger notes, in connection with the fourth talk to the club "Amigos del Arte."

A telegram to the Świeczewskis.

Prepare the radio texts.

Correspondence with publishers.

The French translation of *Ivona* (get it moving). I have no idea— whether this list is boring or interesting.

# Friday

*He doesn't know! This is how corrupting the weight of his burgeoning "I" has become —and this growing "I" is muddling his relationship with the world more and more. Outside of the physical illness which he mentions to justify why he wrote so little, there is the other infirmity which is even more painful: he really does not know what to do with the Gombrowicz who appears to him from time to time in foreign newspapers, already quite international, European, already (almost) cosmopolitan. An infirmity all the more humiliating because this kind of trouble is so typically Gombrowiczian —what is more his, as a theme and problem, than the burgeoning of his personality inflated with fame? Yet it is exactly this that increases his feebleness —because this obligates —and it is not appropriate for him to set off on well-trodden paths with an issue so very personal, so lived through, he must find his own solution here to the question of "how to be great?" he should give a completely singular answer. Well, certainly! He will not, of course, resort to well-known "solutions" of the famous and glib greats; not for him, for example, the affected mastery of Anatole France . . . yet Dostoyevski's greatness, simple and rustic, sly but passionate, is also useless . . . after all, it is completely alien to him. And what of Goethe's Olympus! Erasmus or Leonardo? Tolstoy from Yasnaya Polyana? Jarry's metaphysical dandyism or Lautréamont? Titian or Poe? Kierkegaard or Claudel? No, none of this, none of these masks, none of these scarlet cloaks. . . . One has to create something of one's own . . . except that greatness is an old wh——e, and one of the unfailing lures of art, so it has already been used a hundred times, in various versions. Greatness that is pathetic and humble, clownish and cynical, zealous and brutal, Christian —pagan — lyrical —and dry —and mathematical —is well known. . . . but each of these timeworn odalisques danced in her own way.*

*Of all these styles of greatness, proposed by so many masters, the closest to him was perhaps the one that Thomas Mann worked out for himself in the course of his long career. For Mann was able —in the spirit of his epoch —to link, better than anyone else, greatness to illness, genius to decadence, superiority to degradation, distinction to shame. He approached that mad harnessing of opposites with a sincerity that aroused trust . . . and at the same time, he treated this shameful contradiction not as something deserving revulsion and condemnation but as something passionate and intoxicating and so worthy of love that the great artist in Mann's rendition is repulsive and ridiculous, but also marvelous and attractive . . . like a lover. This "justice" of Mann's in arranging light and shadow, this profound intelligence in grasping the problem, appealed to Gombrowicz more than he could say and in conversations he would often*

*refer to Mann and to the very lovely contours of the story "Tonio Kröger,"
in which he, Gombrowicz, quickly recognized his fate and vocation. As
years passed, however, it became even clearer to him that Mann's honesty,
integrity, and openness were just one more form of coquetry and one more
way of forcing—under the guise of honesty and even humility—others to
acknowledge his own right to glory. Indeed, this unmasker of dirt and
poverty exploded and revealed, as it turned out, only in order to furnish
himself with a more solid, durable monument grounded more firmly in
reality and awareness. And more and more clearly could one hear in
proportion to the growing of Mann's work, behind that unmasking icono-
clasm of the revolutionary, a ponderous rhetoric, enamored of stateliness,
wheedling with its mastery, majestic, and purple as a cardinal. Ah, Mann,
you old strumpet! So this is the coquet you are?!*

    *What should Gombrowicz have done then? Could he have, leaning on
Mann, conquered him—become a new Mann, a more advanced Mann?
More modern by one generation? In short, was Gombrowicz supposed to
play, in regard to Mann, exactly the role that Mann had played in relation
to his forerunners—should he have ruined Mann's greatness dialectically
in order to found a new one on a higher level of consciousness? Our
candidate for master was not deprived of merits that could have ensured
him instant success in this regard; he had a new honesty at his disposal,
and even a new shamelessness—resulting from his slogans that pronounced an eternal breach between man and his form and, as a consequence, allowed one to approach these extreme issues with an ease probably
unmet with until that day. He could, for example, have described in his
diary his own coming into prominence, his entering history, transforming
himself from an unknown minor author into a personality, as if it weren't
about him, as if this triumph were merely the imposition of a new and not
very comfortable "form"—"made for him," and even warping him. To
become great? How's that? What does one feel? How is it that man divides
himself in two and which of these persons is real? He could show (burying
Mann) that greatness is always inauthentic, that man is incapable of realizing himself in a higher dimension, even if his talent is really deserving
of fame and admiration. Confessing to all of the pettiness of his greatness
with a completely unheard-of insolence, boring, tormenting, irritating with
his growing, he could change his confessions into a first-class literary
scandal, and himself into a freakish clown of greatness. Which, actually,
would be completely in keeping with his philosophy of form and would
probably ensure him a fairly original place in the history of twentieth-
century culture.*

    *Certainly—an interesting and attractive assignment! Because this
did not mean at all that he should ascetically scorn greatness—on the*

contrary, this allowed him to surrender himself to it with all his greed, caress himself with his greatness, intoxicate himself, pride himself on it — because the minute he stopped identifying with his greatness and began treating it as something that just happened to him, it lost its intimate and timid character. Self-advertisement was also allowed, for in expounding on these subjects it was impossible to avoid it and this ultimately was also pleasant and even convenient. Gombrowicz was not so naive as to be blind to the unusual artistic advantages of this so free and public intimacy with greatness —for the reader likes glory, prefers a story about kings, princes, or great artists; shoemakers or petty clerks interest him but little, he is an aristocrat in his daydreams and, as we have already said, greatness, that old who——e, or rather courtesan, is a very effective lure and constitutes the sex appeal of older gentlemen in laurel wreaths.

ONE COLD DOG IN SPRINGTIME. Gombrowicz could then really ameliorate his preoccupation with Mann —on the one hand compromising greatness even more; on the other, surrendering to it with an immeasurably greater shamelessness and without that "masterly" pomposity that became Mann's weakness. But something got in the way . . . what was it? To begin with, in actual practice (that is, when our author took to realizing this program in his Diary by including, at first, slight and restrained remarks about his fame), it turned out that the convention forbidding the writer "self-praise" and pronouncing this type of information "boring" is exceptionally difficult to dismiss —much more difficult than if it were a matter of Gombrowicz's usual carrying on about himself (which also aroused considerable resistance). Why did people react so very negatively? It should have been just the opposite. Success, glory, acclaim, growing prestige —this is a tasty trifle; the average reader adores such glories in novels imagined from beginning to end, therefore why not in a real diary, having to do with someone's real destiny, someone's autobiography? Instead they reacted with anger, revulsion, boredom, even genuine embarrassment . . . as if the reader did not really want to hear about all that.

Stranger still was that the reader's dislike was confirmed by the inner unwillingness of the author —an unwillingness that was also unjustified, at odds with the reserves of spiritual freedom at his disposal. Nevertheless this was resistance . . . some sort of unhappiness with himself, similar sometimes to pangs of conscience, and sometimes even to regret . . . bitterness, and boredom, and even displeasure or pain advised don't take this on, leave it alone, don't interfere—let it be. . . . What was going on? Where did this difficulty come from? This protest was not born of intellectual criticism, how much more spontaneous it was . . . it was as if he, in destroying his greatness, destroyed his own youthful dream about himself and as if he were liquidating this beloved, youthful "project" concerning *his own future. Here, therefore, something very personal, lyrical, intimate, stood in the way, something connected with —watch out! —youth and something almost as shameful as love. The situation was becoming scabrous and painful. . . . This was not an intellectual problem, this was something from another realm, of the religious perhaps, or perhaps of love. . . . Love? Youth? Was it possible that the true interpretation of this complex of old men called greatness had eluded Mann, even though he was saturated with Freud's ideas and closer to Freud than to Schopenhauer? And if so . . . what was it that had remained unsaid?*

*—Good —thought Gombrowicz —good . . . the Master in Mann is attractive to a pupil. A pupil "loves" his master. If in an early phase of development the ordinary is attractive, enthralling, then the extraordinary, that which is outstanding, becomes alluring in the later phase. . . . If this is so, if the extraordinary is attractive, why does it reveal itself only as strength —not as weakness? Because —and this is a truth one should not forget —only weakness and inadequacy are enthralling, never power and perfection. And it is true that Freud and Mann knew how to extract all of the biological poverty accompanying greatness, those deviations, the sicknesses of a great man, but what determines greatness in him, genius, talent, the Olympian spark, the flame of Sinai, this is powerful in them, priding itself on all the glories of Perfection and Blossoming. . . .*

*But this does not correspond to the truth (he thought further). Inadequacy is not something that accompanies greatness, superiority; it is its "quid," its substance. Greatness —let us say this at last —is inadequacy!*

*Madman! Madman! He's gotten on his hobbyhorse again! His face, poring over the sheet of paper, has assumed a dramatic concentration, he sought something, something that perhaps was too elusive . . . and perhaps his truth was contained in the pursuit and not in the attainment. . . . Ah, how transparently and efficiently all of this shaped up for him in theory: who was this so-called great man if not the product of unceasing effort, of an artificial engorgement of maturity, of the diligent covering up of his deficiencies, of the forced adjustment to other outstanding people who allowed themselves the same mendacity —and is not greatness an "interhuman" creation like all of culture? In that case he who in the sphere of collective life succumbed to being elevated always had to be below . . . and it is here that greatness, distinction, dignity, and mastery became insufficient, immature . . . secretly affiliated with everything young. . . . Mastery therefore was eternal tawdriness! An eternal feebleness and charm! Yes! But if this were so, why couldn't he, Gombrowicz, find a practical counterpart for this theory, why did this thought become unbearable when he tried to bring it to life in the pages of the* Diary?

*It became more and more apparent to our candidate for master that his formulas did not exhaust the practical meaning of these matters . . . an empty, perhaps "erroneous," perhaps even mutually contradictory meaning. . . . My good God, who will find the right word for the ineluctable, the elusive thought! . . . And it became more and more evident that one cannot show too much of the curtain in a show in which one is appearing — here the play was too passionate, the coquetry was too real, important . . . elementary . . . engulfing. . . .*

*He sought. He looked around for some sort of "solution." But for the time being, he resigned from a frontal attack on these difficult issues in the* Diary, *and from finding his own new* genre *of greatness. He decided to wait . . . to take a closer look at this greatness of his and to determine which kind would ultimately be awarded to him: a difficult aristocratic greatness, incomprehensible to the throng, destined for a narrow group of initiates, or a more popular variety? . . . The only thing he could manage for the time being was the introduction of a "second voice" into the* Diary — *the voice of a commentator and biographer — which allowed him to speak of himself as "Gombrowicz," through someone else's lips. This was, in his opinion, an important discovery, intensifying the immeasurably cold artificiality of his admissions, which also allowed for greater honesty and passion. And this was something new, which he had never encountered in any of the diaries he had read.*

*An interesting innovation, of course. And perhaps more important than it might seem. Gombrowicz had been noticing for some time that great style is not just great, it pokes you in the ribs endlessly, whispering: "watch out, don't miss me, I'm great." A great style possesses its own master of ceremonies, lecturer and commentator. In addition, this division into voices was justified by the very structure of style and firmly grounded in reality. But beyond this — what wealth to be able to speak about oneself in the first and third persons simultaneously! For he who speaks of himself with "I" must, of necessity, lie a lot and leave much unsaid — while he who speaks of himself with "he" and tries to describe himself from the outside will also be wielding only a partial truth. This switching from the "I" to "Gombrowicz" could gradually (in proportion to the perfecting and deepening of this device) lead to interesting results.*

*And it permitted him to praise and unmask himself in one stroke!*

## Monday

A soccer match at the stadium River Plate. About thirty thousand spectators. Warm sun. Suddenly, over stands alive with conversation during the restless wait for the beginning of battle, a little balloon appears. . . . A balloon? Everyone knows that it is not a balloon but a condom, enormously blown up with someone's indecent breath. The condom-balloon, aided by the currents radiating into the air from the heated audience, glides overhead, and when it falls, it is batted back up by the insignificant palms of jokers . . . and the thousands present are riveted to this flying scandal, so horribly visible, so offensive! Silence. No one dares say a word. Ecstasy. Then some *padre de familia,* furious, jabs it with a penknife. It bursts.

Whistles! Howls! An incredible fury shoots out from all sides—near and far—and terrified, the "head of the family" bolts for the nearest exit. This was told to me by Flor de Quilombo alias Florquilo alias Quiloflor alias Coliflor alias Flor-en-coli alias Coli-en-flor.

# XII

## Tuesday

The average educated Argentinean knows well that his creativity is deficient. —We don't have a great literature. Why? Why is there a dearth of geniuses among us? The anemia of our music, philosophy, the plastic arts, lack of ideas, people? Why? Why? It is listless and dull. Why? Why? It is barren and passive. Why? Why? . . . And here the prescriptions begin to multiply: —We live by the borrowed light of Europe. That's the reason. We have to break with Europe, and find within ourselves the slumbering Indian of four centuries ago . . . that is our only source! But the nationalism of another faction is repulsed by the very thought—what, *Indio?* Never! Our incapacity derives from our having moved away from mother-Spain and mother-church. Here, though, the atheism of the progressive left gets feverish, Spain, the clergy, yuck, obscurantism, oligarchy, learn from Marx, you will become creative! . . . while a young man, *fino,* from downtown Buenos Aires, returning from a tea at Victoria Ocampo's, carries a Parisian *revue* and an ornate volume of Chinese poetry.

Pills to cure impotence—ridiculous, thus it amazes me a bit that this discussion has been going on solemnly for decades and has even transformed itself into the main intellectual controversy of Latin America. It is the subject of endless lectures and articles. Believe in the Most High and Catholic Isabella and you will be creative! Implement a dictatorship of the proletariat and the cult of the Indian—and you will see how things improve! But this whining isn't too serious; they need geniuses in the way they need a soccer team—to win a match with foreign countries. The undoing of their spirit is exactly this desire to show the world, to keep up with it. The main concern of these artists is not the expression of their own passions and the building of their own world, but to write a novel "of European stature"—in order for Argentina, for South America, finally to have a presentable work. They treat art like an international sports championship and they worry for hours about why there are so few goals for the Argentine team.

Why are there so few goals? Isn't "we" the problem, that little word "we" (which I distrust so profoundly, which I would forbid the individual man to use)? As long as an Argentinean speaks in the first person singular, he is human, supple, real . . . and perhaps in certain respects, even superior to the European. The smaller the ballast, the smaller the hereditary burden, the less history, tradition, custom, and thereby more freedom of movement and greater possibility for choice; it is easier then to keep up with history. And this advantage would be absolute if South American life were not easy, discouraging effort, boldness, risk and persistence, categorical decisions, tragedy and struggle, any extremity that is the "creating" arena *par excellence.* A soft life softens (why be hard?) . . . everything dissipates. . . . Yet in spite of his lack of intensity, the Argentinean, as long as he expresses himself in the first person, is someone who is not at all stupid, open to the world and sober — and I slowly learned to like and appreciate him. Argentineans often have grace, elegance, style.

Unfortunately, this "I" functions only on the lowest rungs of local existence. They do not know how to get it onto a higher rung — that is, into culture, art, religion, morality, philosophy — here they always switch to "we." But "we" is an abuse. Why, the individual exists in order to use "I"! This foggy, abstract, and arbitrary "we," therefore, deprives them of concreteness, that is, their sanguineness; it ruins their directness, almost knocks them off their feet and puts them in a haze. Then the Argentinean begins to preach about how, let us say, "we" need history because we cannot hold a candle to the other — more historical — nations, and he willfully begins to fabricate a history for himself by erecting monuments to countless national heroes on every street corner, by celebrating a different anniversary every week, by giving lectures, often pompously, and by talking himself into an illustrious past. In South America, fabricating history is an enterprise consuming colossal amounts of (wasted) time. If he is a writer, the Argentinean will begin to consider what Argentina really is — in order to deduce from this what sort of Argentinean he is supposed to be — and what his works should be like so that they turn out sufficiently familiar, national, continental, creole. These analyses will not necessarily produce a novel that fits into gaucho literature; they could also produce a very sophisticated work — but inevitably written according to this program. In other words, this deduced Argentinean will create a deduced literature, poetry, music, a deduced worldview, deduced moral principles, and a deduced standard . . . so that everything fits snugly into his deduced Argentina.

In the meantime, what is this Argentina like — what sort of "we" is this? No one knows. If an Englishman or a Frenchman says "we," that means something sometimes because in those countries people have known for centuries what France or England is. But Argentina? The mixture of races and legacies, the brief history, unformed character, unestablished institutions, ideals, principles, reflexes, a splendid country, it is true, with an abundant future but certainly not formed. Is Argentina chiefly its natives, who have lived here for a long time? Is it chiefly the immigration that is transforming and building the country? Is Argentina precisely this: a combination, cocktail, mixture and ferment? Is Argentina Undefinability? In which case that whole Argentine questionnaire—"Who are we?" "Which truth is our truth?" "What are we striving for?"—has to end in fiasco. For it is not intellectual analyses, but action—action based firmly on the first person singular—that contains the answer.

Do you want to know who you are? Don't ask. Act. Action will delineate and define you. You will find out from your actions. But you must act as an "I," as an individual, because you can be certain only of your own needs, inclinations, passions, necessities. Only this kind of action is direct and is a genuine extricating of yourself from chaos, self-creation. As for the rest: isn't it mere recitation, execution of a preordained plan, rubbish, kitsch?

There is nothing easier than to allow oneself a handful of paradoxes, smacking of the most sober realism. For example: an authentic Argentinean will be born when the writers forget about Argentina . . . when they forget about America! They will tear away from Europe when Europe stops being an issue for them, when they lose sight of it; its essence will reveal itself to them when they stop looking for it.

It is absurd to think that a national identity can be realized from a predetermined program—it must be unforeseen. Just as personality is determined on an individual scale. To be someone is to inquire incessantly about who I am and not to know in advance. It is impossible to extract creativity from that which already is; it is not a consequence. . . .

# Wednesday

However, one could also apply a different method, quite the opposite and closer to what they practice today. It would consist of openly discussing all these concerns (impotence, lack of originality, dependence on other cultures), of seeing them as the subject in order to gain a little distance, to break with them. Similarly, someone who is shy, by speaking of his shyness, can free himself from it, because it is no longer him—it is merely a problem. I know this method well and have recommended it often.

Certainly. But this would have to be presented not collectively but in the first person. "I," "my concern," "my solution." No Argentinean will ask, however: Why is it that *I* am not creative? Their question is: Why can't *we* create? Everything dissolves in this "we."

# Thursday

The awful invasion of stereotypes, theories, abstractions, ready-made forms worked out somewhere else, is a result of their "I" being barely able to stand on its own feet. The invasion is all the more grotesque because abstraction is not in their nature. There is something painful about their need to theorize and their incapacity to do so.

The artists of this country (and the entire continent) cannot take a single step without a crutch—be it Marxism or Paris, ancient Indian digs or Toynbee—dandyism as much as anarchism as much as monarchism (I have seen these types as well). They live on elaborate essays. And because the word inflates quickly in this easy, soft life, all of the -isms end in mere verbiage. The word! Their literature is pretty words. To be an artist it is enough to express oneself beautifully. The most original and independent writer of Argentina, Borges, writes a fine and elegant Spanish, is a stylist in the literary sense (not in the sense of spiritual solutions), and most gladly cultivates a literature about literature, a writing about books—and if sometimes he surrenders himself to pure imagination, it leads him far from life, into a sphere of convoluted metaphysics, the ordering of beautiful rebuses, a scholastics made up of metaphors.

The people who are most alert and most pained by this impotence, for example, the Cuban Piniera, are often too conscious of defeat to be able to fight. Piniera, feeling powerless, pays homage to the Great Absurd, which smashes him—in his art the adoration of the absurd is a protest against a senseless world, his revenge, even the blasphemy of a man offended in his morality. "If meaning, the moral meaning of the world is impossible to attain, I will make a fool of myself"—this is how Piniera's revenge and his rebellion look, more or less. But why does he, like so many other Americans, doubt his own strength so much? Well, because for him it is a matter of the *world,* not his own life. In the face of the world, humanity, the nation, one is powerless, this exceeds one's powers—but one can, in spite of everything, show them a thing or two with one's own life, here power returns to man, although in a somewhat limited dimension.

Some of them—some of the local writers—are endowed with an efficient brain mechanism and precision of expression, and cannot move from where they are only because they have become bogged down in an inherited and obsolete set of problems. This always happens to superficially modern minds. They are constantly seeking victory within the rules of the same game when one should be overturning the chessboard. Coming up with new questions—is the best way of taking care of the old.

Level! Ah, what torment! Level! Ah, how it paralyzes! The main effort is expended on elevating banality and on complicating truisms, as is always the case when one has little to say. This literature, on various social rungs, is always mystification. Each side wants to write a level higher. The provinces do what they can to equal the capital in artificial words. The worst thing is when those at the top, from the highest rungs of the capital, want to make people know who they are—then their inflated and twisted sentences become unbearable and one cannot understand what they are driving at.

An easy life. A provincial life. Here, anyone who has garnered a few prizes transforms himself painlessly into a "master." But "maestro" means both "master" and "teacher." Because no one wants to write for himself but only for the nation (or readers), a South American writer is also often a reader, a master of little guys, a leader, enlightener (generally speaking, it is odd how scholastic this culture is . . . so much so that one has the impression that schoolmarms have shaped the nation). With a little good will, the "maestro" succumbs to the next metamorphosis: he becomes a prophet, seer, sometimes a martyr or hero of America. Strange that in a nation so disarmingly modest there is so much pomposity in the upper strata, almost a childish self-aggrandizement.

# Saturday

Returning to Polish affairs . . . I prefer to play with my enemies rather than destroy them. I have always tried to play with my enemies, even when they gave me no peace.

Today I am amazed by the delicateness of these hippopotamuses—now when I am on top and can crawl under their skin from time to time for the fun of it. How thin their skin is! Occasionally one of these dolts, having not yet caught on to the real, so to speak, relationship of forces, will send a few epithets flying in my direction out of sheer habit—well, let us assume that I am a poseur, jester, zero, a fraud, but if I give him tit for tat, he cries to the high heavens. He is allowed to write that I am a clown, but I am not allowed to write that he is dull-witted. When he gives me a royal working over from the heights of his bombastic vacuity, everything is fine. But I am supposed to sit mum! I am not allowed to utter a word because he is a "critic." And I am not a critic, I am an author, for whom it is "out of place to polemicize," oh, no, what a lack of tact!

When I in my turn take on, just for the fun of it, the criticism of Mr. Critic, without mincing words, a diabolical row breaks out, help, save me, people! That Gombrowicz is a brute, he is evil, no good, how dare he, that conceited so-and-so, that megalomaniac!

Conceited? Megalomaniac? Listen, hippopotamuses: I am not complaining that your professorial or columnist's stupidity has constantly slandered my writing, which, as it turns out, is worth something. You did what you could to ruin my life and you were partly successful. If it had not been for your dullness, shallowness, mediocrity, perhaps I would not have starved for so many years in Argentina and would have been spared other humiliations. You stood between me and the world — a group of omnipotent schoolmarms and publicists — warping, twisting, falsifying values and proportions. Fine, never mind all that, I forgive you! And I don't expect that one of you will grunt out something on the order of a meek "I'm sorry," I know only too well what I can expect from jokers like you.

But how can I forgive your being victorious over me in my ultimate victory over you? Yes. Cheer up. You have been victorious in defeat. You caused my victory to come too late . . . ten, twenty years too late . . . as I am too close to death and it infects even my triumph with defeat. . . . You know, I am no longer so perverse as to be happy at the revenge. Triumph? Megalomania — conceit? You have deprived me even of that — I can delight neither in my exaltation nor in your defeat — how can I forgive that?

# Monday

I like and appreciate Argentina . . . yes, but which Argentina? I do not like and do not appreciate Argentina . . . yes, but which Argentina?

I am a friend of the natural, simple, down-to-earth Argentina of the folk. I am at war with the higher, ready-made Argentina — that awful concoction!

Not long ago one Argentinean said to me: You are allergic to us. But another, Jorge Apalos, wrote to me from Santiago: "You are looking for real value (*lo legitimo*) in this country because you love it." (Love a country? I?)

# Wednesday

Get the government! Everyone is always in opposition and the government is always guilty. After the overthrow of Perón, the idyll took to the streets — joy and visible emotion, banners and all. But this lasted a whole week. After that, twenty opposition newspapers with gigantic headlines sprang up: GOVERNMENT OF BETRAYAL, NEW TYRANNY, DIGNITY OR DEATH, ENOUGH DISGRACE. After three months, poor General Aramburu, the president, didn't have even ten percent of the supporters (it wasn't until he left that they pronounced him a decent man).

When afterward Frondizi was chosen by an overwhelming majority, again joy — and then again after a few months he was a: "traitor," "renegade," "tyrant," . . . These were the more delicate compliments. . . .

The vociferousness of the opposition press is astounding.

The source of these sad phenomena you could probably find in the easy life, in the enormous or sparsely populated expanse, where a person can allow himself a great deal without punishment because ultimately "things will somehow work out." If the private life of an American is still characterized by a certain regularity and if it is still obvious, for example, that if he does not repair the roof, it will rain on his head, then this social, wider, higher political life becomes something like a Great Frontier — one can clamor, riot, and frolic, for where there is no logic, there is also no responsibility, nothing will happen to so vast a country. And so demagoguery, claptrap, political lunacy, illusions, theories, phobias, manias, megalomanias, caprices, and especially the most ordinary *viveza* (we can pull the wool over their eyes but they'd better not do it to us!) abound! One can tell people absurdities strewn with the cheapest banalities and life will never unmask them, because collective reality is *laxer here* — and a blusterer will walk in glory in his old age.

A easy life exudes beneficence, good humor, sentimentality, naïveté, unresourcefulness, delicacy — a softness in which one slowly drowns. But a society that is threatened by softness, that feels the danger subconsciously, wants to defend itself — this is where that famous *viveza* comes from, a little bit of cunning that is supposed to prepare them for life, make reality accessible to them anew, save them from the shame of gullibility and naïveté.

Volumes have been written about the psychology of the South American; they are often metaphysical, almost always too "deep" — knowledge about a man or a nation is not always a deep-water fish — sometimes spiced with a tasty homegrown mysticism (that there is some undiscovered truth in the "silence" of an Argentinean, for example). All right, let it be most profound where it should be, but why should one look for a chasm on the straightaway? Ninety percent of Argentina and South America can be explained by the life these people lead, a life that is, in spite of their complaints, quite easy in comparison with other continents.

# Saturday

This is how they lose themselves in collective reality, how it becomes fantastic to them, impossible to grasp.

In Tandil I speak with the owner of a beautiful villa, the director of a fairly large company, a man of experience. I ask him: what do you think, how many people were killed during the revolution in Córdoba on 16 September? He thinks a moment, then says: — Twenty-five thousand.

Why, only one battle of this revolution took place in the city of Córdoba and only two regiments of infantry, a school of artillery, and two more military formations participated. The battle consisted of firing mainly light weapons and it lasted for two days. The number of fallen was not announced, but if there were three hundred, that was a lot. . . . And this guy tells me: Twenty-five thousand! Twenty-five thousand! What insanity — did he stop to think even for a moment what twenty-five thousand corpses means?

In Goya (Corrientes) when I said that on 16 June 1955 during the bombing of Casa Rosada in Buenos Aires two hundred people died, they looked at me as if I were crazy. In their opinion there were no less than fifteen thousand casualties! Fifteen thousand! I allowed myself to risk the statement that their whole revolution from 1955 did not cost them more than a few hundred lives and most of those as a result of automobile accidents (because a lot of people fled and others chased them). Which offended them greatly.

In Santiago a certain law student at the university in Tucumán assured me gravely that Freud is useless to South Americans. "Because Freud is European knowledge, and this is America."

In Tandil I asked a student from Bahia Blanca, a Communist, if he had ever had a moment of doubt and he answered: —Yes, once. I perked up my ears thinking he would mention the concentration camps, the strangling of Hungary, or the unmasking of Stalin. But he meant Kandinsky, who was ostracized or really shunned for abstract painting. This was the only thing he acknowledged as being out of order . . . a little.

Stupidity? No—they are not stupid. It is simply that the world that exists beyond the concreteness of their family, house, friends, earnings, is dispensable. It offers no resistance. It does not punish for errors, therefore an error does not become forbidding. Ultimately, twenty-five thousand or three hundred is almost the same. In this kind of conversation, they are sybarites, they prefer the pleasant to the true.

The moment comes, however, when Reality bares its teeth. Thus in Argentina—after ten years of prodigality, wage increases, the building up of a completely incomprehensible bureaucratic apparatus, and printing paper money—the bottom of the purse loomed up and a crisis exploded, the likes of which the country had never seen. How difficult it is for them to understand! To this day, the majority are convinced that the government *does not want* to guarantee the people affluence. The political crudity of this nation is glaring; they are touched by Daltonism, they do not know how to distinguish between what is of prime importance in politics and what is secondary and trifling.

Yet they are, from birth, magnificent realists. . . .

# Monday

A few months after my arrival in Argentina in 1939, a small group of minor literati, with whom I formed friendships, began to urge me to give a lecture in the Teatro del Pueblo. At the time, I knew nothing of Argentina. I asked what sort of theater it was. —First class—they answered—these lectures are attended by *the* elite, the crème de la crème! I decided, therefore, to cook up a lecture that was highly intellectual and, after writing it in French, had it translated into Spanish. I entitled it: "Cultural Regression in Lesser Known Europe."

I intentionally did not mention a word about Poland, since this was a tragic time, immediately after the September events. . . . I described how the wave of barbarism that had crashed over Central and Eastern Europe could be used to revise the foundations of our culture.

These beginnings of mine in Argentina today look like total darkness, concealing within its womb a tragicomical *quiproquo*. How did that happen? I show up at the theater — overflowing with people — I read my paper with a horrible accent — bravos — and I return quite content to my reserved loge where I find an acquaintance, an Argentine girl from the ballet, with a low-cut dress and coin necklaces. She had come to admire. I am in the process of taking my coat off the hanger to leave with her when I see some guy get onto the stage and declaim — what a spectacle. I understand nothing and hear only "Polonia." Bravos, excitement. After which another guy crawls up to the podium and fires off a speech, all the while flailing his arms — the public roars. I understand nothing, but I am very pleased that my discourse, which had irritated me like a fly buzzing up my nose when I read it, was causing such a stir. Suddenly — what's this? — our envoy rises and together with other members of the Polish Legation leaves the hall. Oh, oh, something is not right! . . . More speeches, the atmosphere heats up, more clamor, someone turns to me: — Why don't you do something? They're attacking Poland! . . . A fine pickle! How am I supposed to react to a sermon in Chinese?

The next day — trouble. As it turned out, my lecture was used by the Communists to attack Poland. It also turned out that the somewhat communizing "intellectual elite" was not all that creamy, the result being that the attack on "fascist Poland" did not distinguish itself with refinement and stupid things were said, such as there is no Polish literature and that the only Polish writer is Bruno Jasieński.* Appalled, I ran to the Legation — where I was received icily, and suspected of sabotage, almost of treason. In vain did I explain that the theater director, Mr. Barletta, had neglected to inform me that, according to custom, there is a discussion after the lecture (I have no reason to suspect him of deliberately keeping me in the dark; besides, I did not consider him a Communist, as he passed himself for — and to this day passes himself for — an upright, enlightened, and progressive citizen, impartial and just, an opponent of imperialists and a friend of the people; it was only during the Hungarian revolution, when the impartial, just, and noble anti-imperialism of Mr. Barletta inclined him categorically to support Russian tanks, that I lost all vestiges of my faith).

The worst was the ballerina — her rouge, powder, neckline, and coins completed the balance of my misfortune. — What cynicism — they said. — At such a moment! As far as I remember, even the Polish press

---

*Bruno Jasieński (1901–37), Polish futurist poet who switched to writing revolutionary poetry and novels. Arrested in the Soviet Union in 1937, he died on his way to a concentration camp in Kolyma. He was rehabilitated in 1957.

in the United States jumped on the bandwagon . . . but I would have been capable of withstanding this tornado of mad suspicions, accusations, and condemnations, if not for Pyzik! Pyzik, the president of the Union of Poles in Argentina, wrote something in his article that knocked me out . . . to wit, he accused me of *not mentioning a word about the Polish school system.* . . . What???? The school system???? What school system? Why the school system? Ha! That's all I needed—the Polish school system!

# XIII

## Monday

I devoured a few pages with great satisfaction, that he is so intelligent and, bravo, that he reads me so thoroughly, that he is familiar with even the little nooks and crannies of my writings, ah, the critic who *reads,* what a rarity! (I am talking about "Key Issues in Gombrowicz's *The Marriage,*" written by Andrzej Falkiewicz and published in Poland.) But the farther one goes into this forest, however, the thicker the underbrush—and by the time I got to the end of Falkiewicz's essay, I had lost my way . . . I, the subject, I, who should know this territory. . . . So what can I expect of others?

This is disturbing . . . especially since I cannot dismiss it as the clumsiness of the critic, who is penetrating, earnest, unusually subtle. . . . Why the misunderstanding? And if it had been only one of many! But this has happened to me so many times with other critics—that I think it proves not so much the inadequacy of the critics as the perversion of criticism itself, in particular of the most difficult kind, concerning literature that comes into being today, that is, the literature of tomorrow, "modern" literature. I even feel that the situation is perilous, that something must be changed in the method, in the attitude, or in something else. I don't know—something innovative is absolutely essential, like having the authors and critics work together . . . perhaps this would work to pull the wagon out of the mire?

As things are now, the author, though he is alive, has to pretend he is dead. I was once present at a fierce discussion between Kott—and Breiter?—on what X "wanted to say" in his last work. They pelted each other with quotes. I proposed that they put the question to the author over the telephone and even gave them his number. They stopped dead in their tracks and in a minute began to talk about something else. When the problem was reduced to a question over the telephone, it ceased to interest them.

To get back to Falkiewicz—if even he, in my opinion, did not understand *The Marriage* completely, where should I look for the source of the problem? Isn't it because in his impatience he wanted to understand it too profoundly right away? One should advise critics of the

modern and most difficult art not to be so profound right off the bat—
they should be shallow at the beginning, and then gradually and very
carefully should immerse themselves in searching for profundities. My
point is this: each literary work exists on various planes, some closer
and others more distant, but first the story must "move, amuse, make
you laugh," then it acquires various "more profound meanings," and only
in its ultimate sense becomes (if it does at all) precipitous, vertiginous,
and sometimes crazy. One has to establish this rule and adhere to it:
one can speak about the deeper aspects of modern art only after mas-
tering the more immediate, easier aspects which join it to the art that
preceded it.

Falkiewicz began to look behind the curtain prematurely, he neglected to look first at what was happening onstage. He is wrong to say
that *The Marriage* is "unclear and inconsistent"—on the contrary. What
is so strange about a dream (an outlet for daytime worries) that shows
Henry the ruin and disgrace of his parents, his fiancée, the family home?
Is it so strange that in this dream about an inn Drunkards appear and
that these Drunkards begin to persecute the Father when he forbids
them to touch Molly? Is it not logical and appropriate to the situation
that the panic-stricken Father pronounces himself "an Untouchable King"
to elude the touch of the Drunkard? And that Henry feels in his dream
that he alone is responsible for sustaining the miracle or having it totter
into farce—is this not a feeling that often visits us in our dreams? So
isn't his waivering between Wisdom and Stupidity at the beginning of
act 2 understandable? And his new grappling with the Drunkard, who
intrudes once again with his Finger to "touch" the king and then Molly?
But the Drunkard, seeing that he is unable to overcome Henry in open
battle, changes his tactics, proposes to "have a little talk" on the side—
the result of which is that the scene transforms itself into a courtly,
diplomatic reception (has such a change of scenery never occurred to
you in a dream?). And, further on, isn't it the culmination of a psychological process already begun in the opening act when Henry's growing
doubts about the royalty of the king lead, in a more and more muddled
atmosphere of drunkenness, to a coup d'état? When, by reverting to
new methods, the Drunkard arouses jealousy in the new king about
Johnny—is he not consistent in his striving to obstruct the marriage
and "get at" Molly?

The marriage that Henry would like to perform on himself in the
third act is, as Falkiewicz correctly writes, a consequence of his idea
that God did not create man but man created God. This marriage in the
"human church," replacing the former in the "divine church," is the main
metaphor of the drama. When there is no God, values are born of, or

rather between, people. But our hero's dominion over the people must become real—that is why Henry needs Johnny's death, that is why he commands the release of his parents and the Drunkard to pit himself against them in one final clash. And here he collapses. . . .

Is this action so difficult to extract from the text? Certainly, I myself am not without blame. In the introduction ("Idea of the Play"), I wrote: "Everything in the play 'creates itself': Henry creates a dream and a dream creates Henry, the action of the play creates itself, people create one another, and the whole pushes forward toward unknown solutions."*

How careful one must be! I know now that this imprecise formulation can lead one astray. In writing about creating oneself, and especially in saying that action creates itself, I had in mind that one scene often arises from another in a casual way, almost accidentally, and that the drama, as an embodiment of the inner spiritual work of Henry, makes up a canvas of associations that is sometimes absurd and that sometimes eludes form—but I forgot to add that these superficial freedoms are based on the core of the story, which the drama tells, and which in its general outline is not deprived of logic. I did not mention this because it seemed so obvious to me at first.

Falkiewicz grasped this outline, but he didn't follow it to the end. Led astray by my murky information about "creating oneself," he conceives of the drama as an almost completely unrestrained explosion of associations and, as a consequence, seeks justification in the breakneck antics of the latest trends in philosophy, sociology, and psychology even for things which can be explained by the normal course of action. He ponders the existential and antiexistential sense of my laughter, seeks the ultimate contradiction between the problems and the form, analyzes my ties to "dream logic," but sometimes does not notice the most obvious links in the development of the plot. From which comes the moral of avant-garde criticism: beware! Only gradually and with the greatest caution do you descend to the most profound layers of a work— never lose the connections between surface and depths. Grasp the work first in its easiest, its most public form, and then go backstage. Metaphysics, yes, but one must begin with physics. Grasp the work, too, in its connection with the past, with a more classical literature, because ultimately even the most revolutionary outgrowth stems from previous forms the reader is familiar with. And accept the principle that if

---

*The Marriage,* trans. Louis Iribarne (New York: Grove Press, 1969; Evanston, Ill.: Northwestern University Press, 1986), 16.

something finds its justification in the physics of a work, very often it can do without metaphysics. I have often experienced on my own hide that heaven and earth have been moved to explain a comma which simply resulted from the construction of a sentence. . . .

# Tuesday

A few more words about avant-garde criticism, but now in its more journalistic aspect and without ties to Falkiewicz. . . . One must simplify. One must facilitate, simplify things for the reader! You have turned too far away from him, your reviews swell with indigestibles. This is exactly one of those problems of style, one of those real problems of style — which are a headache and silliness itself, and which one haughtily avoids because they are too practical by nature, not enough *à la hauteur*. . . . I, if I cultivated this profession of an avant-garde critic, would stand on my head to change and improve something here, to break out of this deadlock.

Who is this avant-garde critic who writes in a newspaper? Is he an intellectual? An artist? A teacher? A journalist? If he is a journalist, one must admit that he is not enough of a journalist, he does not know how to reach the reader. If he is a teacher, this is knowledge that is far too ranting, condensed, hurried, unclear. If he is an artist, he is not charming enough, he is too heavy, he does not know how to dance. . . . In the role of an intellectual he is reminiscent of goulash, stew, salad, tripe in oil, cabbage and peas. And how often he turns out to be an *élégant* with soiled underwear and dirty fingernails because all of this tends to be poorly laundered, not thought through, and poorly written . . . pretentious shoddiness, terror (of both readers and editors). Snobbery? Why, of course, snobbery. Unfortunately, this is true, this discipline is polluted with snobbery and claptrap. Take a look at the sentences which crush the reader with their *dernier cri* terminology while their construction, punctuation, and grammar are lousy. A magnificent tie worn with a soiled shirt.

The question is, what can one correct here, where should one begin? In my opinion, reform is needed, and it is high time for it. If criticism, especially avant-garde criticism, has become fictional, pompous, deceptive, it is because it is suspended in abstractions, far from any kind of concrete flesh, blood, and bone — these critics wallow in art, culture, philosophy, and other such generalities — well, one can easily drown reality in this and really have a good time! The essence of the problem, then, is breaking with abstraction and linking up to that lost concrete detail. When the critic feels that he is a man writing about another man and for people, when he finds his lost Sociability, he will gain a solid basis for many pressing revisions.

The pseudoscience of today's criticism is becoming unbearable. The schools are to blame for this—high schools and universities—the universities have done a lot of damage by convincing people that one can approach art scientifically. How catastrophic this method of occupying oneself exclusively with the work, torn away from the person of the author, turned out to be!—after this abstraction came others, which separated the work from the author even more, conceiving of it as a self-sufficient "object," conceiving of it "objectively," transferring everything to the realm of a false, lame aesthetic or sociological pseudo-mathematics, opening the gates wide to pedantry and prating analyses as well as to license, dressed superficially in majestic scientific precision. I do not at all demand that a work be interpreted naively through the biography of the writer and that his art be tied to his life's experiences—my point is the principle contained in the aphorism "style is the man," that is, that Chopin's style is the organization of Chopin's soul, and Rabelais's style is the solution to Rabelais's personality. Chopin's romances with Georges Sand interest me little—but beyond Chopin's music I look for Chopin himself; I want to understand the creator by way of his work. Behind the tale Poe tells me I must find the person who tells it, as—understand this—the *only* reality, the *only* thing that is concrete. Thus I draw conclusions about the creator from his work; yet once again this personality of the creator will simplify and open up a work by binding it inseparably to someone . . . to someone's particular existence.

What is this or any other work? "A work of art," "a cultural phenomenon," "an expression of social processes," "a source of aesthetic feelings"—or perhaps it is first of all a person's work, an element of someone's life, someone's spiritual effort. Who doubts that *Hamlet* is not just Shakespeare's reverie but also Hamlet, that is, an imagined character, but as authentic as if he were more alive than Shakespeare . . . in addition, *Hamlet* contains discoveries and beauty that ensure him an existence independent of Shakespeare's. Yet in spite of all that, the truth about Hamlet is that Shakespeare made him up (even though Shakespeare was even more elusive than Hamlet) and it is only this Danish prince, bound to his creator, fixed in his creator, who is one hundred percent real. Do you remember Descartes? When I think of the centaur, I cannot be certain that a centaur existed—the only thing I know for sure is that my thought about a centaur exists. . . . Although Hamlet, the Danish prince, is imagined, the Shakespearean dream of

Hamlet existed and this is the concrete fact that we desperately need. When you begin to carry on about "art," you can say whatever you like—abstractions offer no resistance. When you discover the persons behind the books, however, when your literary world becomes peopled with Tolstoys, Schillers, Balzacs, Ibsens, when style becomes someone's personal style, when you link form to someone's experience, then much of the fog now blanketing our eyes will burn away. No, I do not forget that form and art are born "between" people and not of man; I am very far from granting the creator exclusivity, but if modern criticism is to regain strength, sociability, efficacy within the pale of the human world, we must look beyond the work to the man, to the creator, at least as a point of reference. Not—for heaven's sake—in order to ask "What was he trying to say?" (this would again reduce criticism to the examination of the intellectual, that is, abstract, intentions of the author and, anyway, this kind of questioning is irrelevant in art). But in order for a book to grow out of some sort of—out of someone's—reality, out of someone's experience.

While establishing this kind of contact with the person of the author, should not the critic also introduce his own person onto the stage? Analyses, sure, syntheses, yes, dissections and parallels, well, so be it, but at least let this be organic, red-blooded, pulsating, permeated with the critic, let it be him, his spoken voice. Critics! Write so that the person reading you knows whether you have blond or black hair.

(I dedicate this to Poland. Before the war, while listening to their conversations—when Knowledge, Society, and everything that was social and rational was worshipped, when people turned with fury against the Person and the Personal, when they hated, worse, did not like art for its intimate uncontrollable whisper—while listening to them, to these artist-moralizers, artist-constructors, artist-theoreticians, and poet-mathematicians—I knew already that an incompetent epoch in art was approaching, an epoch full of painful mistakes.)

# Thursday

I ate breakfast at the harbor. A series of scenes expressing one and the same idea. At a neighboring table workers discussed politics; one smarted off, gabbed, palavered, others also smarted off, palavered—at the same time, far inside, the resigned owner tried to convince the waiter of something; the waiter, an old and sly man, but a dolt and a loudmouth, threw himself at the owner excitedly, drunk with his own inanities, deafening himself with his own twaddle. Farther still porters joked, chortling on the subject of a certain part of the body. . . . What idea did this express? An awful one! Probably the one that is most capable of depriving people of hope. . . .

We, the intelligentsia, are guided by the salutary thought that the *lower classes are not crazy.* . . . We, yes, we are condemned to all the illnesses, manias, madnesses, but the masses are healthy . . . and the foundation on which humanity leans is just fine. . . . And actually? The people are sicker, crazier than we are! Peasants are madmen! Workers—pathological! Do you hear what they are saying? These are dark and maniacal dialogues. Illiterates dull not with a healthy dullness but with the ravings of a madman, crying for a hospital, a doctor. . . . Can their never-ending curses and obscenities—and nothing beyond that— can this drunken, mad mechanics of their life together be healthy? Shakespeare was right to present the simple folk as "exotic," that is, unlike human beings.

# Monday

*To the editor of* Wiadomości:

*It is only now that I have had the opportunity to acquaint myself with the fragment of Lechoń's* Journal *reprinted in the sixteenth issue of* Wiadomości, *of 19 April of this year, in which he mentions me and my* Trans-Atlantic. *"Gombrowicz . . . is also a madman, I am sure because I know him. . . .* Trans-Atlantic *is a very seedy story. . . . Amusing enough though somewhat foul-smelling. . . ."*

*Such being the case, I will allow myself to quote the following excerpt from Lechoń's letter to me, received in May 1956, that is, a month before his death:*

*"I will reply in your words 'your soul is somehow familiar to me' and I would like it to give me credit once and for all. If a work of art appeals to me, this outweighs all differences of conviction and even grudges between writers. I think of your works,* Ferdydurke *and* Trans-Atlantic, *with considerable pleasure, as stunning works. . . ."*

*And he continues:*

*"I would like you to know, therefore, that I expressed what I think of you most sincerely and, I think, with all due respect, in an interview published a few years ago in* Wiadomości *and that this is for now my modest* Roma locuta.*"*

*???????*

*(1) Keeping in mind that the above-mentioned fragment of Lechoń's Diary comes from the year 1953, and the letter from 1956, perhaps one could assume that Lechoń changed his mind. . . .*

*(2) Rejecting this explanation, we would have to assume that these passages in the letter are hypocrisy from beginning to end. But to what purpose? This assumption would be painful, since I value Lechoń.*

I include the text of Lechoń's letter because, of course, it didn't get printed without being invaded by the meddlesome pencil of the editor of *Wiadomości*. Namely, the beginning was changed as follows:

*"In his 'Pages from a Diary' dated 1 March 1953 (*Wiadomości, *No. 681), Jan Lechoń writes in connection with my* Trans-Atlantic: *'Gombrowicz . . . is also a madman . . . ,' "* etc.

Holy Mother of God! I can't hold this against them—they sent me the corrected text and I, for the sake of peace and quiet, did not protest—but isn't it just a tiny bit irritating that not even a few lines of a letter written to the editor can be included without corrections and alterations? And isn't this rummaging through letters, not articles, altogether indelicate and rude, especially with respect to those who have covered reams of paper with writing? If only this correction had been made in the name of Holy Grammar! All because I wrote "it is only now that I have had the opportunity to become acquainted with," from which the broad masses of readers could deduce that I rarely peek into that newspaper. Oh well, it is true, I rarely do, but that Altissimo besmirched me. I found out only a few months later and by accident (at the Swieczewskis', while putting on my coat). Of course the fact that the shot fired at me from London reached me so late hardly testifies to the devastating properties of the old culverin, but are the only letters that have a chance of being printed in *Wiadomości* without corrections those exclaiming "I just can't wait to get the next issue, etc., etc.,"? Maybe the letters of praise are also tampered with?

That this was a bullet and a shot that they were aiming at me with the intention of shooting me dead or at least wounding me—I am positive. The shot came after my delightful scrap with a certain Polonist figuring in *World Biography* (New York, 1948). But one must admit they have bad luck. For the heroic attack on the author of the novel *The Quiet of the Forest* allowed me to praise myself until I burst, as I have never praised myself in my life—and now it ends so badly that Altissimo's devastating opinion has transformed itself with the help of a little black magic into the same Altissimo's almost archlaudatory and positive opinion. And I put all the faithful who belong to this little chapel face-to-face with an awful dilemma—for either-or: either Altissimo Poet is enraptured with that seedy *Trans-Atlantic,* or Altissimo Poet is a regular bluffer and a first-class pharisee. Enough. Jokes aside. What sort of magic was this? How could Lechoń make such a leap from abomination to rapture in so brief a time (the interview that he mentions in his letter bears the date 1954, and even then he is speaking of me rather favorably)? There is a riddle concealed here, one that is interesting to a student of literary life.

Perhaps the riddle is confusing only because—like that document from Poe's short story—the solution is staring us in the face instead of hiding in the secret drawer. Why the change of opinion? Because he never had one. Why didn't he have one? Because he never *read* it. I sometimes wondered how it happened that students were perfectly capable of handling the contents of my works while professional literati said the same stupid things over and over again. A student reads, that's all—a literatus looks at, flips through, sniffs out. . . . I sense that Lechoń read me as much as I read his poems . . . but wasn't this the reason our opinions did not dig a chasm between us? . . . After all, his notes were private, he hadn't intended them to be published. Sometimes it's worse. A few years ago, a certain well-known publicist gave me a dressing down in the Polish press on how my *Diary* was terribly provincial . . . that these were merely "endless variations on the subject: Poland and I. . . . " I rubbed my eyes (Had this man written that in a drunken stupor? I don't think ten percent of the diary is about Polish matters), until I figured out that he had read just the few fragments in *Kultura,* which happened to be about Poland, and that from this gnawed bone he had imagined the entire animal.

A few more words about Lechoń. He was an uncreative and unoriginal poet who was too highly esteemed at the beginning—who for his whole life remained nothing but a "promise." An uncomfortable situation that aggravated his innate creative impotence. What was worse, this poet, barricaded in a tower of classicism (the consequence of an excessive pomposity as well as of barrenness; classicism is the "expertise" of artists having nothing to say), completely lost a sense of modern man and his problems (about which, *nota bene,* he knew little, since the paths of human thought beginning with Hegel were almost completely unknown to this Polish head). His life was disloyal, his place in the hierarchy undeserved, his position insincere; none of these things allowed him direct contact with the epoch, with history. He sneaked by. He eluded it and maintained face. At one point he found himself out of it. His whole politics consisted of releasing a "beautiful" poem into the world now and then (so that people would not say, too loudly, that he was finished), as well as of nurturing his social prestige, in which his background, intelligence, and wit were very helpful to him. He also wrote for his "drawer" a diary which was excellent writing and luminous with a natural intelligence, but compromising because of a pathological, almost complexlike, narrowing of intellectual horizons—as if this man preferred not to know, preferred not to see—a melancholy diary, a pitiful incarnation of the Warsaw bourgeois spirit and the cafés of that day. . . . This was how Lechoń tried to pretend that he lived, by reviving a dead world from his youth, from times that had treated him more graciously. . . . Stop! What is this, did I hate Lechoń? Why am I destroying him? Destroying? No! Not at all! Wouldn't dream of it! I value Lechoń! The more reasons I find to denigrate him, the more I value him; I value him in spite of the reasons I have given, I value him because in spite of everything, this was *someone*—this was a personage—no one knows how, no one knows why this profile has become engraved in our memories; the gestures, tone, silhouette, will remain long after everyone has forgotten his work. . . . He realized himself as a person. Even though this man made no significant contribution to Polish progress with even one important poem, one thought, nevertheless he created something . . . he created himself . . . he created Jan Lechoń. And perhaps it is this game with his own nothingness that fascinates me, this realizing himself in a vacuum, that not having even one-tenth of the poetic merits of Tuwim, he was able to distinguish himself in our literary world with almost the same intensity. . . . At any rate, this was a figure to contend with!

A figure, nevertheless, that does not lend itself to what *Wiadomości* does with it, Lechoń as the bard of the emigration—what a bad idea; he was predestined for that chair only by his worst weaknesses, his veneration of the past, his classically Polish romanticism, and everything in him that unfortunately came straight out of *Kurier Warszawski*. It was too obvious that the publicity in *Wiadomości* was dictated more by the megalomania of the editors than by the recognition of Lechoń's alleged greatness—this campaign was inspired by the conviction that the "readers" can be talked into anything—the odor of this conviction mingled fatally with incense and mingles still today. Beyond the *Wiadomości* coterie, no one took up this thesis; Lechoń had miserable press coverage in Poland after his death, even in the camp favorably inclined toward him—the bard remained the local London bard. And it is sad that the man who was a "splendid Lechoń" was made (through unbearable cant) into a "splendid poet"—poor guy, he came out of this campaign on the short end of the stick.

# Tuesday

One more little word about *Wiadomości*. Actually, I myself am amazed and appalled, but this time I must admit that Mr. Zbyszewski is right: this publication was exciting, compelling, and illuminating at one time and Grydzewski was doing Poland a great service. But now?

*For you must know, my dearest crone,*
*That paradise has become a crick*
*Where Jove once ruled from his throne*
*There now rules a pri . . .*

Add a rhyme yourself, my gracious prince! How did this betrayal of Grydzewski by Grydzewski come about? One has to begin talking about this and not for the sake of petty annoyance: today *Wiadomości* is a chapel, museum, mutual adoration society, catalog, album of withered souvenirs, cemetery, armorial, corner for philatelists or billiard players, anecdote, chat, correction, snobbery, little column—but most of all it is the resurrected and, as it turns out, immortal *Kurier Warszawski*. Unfortunately! There is really something that bodes ill in this victory of the Lewenthal family from beyond the grave—who would have dreamed it! This London weekly is the most recent edition of the same indestructible bourgeoisie from Krakowskie Przedmieście.\* And this really is a National Institution whole hog: here the proofreader has triumphed over the writer; the reader over the author; the editor over the writer; the comma and semicolon over talent; form, trademark, pattern over individuality; formalism over art; organization and bureaucracy over flights of fancy, drama, poetry, and life. During the past dozen years of its life, *Wiadomości* has managed to alienate practically all the creative elements of literature in emigration. Miłosz was treated with a boisterous unintelligence worthy of the late Rabski;\*\* a bucket of table scraps was poured over Miłosz's head and he was pronounced a "traitor"—which did not prevent him from affecting the orientation of world opinion toward red terror in Poland more effectively than all the issues of *Wiadomości* put together. Who of today's better authors contributes to this publication? Not only has it been cut off from talent, it has been cut off from living Polish thought. If there is any kind of discussion, effort, struggle, anything at all going on in emigration, it

---

\*Old boulevard in Warsaw.
\*\*Władysław Rabski, second-rate writer at *Kurier Warszawski*.

takes place a hundred miles from *Wiadomości* and its contests: "Whom should we nominate to the Literary Academy?" I, rightly or wrongly, successfully or not, have touched on a multitude of issues of prime importance for us in the course of my writing in emigration—I received not one serious commentary or decent polemic in *Wiadomości* in the space of ten years, nothing except cursory "reviews" which were not as bad as they were shallow, twittering, unwisely nonchalant, and often malicious. Naturally, one should not forget that garbage must be our daily fare in emigration and when it is a matter of critics, beggars can't be choosers—yet if Mr. Grydzewski were able to tolerate modern Polish thought and Polish writing, if he were not allergic to them, *Wiadomości*'s relations with writers could have worked out more pleasantly and the contributors to the publication would have gradually gotten better. The way it is now is pitiful, it really is! In Poland no one is interested in *Wiadomości*, the publication has no political significance at all on a broader scale, it has nothing, absolutely nothing at all in common with the current artistic strivings of the nation or emigration. The only thing that has remained are the readers, still convinced that they are terribly high-minded to be subscribing to this Olympian organ and participating in the contests and polls that are embarrassing testimony to nothing but complete disorientation, an artistic jumble and intellectual hodgepodge, and glaring proof that in the heads of Mr. Grydzewski's sheep absolutely nothing has stirred since 1939.

( . . . I should have chosen a different time . . . it's true, I am giving them ammunition, and to all appearances it looks as if my super-egotistical and solipsistic "I" has attacked them to avenge itself for Lechoń. . . . )

# 1960

# XIV

## Saturday

At around nine o'clock the insistent ringing of the doorbell awakened me—at the door was a short little someone in a big hat—and quietly, almost inaudibly, I could hear him asking for the real estate agent Delgado. —No, he doesn't live here!—I slammed the door. The end. Period. Dot.

And then I could not get back to sleep, so I put on a record with Beethoven's Fourteenth Quartet. Bach? No, not Bach. . . . Actually, I don't like Bach . . . they, modern music, will one day notice through their glasses that Bach was not the right signpost and that he led them to bankruptcy. You adore him because all you can afford is mathematics, the cosmos and purity—oh, that astronomic, pale face of yours nags and torments! You gain the heavens but you lose the earth, you eunuchs! In love with Abstraction, you have forgotten that song served to enchant the female, and nothing will be able to get you out of the Music as such, to which you have devoted yourselves for lack of anything better. The end. Period. As for Beethoven, I have had enough of his symphonies, his orchestra is incapable of drawing me in for good and holding me at bay—but the quartets of his last period, where the sound is difficult, on the borderline and even beyond it. . . . Oh, you Fourteenth Quartet!

If I listen to you so moved, it is probably because you are abundant in sensual delight as much in form as in the violence perpetrated on this form in the name of . . . I wanted to say in the name of the Spirit, but I will say in the name of the creator. For, O crowning glory of the quartets, every moment your four instruments sound in their union, reach for the most intoxicating harmonies, and wind around in voluptuous modulations; and yet, now and again, a severe and even brutal hand violates that delight and forces you to terrifying sharpness, sudden jumps, a hard economy of expression straining for metaphysics, an ascetic expression stretched between the highest and lowest registers, listening with rapt attention to a more distant and higher realization. Suddenly, it got quiet. The record ended. Period and point.

I have to go have coffee.

## 10:00 (In The Café Querandi)

I was drinking coffee, I was eating crescent rolls. And something else. When the waiter walked up to ask what I needed, his hand hung down, quiet, curled up, secret—and idle—until not knowing what to think, I thought about some sort of bush, which I had looked at once at a station, from the window of my train. The hand attacked me in the silence that fell between us. . . . Period. The end. Someone was already walking in and sitting down noisily at a neighboring table—two men— and they asked for dice.

I pulled letters out of my pocket.

"This is a strange example of great intelligence whose object of interest is a field from which he is intuitively cut off. . . . "

"Sandauer est arrivé ici il y a une dizaine de jours. . . . "

"Passing through Kielce, I found Rena. . . . "

"Richter sent me copies of his letters in which he explains all the oddities and problems of this prose. . . . "

## 10:45 (At Home)

The hand of the waiter had vanished and was no more. Until a certain thought from Nietzsche injected it with a dose of splendid existence.

Neske, the German publisher of Heidegger, sent me his *Essais et conférences,* published by Gallimard. The book lay next to the record with the quartet and caught my attention. Why, here in his lecture on Zarathustra, Heidegger discusses the thought that Nietzsche called his "most abysmal"—about the eternal return, "which liberates the spirit of vengeance," vanquishes time that escapes, time that approaches, and imparts to becoming the character of being. *Imprimer au devenir le caractère de l'être . . . telle est la plus haute volonté de puissance.*

I won't let them lead me around by the nose—I am familiar with this childhood, frolicking with Infinity, I know all too well how much frivolity and irresponsibility is needed to proudly enter the terraces of those thoughts-not-to-be-thought and severity-not-to-be-withstood, I know this brilliance! And this Heidegger, at his Nietzschean lecture, suspended over the precipices—clowns! To despise the abyss and not to digest unreasonable thoughts—I determined to do this long ago. I ridicule a metaphysics . . .

. . . which devours me (*nota bene?*).

It is interesting that at the same time and without the least embarrassment I can be a man and a Man. While wondering whether or not to send out the laundry, I am like an arc stretching from there, from the primal beginning, to its latest realizations in what is before me. Not losing a most everyday train of thought for even a second, I am the Mystery of being and its pride, its malady and torment. The bitterness of humanity. The fury of humanity. The unleashing of humanity. The quiet of humanity. The quiet hand of the waiter there in Querandi—quiet and curled up. What is it doing there—while I am here?

### 11:30

If I had not returned to the hand of the waiter, it would have easily disintegrated into nothingness. . . . And now it will keep returning to me because I have returned to it.

### 12:00 (AT THE AMBASSADOR'S)

One of those limpid days with a refreshing heat, deliciously mixing late spring with early summer. The park has become green from the palace to the river, which, as almost always, is immobile and blinding. Breakfast was served in the pavilion, outdoors. Sausage patties—then small and masterly beefsteaks on toast, probably à la Chateaubriand, with artichokes—and phenomenal desserts of cold fruit and cream—add to this a few wines, five butlers.

*Adante scherzo quasi allegretto.* Sun flashing on crowns of fern. Conversation ripples and gleams. And the minister plenipotentiary, an amphitryon, playfully wraps the serpent of conversation first around Spanish bulls, then around Aztec sculpture, Parisian theater, Argentine *asado*. The topiary swans glisten with pearls, while we—the guests, butlers—are like a concert hushed in flawless singing. The French ambassador finds a few kind words for the writer who has paid him a visit, and the flash of a restrained smile appears on the lips of both ambassadors (that is, his and mine). Liqueurs are served.

A diplomatic hand on the arm of the chair, with fingers slightly bent, but it is not this hand but that one, left there as a *point of reference*—a distant flash in the night, a beacon! Farewell, land! I am on the open sea, foam spurting, wind, storm, furrowed waters . . . and the open sea, open thunder and fury.

(Satisfaction that I had not donned my white but cream-colored shirt from Smart—because we ate in the garden—and that I did not have on too ornate a tie, brown, single-toned, rather unattractive.)

## 5:00 (IN THE CAR OF THE EMBASSY ATTACHÉ OFFICER)

She swallowed the hook. . . . What, Olivos already? . . . This old man, his coloring . . . Charlemagne has more in common with me than does Bolesław Chrobry. . . . They will have to grow accustomed little by little to revolutions vanishing into the past. . . . I have not seen . . . in a long time. . . . The dentist . . . Should we go to Tandil? . . . How easy it is to move the world from a standstill. . . . Make a telephone call . . .

## 6:00 (AT HOME)

I am on the open sea again!

She prattled and gabbed without mercy. Until her girlfriends cried: Cut your tongue off! Well, this offended her!

She grabbed the scissors, snip, snap, look, you bad girls: the tongue is on the ground, blood on the lips.

In a corner bar. A seventeen-year-old worker talks to his fiancée on the phone. . . .

. . . Hospital. The right leg shattered. The left cut up and threatened with gangrene . . . ??? What luck! What a coincidence . . . because exactly when he was calling, the Peronist Moya, a militant and a terrorist, was passing by the bar with a bomb under his arm. The bomb mechanism was put into motion unexpectedly. Horrified, Moya threw the bomb helter-skelter, into the bar, and . . .

Without legs. Without a tongue. I read this in the paper.

I was alone, I was sitting on the couch with the paper and before me in the middle of the room were two tables loaded with papers, the back of the chair, a typewriter cover, farther away a wardrobe. I was on the open, open, open sea. What can one do? Pity? I will have pity *here*—and they *there*. . . . Love? I will love *here*—and they *there*. . . . If only our positions didn't bypass each other. . . . A strong wind, dark masses of water that are thrown up and fall back in an uncontained boiling, drowning in one another, a furrowed expanse, an expanse of unappeased movement, no land, no lighthouse and only there, there, there, in Querandi, that one, that chosen hand . . . what is its purpose?

I am very afraid of the devil. A strange confession from the lips of an unbeliever. I am incapable of liberating myself from the idea of the devil. . . . This roaming of the dreadful in my immediate vicinity . . . What good are the police, rights, all guarantees and means of solicitude if a Monster strolls freely among us and nothing protects us from him, nothing, nothing, there is no barrier between him and us. His hand is free among us, the most free of the free! What separates the bliss of the casual stroller from the underground wailing of the voices of the tormented? Absolutely nothing, only empty space. . . . The earth upon which we walk is so covered with pain, we wade in it up to our knees — and this is today's, yesterday's, the day before yesterday's pain, the pain from a thousand years ago — for one should not be deluded, pain does not dissolve in time and the cry of a child from thirty centuries ago is no less of a cry than the one that resounded three days ago. This is the pain of all generations and all beings — not just of man. And finally . . . but who told you that death can bring some sort of peace by releasing you from this world? "And what if nothing but spiders are 'there'?" And what if there is pain there infinitely exceeding anything we can imagine? You don't tremble too much at the thought of that moment because you surrender to the illusive certainty that beyond that wall you will encounter nothing that will be completely ahuman — where does this certainty come from? What authorizes you to have it? Isn't there some diabolical principle contained even in the very womb of our world which is inaccessible to man, inconceivable to the human mind and emotion? Where is our guarantee that the other world is supposed to be more human? Perhaps it is antihumanity itself, the complete contradiction of our nature? But we cannot accept this, for man because of his nature — and this is certain — is incapable of comprehending evil.

Point. I want to believe that in Querandi there is nothing deviating from the most ordinary of the ordinary even though I lack all basis for such an assumption . . . but the presence of evil makes my existence something so risky . . . so disturbing . . . so inclined to the diabolical . . . that in truth it would be difficult for me to succumb to any certainty at all, especially since the lack of data in this case has exactly the same meaning as an abundance of data.

6:30

That ridiculous Leon Bloy! One day he writes in his journal that that morning a terrible cry awakened him, as if it were coming from infinity. He did not doubt that this was the cry of a damned soul, so he fell to his knees and surrendered himself to ardent prayer.

The next day he writes: "Ah, now I know whose soul that was. The press announced that Alfred Jarry died yesterday, at exactly the same hour and minute at which I heard his cry. . . . "

And now for a contrast—the ridiculous Alfred Jarry! In order to avenge himself on God, he asked for a toothpick and picking his teeth, died.

I prefer him to Bloy, whom God supplied mainly with a splendid "absolute" superiority over other mortals. Bloy lived well off the Omnipotent One.

Medieval mind, medieval soul? During the time of Charlemagne the role of the intelligentsia was exactly the opposite of today. Then an intellectual was submitted to the collective thought (of the church) and it was the simple man who thought—empirically, dogmatically—for himself—in practical, daily matters. . . . Today it is just the opposite. . . . Nothing will stop the intelligentsia from running riot any longer . . . (the way communism would like). . . . I have to go see J.

If I could for one moment cope with the whole. To constantly live only with fragments—pieces? To always concentrate on one thing, in order to have all the rest escape? What do I need this Leon Bloy for? And then again . . .

### 8:00 (AT THE CORNER OF LAS HERAS)

I dropped by J.'s but he wasn't home.

I was standing on a stone island in the middle of the street. Evening and early nightfall, lights being born and flickering—and the growing hubbub, cars shoot out next to me, I barely have a chance to look around when two trolley buses turn with a screech, a column of ringing trams approaches, a truck tears out from behind me, I turn around pierced by the whistle of speeding taxis—what madness is this?—still more of this, faster, a high-pitched, earsplitting tone rises from the booming, grating, ringing din, swarming with prickly flashes.

Speed moving into the deep—moments of such velocity that everything wailed, and I lost my footing on the island as if swept up by an undertow. . . . I don't like and I like Bach. I am a "profound nonexpert" of painting. He said ridiculous things. . . . What time is it? It's unfortunate that I lost the letter in French about the translation, when I told M. to leave the table . . . it's good that it happened this way . . . but too bad that . . . What a crater! . . . I have no luck with . . . That bill

... Chlorine—God, save me from the river surrounding me from the outside and the even worse river that rushes in my center—from the inner whirlpool—from my dissipation into a thousand moments. From my own haze! My dust cloud! From the flurry that I am. But I do have a—calm—hand in my pocket.

But what about the hands of these people speeding by in vehicles! Calm. Resting . . . on knees. . . . And the hand in Querandi? What does it do? And what would happen if I knelt before it? If I fell to my knees before a hand? On this island . . . here . . . Well. Yes . . . But what for? No, I will not do this. Of course not, from the beginning I knew that I would not do it.

## 8:15 (In The Tram)

I would call this groping along the peripheries in search of . . . A constant toiling on the borderline in order to . . . An attempt to build . . . An attempt (unsuccessful, as always, as all attempts) to raise there, farther away, some kind of altar, to whatever, in any old place . . . Ah, this kind of grabbing onto any old thing! The hand of the waiter from the Café Querandi!

## 8:30 (In The Restaurant Sorrento)

The waiter comes to the table, I choose snails *à la marinera* and a carafe of white wine, but his left hand is at rest, just like the one in Querandi, although this hand of his doesn't concern me at all—it is important only insofar as it is not that hand. . . . I thought about this a little for my amusement . . . and it amused me that that hand had caught hold of me so easily . . . and also that it grips me harder than this amusement.

To the left and the right the bourgeoisie. The women are putting cadaver meat into the openings of their mouths and moving their mandibles—this goes to their gullet and alimentary canal—they make a face as if they were sacrificing themselves—and again open the opening to put in . . . The men operate knives and forks—among other things their calf muscles are nourishing themselves in their trouser legs, exploiting the workings of the alimentary organs . . . and it would really be strange to conceive of the work of the persons gathered here as the feeding of calves! . . . ? . . . But the apparatus of their movements is set down to the tiniest detail, these manipulations have been shaped by centuries—

reaching for a lemon, buttering pieces of bread, talking in between swallowing, pouring or serving with a conversation on the side, with a crooked smile — the uniformity of movement almost as if it were from the Brandenburg Concertos — and here one sees humanity repeating itself without respite. A room filled with grub, revealing itself in endless variations, like a waltz figure taken up by dancers — and the face of this room, focused on its eternal function, was the face of a thinker.

Yes, but — oh God — this is Sorrento!

This is not Querandi!

## 8:40 (IN THE RESTAURANT SORRENTO)

Why do I feign anger?

Why should it bother me that this is not Querandi?

And why am I clinging to his hand like a drowning man — I'm not drowning, am I? I admit that the hand means absolutely nothing to me. I do not know that waiter personally. A hand like so many other hands . . .

## 9:00 (ON CORRIENTES STREET)

I adore the thing that I myself have elevated. I kneel before the thing that has no right to demand of me that I kneel before it — consequently, my kneeling derives only from me.

My anger is the anger of that sea — an unending expanse, a movement unencompassed by anything — but my secret is the fact that I am located in reality twice. Because I walk along Corrientes Street in Buenos Aires having eaten my supper in the restaurant Sorrento. Yet at the same time, I am there, on the open, open, open, and roiling sea! Tossed by tossing spaces . . . I am on Corrientes and, at the same time, I am in the darkest, interstellar abysses — alone in space! I have just had a pretty good supper and I am cast into infinity, like a shout. . . .

Bah! I chose a hand in Querandi simply to grab hold of something, to feel in relation to something. . . . As a point of reference . . . I chose it precisely for the reason that it has no meaning . . . all directions, places, and things are equally good in my boundlessness, where there is nothing except motion that is becoming. I chose it from the billion things that surround me, but I could have chosen something else. . . . Only now I would not want it to do something to me! To do with me —

or to do to me. . . . Am I no longer alone? Am I already one-on-one with the waiter's hand, which I have chosen . . . are the two of us together?

## 9:10 (CORRIENTES STREET)

I do this only to show how rapacious this parenthetical hand can be in grasping (parenthetically). For my amusement.

## 9:15 (CORRIENTES)

*Gombrowicz felt that he had the right to a metaphysical tempest, to a cosmic catastrophe and a transcendental spine tingle. On the condition, however, that he not betray the everyday.*

*He felt that he had the right to sail on the open sea on the condition that his foot did not leave solid ground, this ground here, in Buenos Aires.*

## 9:20 (IN A BAR ON THE CORNER OF LAVALLE AND SAN MARTIN)

A discussion with Gomez on the subject of Raskolnikov (because one of them, Goma, or perhaps Asno, is reading *The Possessed*).

My view: that in *Crime and Punishment,* there is no drama of the conscience, in the classic, individualistic sense of the word. This is what I lectured to them about.

—At the beginning of the novel—says Gomez—Raskolnikov commits a crime. At the end of the novel he voluntarily turns himself in to the police and confesses the crime. What is this if not his conscience?

I: —Not so simple, *niños!* Look closer. . . .

Raskolnikov does not experience pangs of conscience. In the last chapter it is clearly stated that he regretted only that he "was unsuccessful"—this he considered his sole transgression and in the throes of this guilt, no other, he bowed his head before the "absurd" sentence that overtook him.

If he lacked conscience—what force possessed him therefore to give himself into the hands of the police? What sort of force? The system. The system of almost mirrored reflections.

Raskolnikov is not alone—he is situated in a certain group of persons, Sonia . . . the investigating magistrate . . . his sister and mother . . . his friend and others . . . that is what his little world is like. His own conscience is silent—Raskolnikov, on the other hand, suspects that other consciences will not be silent and that if those people found out, they would condemn him as a criminal. He is hazy to himself, and haziness is allowed everything. But he knows that others see him distinctly, more sharply though superficially, and, for them, judgment of him would be possible. Well—for them—he would be something of a criminal? It is from this suspicion that a feeling of guilt begins to crystallize, he slowly sees himself with the eyes of others and he sees himself a little like a criminal—and this image of himself he communicates in thought to the others—and from there return the even more distinct face of a murderer and the damning verdict. But this conscience is not his and he senses this. This is a specific conscience, arising and growing between people, in a system of reflections—where one man sees himself in the other. Gradually, in proportion to the swelling of a bad self-image after committing the crime, Raskolnikov makes them his judges more and more—and his guilt outlines itself more and more boldly. But I repeat, this is not the verdict of his conscience—this is the verdict that has risen from a reflection, a mirrored verdict.

As for me, I would be inclined to think that Raskolnikov's conscience manifests itself in only one thing: when it surrenders to that artificial, interhuman, mirrored conscience as if it were his rightful conscience. Herein lies the moral: because he who killed another human being now fulfills the dictate born of human association. And he does not ask if it is just.

12:10 A.M. (ON THE WAY HOME)

I could have told them. About the hand. I didn't.

12:20 A.M.

Yes, yes . . .

My good God, the things one says!

One says whatever comes to mind. This mechanism of speaking . . . astounding! When and how do I plan the sentences I utter! How do I know what I want to say, if I do not consider it for a moment in the brisk course of my speech? When beginning a sentence, do I know how it will end? How the words choose and round themselves . . . the thoughts . . . ?

Yes . . .

But better yet, explain why, in saying so much, you told them nothing about the hand, about the hand from Querandi?

I could have said something. But I didn't.

Whereby it became more secret.

And in its own way that *reflex* . . . this *reflex* . . . is a mirrored conscience, created from reflections . . . but this is, after all, similar to creating for oneself the hand somewhere on the outside, beyond . . . as if on the strength of the reflex. . . .

### 12:30 A.M.

How his conscience built itself up (Raskolnikov). Just as this hand is building itself up.

It is like a parasite. Now it is feeding on what I said about Dostoyevski—it will not rest until it sucks from my words . . . everything that it needs. . . .

For what?

Polyp! It sucks, exploits, in order to construct, to construct there, beyond my limit. . . . It is indefatigable!

I have to finish these notes and send them off tomorrow so that they will make it to Paris by the sixth.

The sixth—the sixth—it is not yet here, it will be, but here it is . . . like the hand!

Again!

### 12:50 A.M. (AT HOME)

Where can it be right this minute? Still in Querandi? Perhaps it is already resting and sleeping in some apartment, on some pillow?

Futile hopes. There is no way to take advantage of its sleeping, to be rid of it. . . . The more it sleeps, the more alert it is. The less it is, the more it is.

Let us note: It seemed so calm when I saw it for the first time, in Querandi . . . but it is becoming more and more possessive . . . and I myself no longer know what could stop it there, on the periphery . . . where I end.

# XV

## Tuesday

1939–1959.

A little history? Polish history? I follow it so little, I seek it so feebly (it peeks in at me)—I look at it from afar, as at a chain of mountains. Should I speak of it? But history is—after all—precisely a viewing from afar!

How have these roles finally organized themselves? Who has lost, who has won—Poland or the emigration? Where has Poland finally decided to settle down—in Poland or in "the hearts of émigrés"?

Admit it: the emigration is one big dud; this 1939 version is a failure. Something broke down in its dynamics—it has not fulfilled its historical task. Riddle: what is the difference between an emigration and a can of sardines? Emigration does not benefit from hermetic isolation.

In the meantime, you (it is obvious to whom this "you" refers) worked only for one thing. An aseptic cleanliness so as not to allow any bacillus! To preserve the past! To preserve an unadulterated past! To this end you have become Guardians. And the holiest of your shrines is you yourselves, just as when you drove away on the road to Zaleszczyki from that happy twenty-year period. I will not waste words on well-known topics. Conserve! Preserve! Be a statue changing into bronze, this distancing, running away! To live for the past! To live for now so that in the future one can resurrect the past. Not to allow the least little scratch to appear on this armor of loyalty.

Existence is like a river—this river, when it encounters obstacles, immediately begins to seek other beds and bursts through wherever it can, opening new outlets for itself sometimes in directions it would never have imagined. Our emigration has little in common with a river. It has run into a wall and waits for it to topple over: to this day, it stands and waits. It tries to replace natural movement with massages. And in the course of twenty years you have not been able to muster anything unpredictable, you have not surprised History with anything. This docility testifies to your good upbringing, but it is incapable of reconciling your Nemesis, who values tough guys with . . . Never mind, let's drop this!

Politeness! You are cultivated gentlemen!

# Wednesday

What has happened in the life of the twenty-year-old written word in exile? Writers? Works? Ideas?

I occasionally visit the archboring Argentinean literati, where the conversations begin: *—Que nuevos valores surgen entre Vds.*? What new talents are appearing among us? I could answer this question for hours! Well, because there is Józef Mackiewicz, Czesław Straszewski, Nowakowski; there is Bobkowski's prose and Baliński's poetry—all of this was really born in emigration—as were so many truculent publicists, so many other artists, whom one is not allowed to omit. . . . And would it be right to forget about all these valuable works which writers prominent before the war have added to their achievement? Really! "The literature of exile has left a beautiful legacy . . . ," etc., etc. Sure, sure. But . . . from a historical perspective? . . .

As long as we are speaking about history—what sort of historical task stands before Polish art and Polish thought?

Nothing complicated. Actually, a very simple task: to live, to live at any cost. Not to die! Let us admit that this is quite an elementary program, with a few additional points, such as: do not be a statue, do not be a mourner, do not be a gravedigger, do not recite, do not repeat yourself, do not inflate yourself, do not belittle yourself, do not thunder and roar, do not make jokes. And most of all let's have—a revision! A revision of everything we possess and a revision of ourselves, too. If everything around us is changing—how can we alone remain fixed in an undisturbed identification with what created us, and which therefore no longer fits into the present moment?

# Friday

In one respect, one has to admit that they were intensive. Their barricading and holing themselves up in anticommunism, their war with red Poland.

At least they were able to muster something in themselves. Except . . . on what level does this work take place? There should be, for God's sake, some sort of difference between a political (and propagandistic) anticommunism and the anticommunism of a thinker and poet. The contest between a literature in exile and the enemy does not necessarily have to be reduced to crying "thugs," or sneering, wailing, ridiculing, and cursing. There is room, beyond this easy stuff which quickly absorbs all the ready strategies, for an intellectual and spiritual effort in proportion to the most powerful jolt accorded us since Poland became Poland and worthy of one of the boldest adventures mankind has encountered.

But they would have to strike a most painful blow at themselves — without this, not a step forward. They would have to begin by treating communism with goodwill and even friendship . . . they would really have to feel themselves "comrades." And the second part of this self-inflicted violence would have to be, as much as possible, even more contrary to nature, for they would have to treat their own persons, as well as everything that formed them, that is, all of their history up to now, which is the history of the nation, with hostility. A trifle! Get fraternal with the Kremlin and push away your most valuable treasures — this is what is being demanded of you!

How do you propose to *get at the enemy* without having first penetrated his reasoning in complete goodwill, and without examining his ideal in utmost seriousness? He must be understood even in his venom and dirt (which are inseparable from his virtues) — only then will your blows hit their mark. But perhaps this exceeds your strength? In that case only cold objectivity and justice remain, which see the crimes on both sides of the barricade, a judgment of your own sins so severe it would give you the right to settle accounts with someone else's.

All criticism of communism would also have to be joined to an examination of one's own conscience, an examination which would not retreat before the truth. Who of you has been able to do this? Only Miłosz possessed this coolness — he and Mieroszewski, who introduced a cold sobriety into politics. Besides them? It would be looking for a needle in a haystack to find in your twenty-year-old poetry and prose a struggle that steadfastly seeks the opponent on his own turf — seeks, finds, strikes. Emigré literature has acted differently . . . consistently . . . and, unfortunately, predictably. When they throw you out of your home, what are you supposed to do? (1) Moan and groan. (2) Reminisce. (3) Inveigh against others. (4) Proclaim your innocence. This program has been implemented and it deprives our polemic with communism of its class, stature, and creativity.

Most of the literature under the leadership of the "bard" — (and why not!) — Lechoń and the editor Grydzewski serves this purpose. The remainder of this writing exists in order for writers to prove that they are still writers—and exactly the kind they were before. Oh, this *status quo ante!*

I am intentionally not being more precise about whom I am referring to as "you." Everyone, with very few exceptions. The truth will out.

# Saturday

Moreover I will note that they have not fulfilled two fundamental intellectual tasks earmarked for them by History: to become more familiar with Marxism and to get closer to existentialism.

One might believe that these two do not have much in common— nevertheless, it is only the two concepts together that really introduce the epoch. Except that . . . Hegel is as necessary to Kierkegaard as he is to Marx. And you won't be able to crack Hegel without the *Critique of Pure Reason.* This in turn derives a bit from Hume, Berkeley, and further back it would be necessary to know Aristotle and maybe even a little Plato; even Descartes, the father of modern thought, would come in handy and all this as a prolegomena to phenomenology (Husserl), without which one cannot read *L'être et le néant* or *Sein und Zeit.* I do not want to frighten you with titles or names. I don't make a philosopher of myself, as I am a poet and I have an inborn *abschmack* for abstract thought. But these names and titles indicate the horizon of a second-year philosophy student—and, I ask you, would many of our thinkers be able to handle this exam? Thus they have nothing to offer. You want to fight using your complete ignorance of the modern view of the world and man, of the intellectual development of mankind in the space of two thousand years, with a muddled head on the subject of the most crucial moments of human consciousness—this is what you want to fight with? One senses in everything you write the lack of exactly this most general philosophical orientation, you know all the letters of the alphabet, except your ABC's.

It is not really a matter of intellect, however—one has to listen and to feel one's way into the newness of the world that is coming into being, into its taste, style, rhythm, passion. These artists weren't tempted. The emotional breach between this group of consistent conservatives, buttoned to the last button, and modernity (I know that this word is forbidden and that in saying it I may be accused of snobbery) has the proportions of the Cologne cathedral.

Catholicism! Well, what is one to do, Catholicism! He who knows everything and listens to all the rest between yawns . . . the blinders on Polish eyes which do not allow them a glance sideways. . . . I repeat, I am not an enemy of Catholicism, I am an enemy only of its function in our culture and not just as of today. But your liberalism, scientism, socialism, etc., are equally poorly acquainted with what I would call the disposition of the modern sensibility. You simply do not know what is going on and in which church the bells are ringing. After twenty years of direct contact with the West, you know less about it than people know in Poland!

Let us assume that I am mistaken, that existentialism is not worth much and that Marxism is defeated. . . . Terrific. But how do you want to despise them if you know them only superficially?

# Monday

Originality has never flourished among Poles. A nation almost always inseminated, almost never inseminating, which introduced so little into universal culture, did not feel creation, did not understand it. To us, creativity is something rather distasteful. In art, we appreciate only good secondhand work.

Hence the tragicomic situation when all the Lechońs were backed into a corner: now you must drag something out of yourself, take a leap, have an inspiration, idea, something unexpected and unusual in order to steal the initiative away from History. They replied by reciting all the works they knew up to now plus new ones, which were exactly the same, word for word. All in beautiful, cultivated language, exemplary syntax, dignity and commas intact.

I am far from demanding that each member of the Writers Union in London become a fire-breathing volcano. But let at least two or three of them try. Even unsuccessfully.

It seems to me that you were doomed by the righteousness of your suffering and the decency of your intentions. And, then—you are so charming!

# Wednesday

*In the emigration*—said Wittlin—in an instructive lecture entitled "The Sorrow and Grandeur of Exile" given at a congress of the P.E.N. Club in Exile—*there almost always occurs a confusion of concepts and criteria. There are no real yardsticks for measuring the true value of a writer's work. It is mainly sentimental considerations, obsolete myths and the obsolete laws of national aesthetics —observed by the old emigration when judging its "bards" —that determine this value. This confusion was especially irksome to the Polish emigration during the last war.*

Wise words. But the less life one has, the more difficult it is for this kind of natural selection. *Wiadomości* became the ideal expression of a mediocre demise of the emigration, it would be hard to come by a more polished, pressed, groomed, spruced up, and *comme il faut* graveyard. *Wiadomości,* along with the whole group of London blithe spirits, snobs, Englishmen, Europeans, foreign affairs deputies, Polonists, aesthetes, connoisseurs. Fear grips me at the thought of what would have happened if *Kultura* had not appeared on the horizon by some happy miracle of dialectics, as an antithesis. Think for a moment how we would look without this Parisian monthly. Mieroszewski, of course, would not have been allowed into *Wiadomości,* he would have been sentenced to writing columns in minor newspapers and this most sober and most open mind (which has already attained a prominent place in the history of Polish political thought) could not have galvanized and uncorked our eternally bottled up "conceptions." Not to mention Miłosz, whose *casus* is glaring and obvious. Jeleński! I don't know how it happened, but I think that Jeleński without *Kultura* would not have become the one Polish publicist and essayist really at home in Europe; he would not have penetrated the real French elite. Most certainly, because of those "sentimental considerations, obsolete myths, and the obsolete laws of national aesthetics" that Wittlin mentions, Jeleński's supple intelligence, for he knows European literature better than any other Pole, would not have gained entry to Grydzewski's Olympus and he simply would not have had a place to begin his literary career. And—so as not to cite any more names—many other new things introduced by *Kultura* on the social, political, artistic front—where would all of that have gone? And last but not least, how would our coexistence with Poland look—why, *Wiadomości* and its group are like the Great Wall of China— do you remember the resolution of the Writers' Union in London forbidding publishing in Poland, that monumental resolution, the epitome of absolute incompetence?

# Wednesday

Why have I broken with the discretion that characterizes me, and why am I somewhat embarrassing and even downright provocative? I am not doing this for the fun of it. It is a matter of creating a polarization, a line of demarcation. All that is alive has been sitting in the morgue for too long. Life must feel itself alife; it must experience its own ruthlessness, asperity, vigor, and commence clearing a way for itself.

## Friday

I will cite Wittlin again:

*The writer-exile lives in a restricted society in which it is not easy to create, let alone publish, revolutionary works. A restricted society such as this most willingly lends an ear to that which it has long known. . . . Therefore, it is difficult for an émigré writer to impose his own taste and novelty on the emigration.*

*Woe to him if he yields. Because if, in a normal society each artist is threatened by the danger whose name is "desire to please," that danger is one hundred times greater in a restricted, ghetto-like society. . . .*

There you have it! And one should not ingratiate oneself, this would not be healthy in a "constricted, ghetto" society. Better would be the brusqueness of honesty, even though it might not be to the taste of those who for two decades have sprawled in their sinecures, taking advantage of the fact that "a constricted society such as this most willingly lends an ear to that which it has long known."

The dividing line! The line between movement and the "feigning" of movement!

## Saturday

What a shame that we don't have a Sandauer! He would come in handy with his "No Reduced Fares" stamp. At least Poland was able to come up with a Sandauer—this alone indicates how far they were able to surpass the immobile shallowness of the emigration.

How so? Surpassed? They, bound, and you, in completely unhampered freedom? Impossible! Irritating! Indeed! As one can see, prison is not the worst place for a spirit that becomes vigorous only under lock and key. Whereas it is so easy to dissolve in the boundlessness of freedom—like a piece of sugar that has fallen from a ship into the ocean.

In a certain sense Poland and the emigration are sick with the same disease. For if the emigration sinks into artificiality, as a consequence of its being cut off from the nation, then it is also true that artificiality in a more brutal dose was imposed in Poland by a theory as rapacious as it was false. In emigration one exists in a void, bereft of the contact with life that tests and renews. In Poland everything is also tainted with fiction, but because it has been separated from the world, from the free play of values, Poland has turned into a closed system, subject to special laws. In these conditions it is not difficult to find criteria in art: everything there, in Poland, or here, with us, that invokes reality, life, truth, not the relative and provincial but the universal and ultimate truth, is valuable and even priceless; everything that in its essence is owed to the existing state of affairs and rests on deceit as on a throne is miserable and flat, cunning and mediocre.

Before me on the table is Sandauer's book *No Reduced Fares,* containing his all-out attack on contemporary Polish writing. I said "all-out" even though the bloodthirsty Sandauer limits himself to devouring Adolf Rudnicki, Jerzy Andrzejewski, Jan Kott, and a few others. But basically this book is, from first page to last (it doesn't matter whether it is glorifying Bruno Schulz or trouncing Kott), a blow aimed at the game — the game according to the agreed-upon rules of Polish literature.

Didn't he get a little carried away when butchering Rudnicki? Is Andrzejewski really so awful? The issue is not them but rubbish as such and the dubious distinction of this literature. I am not inclined (like Sandauer) to blame their shabbiness exclusively on the period of muzzle and terror. First of all, this all ended quite a while ago, and, second, art, being a metaphor *par excellence,* bears all kinds of inquisitions quite well. Third, it would probably be enough if art in Poland, even without touching politics, would manage to produce even one truly profound and authentic individuality — this immediately infects, forces people to exert themselves, dictates a standard. Their miseries are a result not so much of their situation as of their being unable to look their situation in the face. Yet how do you want them to look it in the eyes, if they have gotten so entangled in it? They did attempt — for all their concern about the spiritual and artistic values they represent — to come to terms with the situation somehow, which, after all, *entre nous soit dit,* worked in their favor to a great degree by removing the competition and introducing a discount fare. The only recipe for good writing is to get at reality through convention, to get at the ultimate reality via conventional reality. But they? So entangled, so embedded in their own history, steeped in it up to their ears, they, the actors in this play — how were they to go about acquiring distance? Even the enemies of communism, such as Hłasko, are embedded in communism for — in an artistic sense — they live off of it . . . and Sandauer was right to include in his book a brief exposé of the career of this talented author, touchingly helpless, incapable of getting his troubles under control intellectually, disoriented, primitive, doomed to elaborate on a few naive themes. Hłasko: interesting, but only as a product of communism—also a son of everything shoddy and one of its constituent parts.

If this is how it is, why did I say that they have outstripped the emigration?

Because they—in contrast to you, here—are tired of the rubbish. Sandauer's tone—that cool determination in unmasking—is not a coincidence but a necessity, and he must have many, many readers in Poland (sometimes a book is not printed in large editions, but its tone is passed from mouth to mouth like "village news"). Sandauer does not altogether appeal to me, he is too cerebral, his intellectualizing is dry, without suppleness, and sometimes even seems lame, but one must admit that no one has inserted his finger more unceremoniously into their throbbing wound. He said what could no longer remain unsaid; he found within himself stores of honesty, ruthlessness, harshness which are absolutely essential and vital for the future development of Polish literature. It is not just a matter of this or that particular opinion, which may sometimes be wrong. In this book, for the first time since the war, one hears the voice of a *clerc*, returning Poland to Europe (which does not mean: to European capitalism).

# Sunday

*For Gombrowicz, Sandauer in Poland was what Jeleński was on European soil. Jeleński and Sandauer: both pushed him to the top with indefatigable industry, which he admired (because it was practically inconceivable to him that one could muster something more than acknowledgment—which obligates one to do nothing—in relation to someone else's works). Nor could he conceal from himself that* Ferdydurke *is mentioned a lot in the pages of* No Reduced Fares *and that, for Sandauer, it became a point of departure in his offensive on Polish writing. And,* entre nous soit dit, *a book that devastated those around it to establish the ruthless preeminence of Gombrowicz's achievement as a writer could not help appealing to him.*

*Did it please him? Why, certainly. So what? Was this reason to refrain from talking about Sandauer? He felt that it would be enough to let these debts be known in order to purify himself. When this complex was admitted, it lost its sting.*

*After all, he saw more and more clearly that his understanding with Sandauer was far from perfect, encompassing only part of his works and his person. One could not expect Sandauer to have the extraordinary receptiveness and sensitivity that allow Jeleński to grasp things in midflight — Sandauer was a species of beetle, an individual marching to his own drummer, a mastodon, crustacean, monk, hippopotamus, crank, inquisitor, cactus, martyr, crocodile, sociologist, and avenger. This lone man took from him —from Gombrowicz —only what fit him and in the long run, who knows, one even had to count on the possibility that this ally might change into the enemy . . . this turn of events, although not too likely, was not out of the question. . . .*

# Tuesday

To me, it is clear: in spite of its impoverishments, the higher stratum in Poland is superior to the émigré elite in matters of intelligence and enlightenment.

While the emigration has wasted the bulk of opportunities and riches that the wide latitude of the West has given it, the Poles have at least been able to exploit some of their advantages. What sort of advantages? First, the inner, secret, almost conspiratorial, individual maturing that inevitably occurs in an atmosphere of being stifled, in an atmosphere of violence, persecution, and complication—not to mention catastrophes, horrors, blows, defeats. All of this taken together has sharpened them as much as the softness and monotony of the emigration (whose only struggle is the struggle for money) have made émigrés emblems of the ideal bourgeoisie. The affability of the official tone in Poland is accompanied by an awful dissonance somewhere deep inside—a dissonance as dynamic as it is bitter. Disillusionment—a series of disillusionments—is probably the advanced instruction they have received.

Let us also remember the renewal that is always brought by a revolution, even a bungled one. The social reconstruction had to bring with it changes in intellectual and spiritual perspectives. The new materialistic evangelicism was after all a jolt, a jolt out of the narrowness of Catholic tradition, which had become so inhibiting in Poland that only now is the legacy of the Jesuit boarding school being eliminated. This is how Marxism has compromised the Church while compromising itself, after having revealed itself as no less rigid and dogmatic. On the other hand, the Nation has also been questioned (I am speaking of the upper class), because its weakness has been revealed and because in the new political constellation of Poland the issue of nationality has less and less to say. It seems, therefore, that on the corpses of Dogma, of Philosophy, and of Ideology only Science and Technology can proclaim their kingdom. But Technology and Science are barely inching along in Poland, something is plugging along here and there — too clumsily to be able to become even the semblance of life's profound daily contents. Degradation is common, it has encroached upon all areas and it has disposed of all the gods — hence their disillusionment, hence their wisdom.

This wisdom, however, is specific . . . not to be revealed. For political reasons? Not only. These people are like children who would like to build a new edifice with only a pile of blocks left over from a lot of previous birthdays; they build something inharmonious, with castle vaults, the facade of a Swiss house, a factory chimney, and a church window. Poland is full of clutter and her intellectual life consists of flinging platitudes at one another — those from before the war and those that were inserted into their mouths after the war. In listening to these learned discussions we sense a poor education, even a poor upbringing, but most of all the absence of a style that would allow these fine talents to achieve something every once in a while — everything is a junkyard, chaos, ineptitude, and dirt. So much dirt! So much garbage! Nevertheless, the underground pressure of their restless, tragic, brutal, disillusioned intelligence seems to me infinitely stronger than before the war, and will probably one day make its way to the surface.

# XVI

## Tuesday

Art is aristocratic to the marrow, like a prince of royal blood. It is the refutation of equality and the adoration of the superior. It is a matter of talent, even genius, or superiority, prominence, uniqueness; it is also the harsh creation of a hierarchy of values, cruelty in relation to that which is common, the selection and perfection of that which is rare, indispensable; it is, finally, a nurturing of personality, originality, individuality. No wonder, then, that the magnanimously endowed art of the People's Democracies is a mountain that gives birth to a mouse. This costs cool millions and all this "production" boils down to nothing but gab.

Gab. When I happen to cock my ear in the direction of Poland, this is what I hear — gab and more gab. They are terribly garrulous. Their books are like their literary press, and their literary press is like their coffeehouses — everything is dripping with chitchat, bursting with blather. I don't know a single work of theirs that I could recognize as being born in silence. Nor do I know a single author (except for maybe two) about whom I could say: he doesn't write on the sidewalk or in a café attached to the sidewalk. Even the works of people who have been isolated for some time have in them this peculiar sociability, characteristic of persons who do not own their own apartments (spiritually speaking; I am not speaking of a kitchen and bathroom). Listening to the café hubbub they create, one could claim that all their voices have more or less the same intensity; they also have the same "color," as musicians say. There is such a cacophony of voices and instrumental groups that the trumpet is indistinguishable from the flute and the double bass flows together with the oboe. Altogether it sounds like an orchestra, pardon me, like a café — yes, there is no question about it, modern Polish literature is not only great babble but a great "locale" with pastries, demitasses, and souls.

I would make a face at them today and call out "tsk, tsk" — because, formerly, before the war, for the heroic Polish left, I was a coffeehouse literatus worthy of condescension . . . but now the roles have been reversed. It is obvious that their truths have been hammered out over a demitasse (hey, do people still say this?), that their poems are washed down with tea, that their essays are like a layer cake and their novels like "napoleons" (hey, do you still use this word?). Not that they are too sweet. The matter is more peculiar than that. As you know, a man feels different whether he is, for example, in a dark forest, in a manicured French garden, or on the fortieth floor of an American skyscraper. For an expert like myself (for I have worn my teeth down to the gums in cafés), there can be no doubt that their sense of well-being is the sense of well-being of café habitués. There is in them, how shall I put it, this little aftertaste . . . the limits of their personality are exactly the distance "from one table to the next." In vain would one seek in them a holy thicket or the expanse of a meadow. There isn't a penny's worth of the dramatic ferocity of a loner like Kant or Proust. They lack the metaphysical anxiety born of a concentrated silence. They lack the religion revealed in a burning bush. They lack the method, hygiene, discipline that characterize science laboratories. Each of them ends close by—where his neighbor begins—they are limited by each other, by their own company. Of course they know all this and they do what they can *not* to be a café; but their spiritual convulsions exist so that they not be a café, the result of which is that they again become a café, inside out. A vicious circle.

Even before the war, the excessive domestication of literature in the cafés Ziemiańska, Ips, Zodiac, etc., was disturbing. A café is dangerous because it creates its own world; a café, even a Parisian café, is always local and so provincial. Sandauer's achievement will go down as the discovery of the forbidding percentage of cafés and, what goes with it, the provincialism in the work of an eminent Polish writer, but in my opinion it would be better to praise this writer for a creativity that is so typical and representative. How is one to be cured? There is only one means of escape. Immediate departure abroad, to the other side of any border (as long as one gets across). This is inopportune because of the difficulties caused by the authorities in getting a passport—but let us not forget that a writer can leave on a book, like a witch on a broom. Do you get my advice? A Polish artist, if he wants to achieve something, has to leave, leave spiritually, leave without budging an inch—and he has to leave for the mountains. The Polish plain is in every respect moving but for an artist there is nothing like mountain air, sharp, sharp mountain air, accompanied by such unevenness of terrain that someone is always looking at someone else from above or below—is this clear? Move out (in spirit, not budging from the spot) into a blessed land, which swells beneath your feet, stiffens, grows and rises. Or in other words: if you want to cultivate art, you have to lean on art, move out to seek the highest art of Europe, and recover in its nature your own nature as an artist and bind yourself to it. . . .

I would refrain from these suggestions if communism had not revealed art and literature to be in a state of such advanced sclerosis . . . one must admit that although communism is not always sclerotic, in such "cultural" matters it suffers from an incurable stiffness and clogging of the arteries. In other areas it is innovative—here it is heavy, blind, unintelligent. If Communists wanted to approach art less brutally and dully, they would have to understand that one cannot change art in its very essence—that it, like certain shrubs, is a high climber. There is little in humanity that is as uncompromising as the artist. It would be wisest, therefore, to leave artists in peace and allow them to be like the aristocracy of old, in keeping with their vocation. This kind of aristocracy is conceivable and acceptable within Marx's system. But Communists preferred to "level" art by stomping on its face. Too bad, but in these "civilized" conditions only one thing remains—to emigrate in spirit as quickly as possible—but, of course, I give this advice only to the two or three authentic princes divinely ordained, the remaining thirty thousand democrats, engaged in dabbling, can do what they want, because it is of no great importance.

# Tuesday

All of the (monstrous) Communist disasters in treating art derive from their incapacity to understand its reasons for being.

The power of art, its capacity to resist, its perpetuity which always renourishes itself, derive from the fact that the individual expresses himself through it. Man. Individual man. Science is collective just as reason and knowledge are not private property; truths arrived at by reason, abstract truths, are passed from generation to generation and a scholar is like an architect who adds one more brick to the edifice built by his predecessors. Philosophical, conceptual truths are no less abstract and no less Communist—they are thereby common (as long as the philosopher does not become an artist, which often happens).

On the other hand, when you step onto art's terrain—watch out, Communists! For this is private property, the most private property man has ever achieved for himself. Art is so very personal that each artist begins it from the very beginning—and each creates it in himself, for himself—it is the vent for one existence, one destiny, a separate world. In its effects, in the mechanisms of its effects, it is social; in its conception and spirit it is individual, separate, concrete, unique.

What would happen if you liquidated art, Communists? Nothing, you say? Human progress would not be hindered, there would be no void, no silence, the loud voices of Science, Philosophy, the Party, maybe even of Religion would still ring out, each day would bring new discoveries. Surely. . . . But are you really prepared for one major sacrifice? From then on, there would be no way of knowing what a man thinks or feels. What the individual man thinks or feels.

It would be unbearable. But why shouldn't Communists be capable of acknowledging a separate place for art and respecting its needs? They will need this kind of preserve, they could allow (others, but also themselves) this kind of private property and this kind of aristocracy. Why don't they do this? I don't know. Doesn't the established pattern allow it?

# Wednesday

Councillor Podsrocki of *Trans-Atlantic* reminds a person I know, I am told, of a comical personage, the councillor Korczyński. This Korczyński was, around 1947, the secretary of the Legation that sailed into Buenos Aires from Warsaw under the leadership of Minister Szumowski. A secretarial figure, bureaucratically diplomatic and Galician to boot— extremely good material for vaudeville. And he wasn't the only one at the consulate who roused one's sense of humor.

# Thursday

Ah, a Polish teacher! In answering Mr. Grabowski, I thought he was a mere columnist, even though he had the air of a teacher of Polish. And my feelings probably did not lead me astray, because his reply brought the proud admission that he was the son of a professor (history of literature) and then—how inestimable, delightful, and typical the passage—that he was used to evaluating a work of art methodically, according to three considerations (I no longer remember what they were, but I read them with great enthusiasm).

Alicja Lisiecka, who carries on about Sandauer in *Nowa Kultura* ("Jubilee of Criticism"), also, unfortunately, smells like a Polish teacher. Her piece is a little too smart-alecky, academic, and professorial, like a bullet that misses its mark. (P.S. Strange. Another article in *Życie Literackie,* also about Sandauer, also schoolmarmish and like a schoolteacher's, but not by Lisiecka but Lisicka and not Alicja but Teresa. What is this: a holy professor in two persons? Could it be that she splits herself in two like an amoeba?)

# Friday

Byron and Debussy. These revolutionaries from years ago are worth envying. They at least had something specific to destroy, they had a distinct, solemn enemy they could strike down. In our times the revolution has penetrated everything and there is no longer anything shocking. The scandal has exhausted itself.

But today Byron's letters are richer in dynamite than *Childe Harold's Pilgrimage,* than *The Corsair,* than the works that were intended to be revolutionary. And Debussy? Doesn't his conservative stubbornness, his peculiar classicism, appeal to us at least as much in his partiturs as his "modernism" does?

# Sunday

Guitarra was taken to *colimba.* "Guitarra," as the name itself indicates, is a guitarist, whom I came to know in Tandil when he played Bach and *Suite en ré,* whose author is probably Visée. And "colimba" is military service. Later, during successive meetings, I read from his face all the horrors of the torture—which in Argentina lasts for well over a year in the army and two in the navy.

Is it possible to reconcile the barracks with democracy? With constitutions guaranteeing personal freedom and dignity? With the declaration of the rights of man? They put a twenty-year-old boy, who has committed no crime, into this concentration camp, worse than a prison (because in prison there is no sergeant who takes you for a gallop; because prison, unlike the barracks, is not determined to break down your being; because prison is incarceration but not harassment day and night). One or two of their most beautiful years must be given away to the Sergeant. They are lucky if they come away unscathed (and no one pays reparations). The inevitability of this ordeal poisons their youth long before the fatal date.

How does one explain that the wrong of some individual Dreyfus or some other lucky fellow becomes a problem of conscience and provokes something like a civil war, while annually depriving ten million boys of their most elementary rights (sometimes together with their lives) gets swallowed so easily by our humanitarian throats? Why does no one protest, neither the parents, nor they themselves, nor, finally, any of these sensitive consciences of humanity who are always ready to rend their garments.

If you are curious to know who is at fault, take a look around . . . yes, it is, it is . . . age (this hidden spring of social life). Twenty years old! *Colimba* is where two types of violence basic to society take place. The violence of the more enlightened upon the less enlightened and the assault of the older upon the younger. Here an officer, more aware, grabs half-illiterates by the throat, here the older grabs the younger by the hair. We live tempered lives, in an atmosphere of mutual respect, but somewhere there must be a little cranny where the superior meets the inferior, the older the young, oh, just like that, without inhibitions or restraints.

Flor, Marlon, Goma, and others, already liberated, told anecdotes from the *colimba* yesterday—hair-raising!

What would happen if a law was announced sentencing a person who completed, let us say, his fortieth birthday to prison for a year? The general protest would lead to revolution in a second. But the *colimba*? Well, people have been used to it for centuries. And, after all, this age . . . The age of complete, yet still childish physical prowess makes it easy, enables . . . the concentration of many lives in the fist of one officer, as if it were the fist of a demigod.

# Tuesday

Today I awakened in the delight of not knowing what a literary award is, that I do not know official honors, the caresses of the public or critics, that I am not one of "ours," that I entered literature by force—arrogant and sneering. I am the self-made man* of literature! Many moan and groan that they had difficult beginnings. But I made my debut three times (once before the war, in Poland; once in Argentina; and once in Polish in emigration) and none of these debuts spared me one ounce of humiliation.

I thank Almighty God that he got me out of Poland when my literary situation began to improve and cast me onto American soil, into a foreign tongue, into isolation, into the freshness of anonymity, into a country

---

*"Self-made man" in English in original.

richer in cows than in art. The ice of indifference conserves pride quite well.

Thanks be to you, too, Almighty God, for the *Diary*. One of the most dramatic moments in my life happened ten years ago when the first fragments of the *Diary* were being born. Oh, how I quaked! I cast off the grotesque language of the works I had written to that point as if I were taking off armor—this is how vulnerable I felt in the diary, I was so overcome by the fear that I would emerge pale in these simple words! Was this not my fourth debut and the most dangerous of them all? But afterward! What security when it turned out that in a tight spot I could comment on myself—that is exactly what I needed: to become my own critic, my own annotator, judge, director, I needed to deprive others of the power to decree sentences . . . that is when I truly won my independence!

I owe much to a few writers who supported me, beginning with Bruno Schulz, who is very well known today. But it was only when I really started to write in the *Diary* that I felt I was wielding my pen— a wonderful feeling, which I got from neither *Ferdydurke* nor any other of my works of art, which seemed to write themselves . . . somewhere beyond me. . . . From then on, my pen began to serve me. . . . It was as if I were accompanying my art all the way to the point where it dropped into another person's existence and became hostile to me.

# Tuesday

*Gombrowicz felt that exceptionally malicious circumstances forced him to such directing of his personal drama in the* Diary *(although perhaps it was also justified by the spirit of his writing, in which the idea of directing and the figure of the director appear so often)—therefore, no one ought to reproach him for this. He wrote in conditions that were downright stifling— gagged in Poland, cutoff from the world at large by his exotic Polish, choking in an émigré narrowness. This is how his unfortunate works were born—not easy, after all, not easy to the point that even in the very center of Paris they would have to fight hard for recognition.*

*It is a measure of the unbelievable shallowness of the Polish minds with which he had to contend in the suffocating emigration that even his* Diary, *so much easier to understand than his earlier works, did not often penetrate their brains. He was labeled "egotistical"—and* Schluß! *that settled it! It never occurred to the majority of these émigré readers and critics—scholars of Polish literature, poets, writers, intellectuals—that one could speak about oneself in various ways, that his "I" in the* Diary *is not the "I" of a trivial egoist, or a naive Narcissus, but of someone who realizes what is going on . . . that if this is egotism, then it is a methodical, disciplined egotism testifying to a high and cold objectivity. They saw only the pattern. And furthermore the outcry: —Egotist! Conceited! Tactless! Aggravating, angry, unlikable!*

*It is true that Gombrowicz sometimes teased the emigration on purpose. —I tease it so that it will not throw itself at me—he once said; for he claimed that Stupidity is an exceptional beast, one that cannot bite if it is yanked hard by the tail.*

# XVII

## Friday

Beethoven's form and its drama in history.

For some years I have been existing beyond music. I have become unaccustomed to it. As for Beethoven, I devoured him with pleasure in my youth just like everyone else, but later, what do you expect, he had settled in my ear too much and a time came when his "phrase" came close to being trite for me. And all these revelations—Beethoven's "thought" and his ecstasies and demonisms and lyricisms and the very outline of the theme, harmonies, modulations, transformations—I already had everything in me for good . . . only echoes reached me from the stage.

Nevertheless a few months ago, I began listening, by accident, to his Quartet in F Minor, the eleventh—and I don't know if I was particularly craving music that day or if perhaps I was simply won over by the polyphonic riches of the quartet as a string group, always so inexhaustible . . . immediately the next day I bought myself records with these quartets of his . . . and I drowned. E-flat major, E minor, C major, C-sharp minor, F major, A major, G major—quartets! Sixteen quartets! It is one thing to dip occasionally into one of them, in passing, and another to step into the building, to immerse oneself, to wander from hall to hall, wander in the galleries, take in the vaults, examine the architecture, uncover the inscriptions and frescoes . . . with a finger to one's lips. Form! Form! It is not him I look for, the building is not full of him, but his form, which I get to know in the course of this gradual self-composition of adventures, changes, acquisitions—similar to creatures human and nonhuman from ancient fairy tales. As if through a fog, constantly losing my way and with a finger to my lips, I move from "adagio molto e messo" from the seventh to "molto adagio—andante" from the fifteenth, or, too, pensive, I examine how and why Haydn's sun from the time of his youth returns so strangely at the threshold of death, in the last rondo and in the andante in F major? How and why? An unclear question—undelineated answers—dissolved in a musical noise, like the noise of a river—this is not an area of clear contour—and one cannot do more than ask, than answer, while constantly searching with a finger to one's lips, constantly losing one's way.

Certainly, if not for that elegant sound of four stringed instruments, if not for that polyphonic quartet refinement, thanks to which all music that passes between these four instruments undergoes an inordinately subtle transformation, I would not have gone crazy about Beethoven so unexpectedly. But he also interested me as a problem. . . . I thought: this music is probably one of our greatest compromises in the area of art . . . its history is the history of the dirty trick that was played on us . . . its history is the history of our defeat . . . and this old, easy Beethoven is one of the most difficult nuts to crack, today, in the day of Schönberg.

For in art nothing is as difficult as easiness. For art becomes more and more difficult in proportion to its development; easiness is then contradictory to its tendency, easiness remains behind, easiness dies, is taken care of—keeping easiness alive is then contradictory to the natural evolution of art.

And one more thing, before I get to Beethoven: as everybody knows, music is almost exclusively a form, pure form, which develops by itself, with its own logic, from generation to generation. A composer, depending on his era, finds an existent musical language with which he must express himself.

Let us now take a look at musical form from the Mozart-Beethoven period. Forests, groves, streams and pools, flowery meadows and fields rustling with wheat—freshness, lushness, youth, splendidly fertile ground—this is natural music, as God ordained, whose rising force one had to stop. What a wealth of singing! What a flood of harmony! During those blessed times, O musicians, Form was gracious to people. And Beethoven, happy fellow, arrived in the world exactly at the close of this period, when naturalness began to exhaust itself and artistry was gaining momentum. What a happy moment, musicians! Joining nature and art so attractively, as in his transformation of the sonata form, already fanciful and disciplined, yet still direct, fresh. . . . These idylls of art with nature rarely happen to humanity, and humanity, having once experienced them, does not forget them for long centuries. . . .

But Form wouldn't be our curse if it allowed this romance to endure for any length of time. It began to fulfill its ominous destiny. The virgin soil of Mozart and Haydn began to exhaust itself. Chopin and Wagner understood with horror that they could not cultivate the same ground, something repulsive—satiety—stood like an angel with flaming sword in their way; they then found other lands which had lain fallow—but they turned out to be worse. Unhappy Wagner had to complicate his mighty musical invention with the intellect just so as not to follow in the footsteps of those masters—what an autocatastrophe, musicians! And Chopin, exploiting his discovery—the different treatment for piano—to its maximum, discovered his own row from which he did not budge, happy that he possessed at least this farmstead. For these people, music begins to contract violently, limit itself, concentrate, make itself difficult, this is no longer Beethoven's evening stroll but hard labor, digging the well, irrigating the land. What then of Debussy or Stravinsky, and all the others later, cast out by music, by Form, and even further on, where there were clods, crags, fallow ground—laborious, grim effort, in the sweat of one's brow, the acquiring of bloody, meager fruits, isn't this true, musicians? They could delude themselves, like Debussy, that they were getting out from under the tyranny of classical rules into freedom—it is true that these few freedoms, fought for in agony, were accompanied by the growing pressure of Form, but an (already) inhuman and cruel Form, acting against our humanity. Did not this worthy-of-our-pity Debussy say that music should be esoteric and accessible only to the chosen? to specialists?

Yes, a glaring example, one of the most glaring in the entire history of culture, that "form deforms," turning against man. The history of music of the past one hundred years is the almost clinical history of suffocation. I do not deny that this slow choking of the soft body in the harder and harder armor of form does not lack its lofty and insightful moments—for even wanderers who are exiled by hunger from their native land and who take on the desert and wild regions often have stunning experiences, an unusual revelation—the exiled spirit, wandering spirit, attains in such extreme circumstances a store of new and raw material, which one would search for in vain at home. I do not treat this wealth lightly and even someone as good as Schönberg—his face twisted with lack of joy in a feeling of tragic obligation and tragic fate, pushing on toward a complete realization of his demonic destiny—fills me with as much pity as respect. But how far you are, O torture, from the happy days of Merciful Form. The most scathing absurdity of these martyrs is that they do not express what they live. When Form turns against you, you experience awful and poisonous states. The pleasure that you desire to create torments you and humiliates. Your lungs lack the air that is called joy. Everything becomes an effort and you are like a high jumper who puts the bar higher and higher in order to jump higher still. Mysterious powers force you to seek, not what tastes good to you, but taste, and your shame is that you must completely support and confirm that which is killing you.

# Saturday

Tchaikovsky's artistic defeat is proof that in art one can neither go back nor lower oneself—a backward direction and a downward direction are not allowed. The unbearable stench penetrating his work, of something like the inessential mixed with something "that was," ex, buried, and now artificially blown up, the feebleness of the melodiousness that has seen its day! And what can one say about Shostakovich? Folklore, melody, anecdote—no, returning is not allowed! Making it easier is not allowed! One is not allowed to lower oneself! Up, crawl up, without respite, without looking back, even though you might have to break your neck, even though, at the top, there may be nothing but rock.

Today Beethoven is an inaccessible yardstick. The most precious thing about his song derives from the impossibility of its ever being repeated.

# Saturday

This tragic exodus of modern composers is not only a matter of gradually making barren our musical ground—everything in our culture, all of its mechanisms, counts on this pushing out to the extreme or up to the top. . . . Nietzsche's and Ortega's opinions about Beethoven interest me, for example, because I deny them freedom. These are forced opinions, the kind that "speak themselves" as if against the will of the person who utters them. This is a little like a totalitarian system: everything must support the dominant tendency.

Nietzsche (in *The Gay Science*):

He says first that vulgarity has visited German music—a bourgeois, revolutionary vulgarity, intolerant of "nobles," especially in their embodiment of *esprit* and *élégance*. "If you want to imagine the human being that goes with *this* music, merely imagine Beethoven as he appears beside Goethe—say, at their encounter in Teplitz: as semibarbarism beside culture, as the people beside nobility, as the good-natured human being next to the good—who is more than merely a 'good' human being—as the visionary beside the artist, as the man in need of comfort next to the man who *is* comforted, as the man of exaggeration and suspicion next to one who is fair-minded, as the mope and self-tormentor, who is foolishly ecstatic, blissfully unhappy, guilelessly extravagant, presumptuous and crude—and in sum, as the 'untamed human being': that is what Goethe felt about him and called him—

Goethe, the exception among Germans. No music of his rank has yet been found."*

Interesting. Because this is, on the one hand, aristocratic, profound, refined, but on the other is a glaring lie and quite a coarse simplification. To furnish Beethoven's music with Beethoven's nose — to humanize it to the point where it almost has the shape and gesture of the person? One could say to me: how's this, why you yourself have often said that one must seek the creator behind the work? Yes, but not so simplistically! A creator, in my opinion, should be only "one point of reference" for the critic, the work can be bound too closely to the creator only by someone who does not know how much in art "the language deceives the voice and the voice deceives the thought." And in music this kind of naïveté is almost inconceivable because here form reaches the highest degree of objectivity. That Nietzsche! To make the transformation of a theme in a symphony dependent on the expression of the eyes or the manner of bowing! To accuse of "unrefinement" someone capable of refining the fugue! To deny self-control and style to someone whose profession it was to saturate an aristocratically cool form with emotion! To imagine that Beethoven, consumed by the most specific musical assignments, such as the shaping of a theme, the extracting from it of all its possibilities, following it through tonalities, such as the organization of harmony, in short, all the work of composing, which ultimately relies on drawing out of the musical embryo a few new elements of form which then later "work together," blazing their own trails . . . to imagine that the Beethoven who lived in this kingdom of sound was also supposed to be a "soul" in the ordinary sense of the word while he worked!

And why does Nietzsche add to the music the not necessarily handsome nose of its creator, instead of adding the music to the nose? Are the variations from the Thirty-Second Sonata really supposed to be barbaric because they were composed by a barbarian quite shocking when compared with Goethe? It would probably be simpler to recognize that the barbarian who wrote these variations was not a barbarian. The author of the fugue from the Quartet in C-sharp Minor a plebeian? A bourgeois good old boy with the adagio from the *Hammerklavier* Sonata in his head? An eccentric dreamer, hammering out the architecture of the Fifth Symphony? A simpleton with ideas from "adagio molto e messo"?

*From Walter Kaufmann's translation of *The Gay Science* (New York: Vintage Books, 1974), 159.

Why does Nietzsche fall apart when he gets to Beethoven?

But let us take a look at what Ortega y Gasset, that modern *porte parole* of the latest generation, has to say.

"The same distance that exists between Bach and Beethoven exists between the music of 'ideas' and the music of 'feelings.' "

"Beethoven takes for his point of departure the real situation in which life places him—the absence of his beloved, or the absence of Napoleon, a spring day in the country, etc.—this situation unloads in him streams of feelings, sorrowful or tempestuous. . . . " "This same procedure proposed to Bach would be interpreted as impertinence. . . . "

And further:

"Romantic musicians, including Beethoven, devote themselves to expressing the coarse feelings that visit the decent bourgeois."

And he explains that common, lower feelings exist, as well as the higher, more refined ones—that Beethoven is the bard of exactly this inferiority, but that Debussy is "a real artist"; even if he experienced such common, average feelings, he would stifle them in himself, ashamed—he would allow only refined, artistic experiences deriving from the higher sphere of the spirit to be heard. That is why—concludes Ortega—a musician like Beethoven writes the *Pastoral* Symphony and a musician like Debussy, *The Afternoon of a Faun.*

It is enough to repeat what I said a minute ago about Nietzsche: why, when Ortega touches Beethoven, does Ortega fall apart?

Is it really "the absence of a loved one or the absence of Napoleon" that constitutes a point of departure for Beethoven's works? So "common" feelings are deprived of the right to greatness in art? Does Beethoven express feelings in his music? Isn't it really peculiar, bah, even offensive that one speaks about Beethoven in this way? Why do people speak only of him in this way? And how does one arrive at this kind of listening to his music? Why him exactly? Why is Ortega in top form, sensitive, knowing and not stupid when he listens to Stravinsky, but Ortega listening to Beethoven totters down to the level of an ordinary engineer, a romantic lawyer, a sentimental hairdresser, and looks around after his lover, after Napoleon, humanity, destiny, or a stream in the woods? Why, I ask, doesn't he listen to Beethoven in the same way he listens to Bach?

Why? But let us also add that these are not the private perversions of two wise men. The dull-witted, the dull-wittedly malicious approach to this artist becomes a feature of our times. These commentators! Even Wagner said the first thing that came to his mind. In the last chord of the andante from the Thirteenth Quartet these jackasses want to see "the laughter of Bettina Brentano." Those two musical Tartarins,

Romain Rolland and Herriot, dream of battles, sylphs, gnomes, or even "giants throwing mountain crags." And particularly repulsive is the fate prepared for the splendid Quartet in A Minor, opus 132. This quartet has been labeled the "convalescent quartet." It was generally agreed that the first allegro was illness; scherzo—the recovery; adagio, molto, andante—the thanksgiving hymn of recuperation; the final allegro—health and happiness. This precious quartet about a clouded, desperate sky, whose first allegro always gives me a precipitous jolt—namely, that after the modulation there enters another theme—they have dressed in a bathrobe, slippers, nightcap, and stuffed with pills.

But these oddities, mistakes, stupidities, or brutalities do not take place exclusively in the higher strata of the musical world. The average listener's attitude toward Beethoven, the attitude of those attending concerts, is tainted with disease. At the beginning, an honest and joyous love, there are no tones of God above him then, no style grabs you this way. . . . Then the young student experiences his idyll with form and wallows in delectation. This, however, does not last long . . . the hearing becomes accustomed, satiety follows—too bad, too bad! Splendor becomes too intimate, it wearies.

And together with the melancholy boredom of exhaustion, the pressure starts to get annoying—from where? From the air—the pressuring, all-pervasive suggestion that of all the creators it is exactly this one that is "in bad taste," that is too easy. . . . A malicious ease turning itself into difficulty! Bach, Chopin, Schubert, even Mozart—well yes! But not Beethoven! From then on, therefore, music becomes a steep staircase leading upward for our student, a difficulty that surrounds him; it is as if he, in casting off delight, were entering another realm, raw, hard, dry, bitter. And finally the highest initiation appears, the tragic Moloch and tyrant: Bach!

# Monday

Bach is boring! Objective. Abstract. Monotonous. Mathematical. Sublime. Cosmic. Cubic. Bach is boring!—This is how the worst of heresies sounds, which can deprive one of respect in the musical world.

Take a close look at the priests of Bach's mass, look them in the eyes: obduracy, concentration in abstraction, severity, just like the one that offered the bodies of young children to the gods.

Now is the time to answer the question: why do people want to destroy Beethoven, why is every absurdity allowed as long as it is anti-Beethoven, why is a strangling net woven of naive compliments and reproaches? Is it perhaps because they don't like Beethoven? Quite the contrary: because this is the only music that humanity has been successful in creating, because it is beguiling. . . .

He captivates us and that is why we must revile him.

This will be a paradox only for the person unaware of the danger of the situation—that we are under Form's sway, which exists according to its own laws, independently of us and our tastes. This form—the musical form in a given case—must develop; therefore it must shatter all of its attainments up to now; and specifically those that have enchanted man, those that humanity has fallen in love with, those . . . that are riveting . . . and that is why Bach is raised onto a pedestal—because they don't like him, or they don't like him too much—and this creates the possibility of development, here form does not fit man well, here, therefore, something is left to be done between man and form. Modern music, based on Bach, can still live and progress. And that is why in Bartok's six quartets, whose ties with Beethoven's last chamber phase are very strong, Bach dominates in spite of everything. And Schönberg?

But how sad this is! How unenviable our fate!

We are condemned to revile our most genuine delights and to think up other, revolting ones which torment us, which we cannot bear—and, what's more, we are forced to admire them as if this were our true love—we are artificial in this self-abuse, artificial and poisoned, with a tormenting, repulsive art which we are not allowed to vomit up!

# Tuesday

*Ways of listening to the quartets.* —Sometimes I try to tie them with another age, even with another sex. I try to imagine that the C-sharp minor was composed by a ten-year-old boy or by a woman. I try, too, to listen to the Fourth as if it had been created after the Thirteenth. In order to gain a personal attitude toward each of the instruments, I imagine that I am the first violin, Quilomboflor plays the viola, Gomozo is at the cello, and the second violin—Beduino. It is also splendid to listen to the quartet as if it were one instrument—then one values the expansiveness of the scale and the richness of color. I think of names for them: the Eighth, for example, I call the "raspberry" (because of the tonation in the first allegro) and the Fourteenth the "Nietzschean" (because it is so borderline). There are no childish things that will not serve to excite the feelings.

# Friday

*Native Realm* (I agree with Mieroszewski) lacks that something which in Aristotle is called *quid*—it doesn't get to the heart of the matter, doesn't answer the question "what is this about" and also "what is the reason for it." Once I sailed along the Paraná like this: early dawn, neither day nor night, just fog and the movement of the all-encompassing, rustling water, sometimes a specific object would appear in these whirlpools—a board, a branch—but it made no difference because it was immersed in a thrust so universal that it took away your consciousness.

Miłosz, who is immersed in Life and in History, will say that there is no greater falsehood than the definition that the only truth is the one that cannot be encompassed. Naturally. Except that . . . in reading Miłosz I recommend caution, for he is—I believe this—personally interested in blurring contours.

To me Miłosz is one of those authors whose personal life dictates his work. It is not always this way. If my life had turned out differently, who knows if my books would have changed. But Miłosz! Except for his poems, all of his writing is tied to his personal literary situation, that is, to his personal history or to the history of his times. Gradually he turned out to be almost the official informant on the subject the East, at least, the Polish informant; all of the prose he has written to date is devoted to this subject. This is not art for art, this is art for the West. This has its consequences. Among them the fact that if Miłosz cares for his prestige, he cannot be shallower in his information than the French or English; on the contrary, he must be more profound. And if Miłosz cares about the productivity of his subject, among other things, he should not deprive it of greatness or danger. . . .

Here already one discerns the outlines of certain pitfalls. . . . Let us add one more, deriving from the very nature of the East: namely, the East has always oscillated between extremes for which the principle of *tertium non datur* governs. If we do not see the terrible profundity of this, it becomes terrible shallowness instead. If not loftiness, then flatness. But let us add one more danger, quite typically Polish, deriving from the intermediary Polish situation, thanks to which our country is a little bit of a caricature of the East as well as of the West. The Polish East is an East dying in contact with the West (and vice versa), which results in "something being amiss." Let us then imagine Miłosz's troubles when he writes about Tiger,* for example. The issue is whether or not this Tiger is really a tiger or merely a meowing tomcat prowling the rooftops. Is there a real riddle to him or is he one more lush from that fabulous Polish inn called "Under the Dead Cat and Dog" ("Under the Dead East and West")?

Miłosz's troubles are augmented by his being from this very same inn. One of the most interesting, subtle, and even moving aspects of Miłosz's prose is his personal tie to the Polish flea market—one feels that for all of his Europeanism, he is one of them. . . . While recently admiring Wajda's wonderful directing in *Ashes and Diamonds,* I thought about Miłosz and his Polish homeland. How difficult it is to write a synopsis of *Native Realm* because one is its son and come what may, one sails on its waves, immersed in its murmur and fog. . . .

But the strong point of *Native Realm* and a guarantee of its modernism should be nothing else except that here it is not a Pole writing about Poland and the East, but a man writing about the Pole in himself and about "his" Europe. A program like this is almost Husserl or Descartes. Yes, except that they were philosophers and did not scorn abstraction, whereas Miłosz-the-artist and existentialist fears it like wildfire, because he knows that it kills art. He avoids formulas, and so there is no way that he is going to get out of the river to have a look at it from the shore; he immerses himself in its muddied waters, he engages himself personally in his description all the time and then he stops being a man; he again becomes a concrete Miłosz. . . . And this is where the balancing act of this scrupulous writer begins: "Haven't I denigrated myself too much?" "Haven't I raised myself too high?" "Haven't I denigrated them too much?" "Haven't I raised them too high?" From wave to wave, from top to bottom, bottom to top—the dialectical seesaw. Noise. River. History.

---

*Tiger (Tadeusz Kroński), name of a character in Miłosz's *Captive Mind.*

# XVIII

## Friday

Roby has come to visit from Santiago. He is the youngest of the ten brothers S. Two years ago I spent a few months in this Santiago del Estero (1,000 kilometers north of Buenos Aires)—at the time I looked at all the fads, irritations, and inhibitions of this backwater, stewing in its own sauce. . . . The bookstore owned by the so-called "Cacique," a member of that numerous family S., was the collection point for the spiritual anxieties of this small town, placid as a cow, sweet as a ripe plum with its earth-shaking and earth-making ambitions (I am speaking of the fifteen people who met regularly in the Café Aguila). Santiago despises the capital, Buenos Aires! Santiago feels that only in it, in Santiago, is the authentic (*legítima*) Argentina preserved—that all the rest, there in the south, is an assembly of half-breeds, gringos, immigrants, Europeans—a mix, dirt, garbage.

The family S. is a typical specimen of Santiago vegetation, transforming itself with an inconceivable twist into impulse and passion. All of these brothers are of saintly goodness and do not lack that sugarplum sweetness—they are a little like fruit ripening in the sun. At the same time, mighty passions from somewhere, some substratum of a telluric character, galvanize them, their torpor gallops, touched by the madness of reform, creation. Each is a sworn adherent of a different political tendency, thanks to which the family does not need to worry about the frequent revolutions here; whatever happens it will always be the triumph of one of the brothers, the communist or the nationalist, the liberal, priest, Peronist. . . . (Beduino once explained this to me.) During my stay in Santiago two of these brothers had their very own press organs, published at their own expense by the dozens: one published *the* intellectual monthly, *Dimension,* and the second a newspaper whose job was fighting the local governor.

Roby . . . Shortly before his visit to Buenos Aires he surprised me—we never wrote to each other—with a letter from Tucumán in which he asked me to send him the Spanish edition of *Ferdydurke.*

*"Witoldo, something of what you say in your introduction to* The Marriage *has caught my interest . . . these ideas —immaturity, form — which seem to be the groundwork of your work and have a connection with the problem of creativity.*

*"Of course I didn't have the patience to read more than twenty pages of* The Marriage. . . ."

Further on he asks for *Ferdydurke* and writes: *"I spoke with Negro* (this is his brother, a bookseller) *and I see that you continue to be chained by your European chauvinism; the worst thing is that this limitation does not allow you to attain the deepening of that, so very interesting, problem of your writing. You don't seem to understand that the most important thing 'currently' is the predicament of undeveloped countries. From knowledge of this you could extract basic elements for whatever you intend to do."*

I am on intimate terms with this puppydom and I let them say whatever they want. I also understand that for all practical purposes they prefer to attack first — our relations are far from a mawkish idyll. Nevertheless, the letter seemed to me too smart-alecky — well, how dare he? I answered with a telegram:

TO UNDERDEVELOPED ROBY S. TUCUMAN — DON'T TALK NONSENSE. CANNOT SEND *FERDYDURKE.* WASHINGTON FORBIDS IT. NATIVE TRIBES ARE BANNED FROM READING IT TO RETARD THEIR DEVELOPMENT, SENTENCE TO ETERNAL INFERIORITY — TOLDOGOM.

The telegram was put in an envelope and mailed as a letter — these are actually letter telegrams. Shortly thereafter an answer arrived which addressed me indulgently:

*"Beloved Witold, I got your short letter, I see that you are progressing, but you are trying to be original unnecessarily,"* etc., etc. Perhaps it is not worth writing this banter — except that life, authentic life, is nothing extraordinarily brilliant and it is important to me to re-create it here not in its culminations but exactly in its average, everyday character. And let us not forget that a lion, tiger, or serpent can sometimes be concealed in trifles.

Roby then came to Buenos Aires and appeared in the *barcito,* where he officiates almost every evening: a boy "strong in color," raven-black head of hair, olive-brick complexion, lips the color of a tomato, blinding set of teeth. Somewhat slanted and hunched Hindu style, robust, healthy, with the eyes of a clever dreamer, gentle and stubborn — what percentage of him is Indian? And something even more important: a born soldier, fit for a rifle, trenches, a horse. I was interested in whether something had changed in the two years of our separation; had anything changed?

For in Santiago nothing progresses. Every evening the same bold "intercontinental ideas" are expressed in the Café Aguila—Europe is finished, Latin America's time has come, we must be ourselves and not imitate Europeans, we will find ourselves when we return to our Indian traditions, we must be creative, etc. Yes, yes, Santiago, Café Aguila, Coca-Cola, and these bold thoughts, repeated day in and day out with the monotony of a drunkard who first puts out one foot and then does not know what to do with the other, Santiago—that cow which chews its cud every day, that nightmare in which one runs at breakneck speed, never changing place.

It seemed to me, however, that it was almost impossible for Roby to protect himself from mutation, even partially, at his age, and at one in the morning I went with him and Goma to another bar, to discuss things within a smaller circle. He went gladly, was ready to talk the night through, and it was evident that "brilliant, crazy student talk," as Żeromski puts it in his journal, had entered his bloodstream. Generally speaking, they sometimes remind me of Żeromski and his colleagues from the 1890s: enthusiasm, faith in progress, idealism, faith in the people, romanticism, socialism, homeland.

My impressions from this conversation? I left discouraged and disturbed—bored and amused—irritated and resigned—and as if dressed down, as if they had taken me in.

This dummy hadn't appropriated a thing for himself since I had last seen him in Santiago. He initiated the same conversation he did two years ago, as if it were just yesterday. Word for word—I saw only that he was better organized in his stupidity, and therefore more conceited and unyielding. And again I had to listen to: Europe is finished! America's time has come! We must create our own American culture. In order to create it, we must be creative—but how is one to do this? We will become creative when we have a program that liberates our creative powers, etc., etc. Abstract painting is betrayal, it is European. A painter, writer, should cultivate American themes. Art must be related to the folk, must be with folklore. . . . We must discover exclusively American issues, etc.

I know this by heart. Their "creativity" begins and ends with these declamations. What misery and penury—I can count dozens who recited this to me and I never heard anything that could not be summarized in the following groan: "We are uncreative, we should do something to achieve originality, personality . . . we should do something. . . ." They don't see the silliness of this griping. They do not know, these childish creatures, that creativity is not made to order. . . . They do not see the grotesqueness of this choir, lowing as far and wide as Latin America:

originality, personality. They see only that Europe creates; therefore, they too would like to do the same—but it has not occurred to them yet that this desire for originality is also an imitation of Europe. They have not yet comprehended the compromise contained in the rhetoric beyond which they are not capable of moving. They do not sense the frivolity expressing itself in the fact that they desire to "live their own lives" not from a real need, but only to rival Europe—which is better! The naïveté of the postulate they propagate escapes them—that "we are supposed to discover and delineate who we are in order to know what we are supposed to create" (for the reverse is true—man, a nation, a continent, only in creating finds out who he is, his creativity precedes him). In short, envy, inferiority complex, shallowness, feebleness and muddle.

Rubbish. There was no way that I could convince him.

—You are a *europeo*. You are in no position to understand us.

Or: —You are not grasping that the consciousness of our historical moment delineates us in our self-creation and in our subconscious mythology (because, of course, this must all be terribly Toynbee, Spengler, Freud, Marx, Jung, phenomenology, Heidegger, Sartre, Sorel). Despair! His passion is draped with every single paper he has ever read. He is so stuffed with "thoughts" that he has lost his taste, hearing, smell, sight, and touch, and—what is worse—he has stopped feeling his own feelings.

Cairo, China, Bombay, Turkestan, and even the Parisian suburbs and London working districts—all that "thinks," all of the inferiority of the world is immersed in this kind of "thinking." How is it that Europe—not this geographic but spiritual Europe—has withstood the onslaught of so many avaricious ferments which have but one goal—to reach Olympus or destroy it? And this has a nasty taste—this spiritual superiority and intellect, the fruit of development, cannot count on obedience, respect, and gratitude, but becomes an object of desire, of a wild greed for its place, its honors. The disturbing taste of this dirty work which replaces genuine effort (of this they are incapable), a compound of passion and deception.

Rubbish. And, let us add, the unheard-of-naïveté which thinks the "creation of new cultures" is easy.

This Roby pushed me into the past. Into Nazism. I remember: the same powerlessness when that Austrian was intoxicating himself on the consolidation of Brochwicz-Kozlowski (in the train that was taking us from Vienna to Tarvisio), the crash of a rotten Europe and the impending triumph of a new spirit. 1938. The same powerlessness in the face of another language, "their" language. The astonishment that rubbish could be so powerful and aggressive. And the nagging suspicion that the quality of the slogans, truths, ideologies, programs, their meaning, their reality, haven't the slightest significance here, as they serve a different purpose; the only important thing—to accumulate people, produce masses, mass power, a creative power. Ah, to be nothing else except oneself, only one's "I"—how beautiful this is! How clear and unambiguous. To stand firmly on one's own feet. You know what reality is—your reality. You are far from the blather, din, intoxication, deceit, declamation, terror. . . . During the interwar and wartime period I lived through the victory of collective power as well as its defeat and breakdown, when again that immortal "I" was reborn. Gradually those fears faded in me—until here again, with Roby, it assaulted me with the same evil smell!

Not a pleasant discovery. You have the impression that once again a monstrous plot is being hatched in order to grab you and subject you to the blind forces of the collectivity and History. Words, ideas, everything then gains another meaning, morality, science, reason, logic, everything, everything becomes the weapon of some other, superior idea, everything is masked, everything desires to conquer you, possess you. What sort of idea is this? You seek it in vain, it does not exist, only the Collectivity itself exists, nothing more, the concentration of people, mass, a creature arisen from the masses, an expressive mass. I sat over a beer across from that student, fetchingly young and so vulnerable, yet so dangerous. I looked at his head and his hand. His head! His hand!

A hand ready to kill in the name of childhood. The extension of the absurdity, imagined by him, was a bloody bayonet. . . . A strange being— with a muddled and frivolous head, with a dangerous hand. The thought occurred to me, a thought neither clear nor complete, which I nevertheless desire to note here. . . . It would sound more or less like this: his head is full of chimeras, therefore it is worthy of indulgence, but his hand has the gift of transforming chimeras into reality; it is capable of creating facts. Unreality from the head, reality from the hand . . . *and the seriousness from one end.* . . .

Perhaps I am grateful to him that he returned my old anxieties to me. The self-assurance of a member of the intelligentsia, intellectual, artist, which grows in me with age, is bad! Remember, those who do not write in ink, write in blood.

# Monday

They do not know that I am somewhat of a specialist in their main problem—immaturity—and that all of my literature is at home in it. It is paradoxical that in South America, Borges, abstract, exotic, not tied to their problems, is a luminary, but I have only a handful of readers. The paradox, which stops being a paradox when one reflects that they can show Borges off in Europe. Not me because I am a Pole. I am not *valor nacional.*

That they do not want to be the darling pupils of alien cultures, I feel is right. And I also agree that they have their own reality and that only in supporting themselves on it can they become someone in the world. . . . But, in my opinion, they commit one serious, dramatic error. . . .

Namely, instead of saying "I," they say "we." We Americans. We Argentineans. When a single man says "we," he is misusing the word, for no one has authorized him to use it, he is allowed to speak only in his own voice. Whoever wants to get at his "own reality" and support himself on it should avoid the plural form at all costs. What is this "our reality"? I can be certain only of "my reality." What is America, Americans? A concept, generality, abstraction. What is the "American reality"? Something that each person can understand as he wishes.

The difference between them and me comes down to their wanting to *first* discover American reality and liberate America from European dependence and only later to produce this new type of "mature" American. This new America, discovered and defined, will create its people. In my view, one must begin with man, the individual man, and I will say more: the development of America can only be the work of people who have overcome America in themselves.

You say that your America is backward, immature? Good. But in that case your first task should be to liberate yourself from its inhibiting influence. As a man, you are just as good as an Englishman or a Frenchman. As a Cuban or a Paraguayan, you are worse. Feel yourself a man, then place yourself above this undeveloped America. Do not allow your milieu and your American way of thinking to shackle you.

Except that . . . this immaturity imposes the word "we" on them. They are in a collective phase and this phase is also South America's so they cannot make their way out of it. "I" is too independent for them, too free. They are "we." They are America. And in being America, how can they progress? They have gotten bogged down together with it in history. Amen.

Much of this could be applied to Poland and Poles.

# Tuesday

On the ship *General Artigas* on the way to Montevideo. Night. Storm. A priest reads the paper. A child cries. Waiters talk in the corner. The boat creaks.

The melody from Brahms's Fourth Symphony, which has been dogging me from the time I left Buenos Aires. I think about Brahms's themes and Beethoven's themes. Beethoven makes a strange impression against the background of Brahms's constant threat that the work will not be organic enough—Brahms's thematics, cautious and *deliberate,* are permeated by a concern for the homogeneity of composition; you can see that this architect is afraid his building might collapse. But Beethoven loaded themes suggested by his spirit into a work with the certainty that whatever is conceived of the spirit cannot be stillborn. And this tearing of Beethoven's theme into a work, as if from the outside, only to sink its roots into it, seems to be somehow singular, singularly bold, captivating, when I recall how Brahms builds up gradually, cautiously from himself and never, so to speak, does he stick his nose beyond himself.

How the wind batters the canvas on the deck! Fatigue. Why does this entrancing melody—the second theme from the allegro of the third concerto—come to mind exactly at this moment? Ravishing.

Why—I would like to know—in musical analyses, in learned commentary, does one avoid mentioning the beauty and charm of such melodies? There is no doubt that when we are still in the beginning phase of listening to the work the overwhelmingly melodious entrance of the orchestra and piano are what they should be: the dominant effect, the most important, most thrilling effect. It is only in a gradual acquaintance with the work that one exhausts their charm; other more complex values then attract our attention. This is why experts are silent about their first impressions. Is it right, though, that a work be judged by an ear that has become weary and is incapable of experiencing the holiness of its first emotions?

The lights flicker. The front wall of the salon rides from the bottom up and from the top down. The ship is blown through and through by the whistling wind. In *Pornografia* I tried to return to such melodies . . . melodic, thrilling . . . alluring. . . .

And not only in *Pornografia.* But in *Pornografia* I was able to get up my courage and I resigned from humor, which isolates.

A waiter brings black coffee. Something knocks against the wall, as if trying to get to my head. What impertinence on my part—to flee to such thrilling-melodic subjects! And today, when modern music is afraid of melody, when the composer, before he uses it, must clear it of attractions, render it dry. It is no different in literature—a modern but self-respecting writer avoids lures, is difficult, and prefers to repulse rather than tempt. And me? I am exactly the opposite, I load the text with tasty tastes, charming charms, I stuff it with excitement and colors, I do not want dry, unprepossessing writing . . . I am seeking the most graspable melodies . . . in order to get at, if possible, something even more "captivating." . . .

Siren. I go on deck. The ship is moaning painfully, it plunges into the exploding water under the dome of a full moon wracked on the surface. God! What pain! What despair! In my heavy, painful striving to rejuvenate, to freshen my art, I have not even refrained from, ah, let us confess . . . boy with girl. Oh, shame! Who in today's literature is bolder? This is my boldness! The river-ocean roars. But, but . . . let us confess on this thundering trail of water, white with fury, unloading its despair under a quiet moon. . . . I, accursed one, could approach their nakedness only in a costume more sophisticated than that worn by the most modern avant-garde, by the driest intellect! I made them parenthetical!

I made them parenthetical; I couldn't sing any other way!

## Wednesday, Montevideo

I stroll in a tidy city, with odd balconies and congenial people. Montevideo. Here the old decorum still reigns after having been expelled from many other parts of South America.

Kind faces, rich apparel, a beach twenty minutes away by bus, this is the life! And if I moved here permanently?

*Avenidas* running into the ocean-river.

The world is written for two voices. Youth supplements the Incomplete with Completion—and this is its brilliant task. This is the subject of *Pornografia*.

One of my chief aesthetic and spiritual tasks: to find an approach to youth that is sharper and more dramatic than that which is currently in use. To thrust it into maturity (that is, to reveal its ties with maturity).

## Thursday

Peace. Anxiety! I am a little disturbed by the complete lack of a "metaphysical spine tingle" in the Uruguayan capital, where no dog has ever bitten anyone.

*Pornografia.* Pulling two older men down . . . into the body, senses, the juvenile . . . when I was writing this, I felt vague. But I needed "physics," it was indispensable as a counterweight to metaphysics. And the reverse—metaphysics cried out for the body. I do not believe in a nonerotic philosophy. I do not trust thought that frees itself of sex. . . .

Of course it is difficult to imagine Hegel's Logic without abandoning the body. But pure consciousness must once again be immersed in the body, in sex, in Eros, the artist must again thrust the philosopher into beauty. Consciousness dictates the conviction that it is final, and its work would surely be impossible without this certainty—but the results of its work can be returned to life, conceived from a different position, by another spirit, here the spirit of art can be of use to the spirit of the thinker. And even if an incurable contradiction between them does exist—are we not a walking contradiction, are we not forced to live the division we are?

That peculiar absolute of sex, the erotic absolute. This divided world of the sexual drive which, because of its division, becomes self-sufficient, absolute! What other absolute is needed when he who desires has drowned in the eyes of she who desires?

Sun. Breakfast with Minister Mazurkiewicz and with the long-time honorary consul in Montevideo, Józef Makowski, who plays host. We fondly remember Straszewicz and other friends.

# Friday

Foul weather rants and raves in all directions. We sit at the Tip Top, Dipa and I, and we drink coffee, staring at the dirty waves under the rain. I look at the paper. Ah, in the evening at the Writers' Union Dickman, who is visiting from Argentina, is supposed to read a paper at a session chaired by an old acquaintance, the Uruguayan poet Paulina Medeiros. We will attend—I not so much to hear Dickman but to see Paulina.

It ended dramatically (all of my contacts with the *escritores* of this continent end dramatically).

We appear midway through the lecture. Dickman is talking about twenty-five years of work as a writer. Uruguayan literati—not one interesting face—and universal courtesy, banality, and boredom hang in the air. I feel that the sight of this mob of writers is beginning to excite me—as always. I am allergic to writers in groups, in their mob aspect; when I look at my "colleagues" all together I get sick. But I don't know if this will be clear, the sound of the word *escritor* in South America is somehow dumber than anywhere else; here the writing profession floats in some sort of special, pompously fictional sauce, highmindedly sincere, rancid and honeycombed. And this ridiculousness, rising like steam from the *escritores,* amuses me. Applause. He is finished.

Paulina Medeiros rises and announces that by happenstance the Union also has a foreign guest, the writer Gombrowicz, whom we greet, etc., etc. — and now perhaps Mr. Gombrowicz would like to say a few words? . . . Silence. Expectation. I admit that I really did act inappropriately. Instead of saying a few pleasant words, that I greet them, etc., etc., I say to Paulina: — That's all well and good, Paulina, but what have I written? What are the titles of my books?

A lethal question, for no one in America knows anything about me. Consternation. Paulina's stammering and blushing, for she's completely taken aback. Dickman comes to her aid: — I know! Gombrowicz published a novel in Buenos Aires, a translation from the, uh, Rumanian, no, from Polish, uh, *Fitmurca* . . . no, *Fidafurca.* . . . I sit in cold sadism, I sit and say nothing; people begin to stir and to leave their seats in embarrassment, when finally the chairman, or the secretary, carries in an enormous book into which Dickman inscribes an appropriate aphorism and I my signature — after which I pass the tome to Dipi so that he can sign it too. Which again sends a ripple of anxiety through the respectful crowd, because Dipi is of draft age and doesn't look like a writer at all. He signs his name with a flourish — his signature is probably the most commanding in the whole book — and I explain that he has been writing novels since the age of fourteen and already has four to his credit.

# Saturday

Straight from the unfortunate visit to the Writers' Union — I am speaking of my stay in Montevideo — we, Paulina Medeiros, Dickman, Dipi, and I, went to a *peña* of poets. This took place in a tiny, pretentious restaurant, where a wall painting added wings to a menu deprived of all imagination. At an enormous table sat about fifty people. Paulina explains quietly: this is a banquet given by the poets in honor of Professor R., this will introduce us to the poetic climate of the capital. Who is this Professor R.? — Oh! — a worthy gentleman — a renowned critic — university professor — author — friend, father, guardian of poets —

who has just received an award for a collection of essays and hence the feast.

Never would I have assumed . . . no, I still do not know America, I do not know it in all of its complexity, its strange mixture of levels, its half-baked quality. . . . What I saw, so terribly provincial, would not have been possible in the worst Argentine backwater, but, at the same time, to my delight, was straight out of the Pickwick Club.

A luxuriant angelicism reigned. Next to the angel Professor R., who smiled, greeted, and charmed, sat another angel, a frisky and ardently poetic old man, so poetic he ran the session, warming and buoying everyone's spirits. Speeches, a poet stands up and lets out a poem in honor of Professor R. Applause.

Right after that a *poetiza* rises and dashes off a poem in honor of the professor. Applause.

Then yet another poet rises and lets fly a poem in honor of the professor. Praise. Applause. It was only then that I realized a strange, uncommon thing not so much out of Dickens but Chesterton: *even if there were fifty of them, all of them were poets and each would launch a poem in Professor R.'s honor* (who discreetly and tactfully let it be understood that it was not he who mattered but the poetry).

I called the waiter to bring me two bottles of wine, one white, the other red, and I began to drain them both! Meanwhile poets were declaiming, R. beamed, angelicism glowed along with all of the virtues practiced in such cases—humility, discretion, but also gentility, emotion, heart, as if it had all been taken out of the sweetest and most poetic dreams of some old maiden aunt: "beautiful" and "pure." When the poet finished, people shook his hand and everyone yelled "bravo!" When, in conclusion, this fat hussy impatiently awaiting her turn tore from her seat and, tossing her bust left and right and waving her arms, trundled out more bouquets of rhymed gentility, I, full of the red and white, couldn't stand it any longer and burst out laughing, stifling my spasms in Dipi's back. He also broke up but had no back to bury his face in and so exploded with laughter right in front of the entire gathering!

Shock. Looks. But here stands the honorable laureate and utters: that he wasn't deserving, although maybe he was, but no he wasn't, although maybe he was. . . . People are moved. Applause. The angel-chairman-poet thanks all present and warms their hearts. . . . The atmosphere becomes so rarified and sweet that Dipi and I dash for the nearest door, stumbling, drunk as skunks, soused, and mighty plastered.

Had I once again compromised Poles in front of foreigners? Give me more, "this is what I like," as Mickiewicz would say! But this is not the point. Something else interests me here. How would these events look from the other, Uruguayan side?

"Indifferent, conceited, and stuck-up European writer demonstrates contempt for the naive, perhaps, but heartfelt freshness of Uruguayan poetry!"

Meanwhile—it was exactly the opposite. I was freshness, sincerity among them and they—what can one say—were a gang of dealers, fabricating an artificial atmosphere of mutual adoration.

This kind of *quiproquo:* a provincial young poet is no innocent . . . while an old cynic fights for the purity of poetry naively, purely.

## Saturday

Gossip in action! While eating supper the next day at the Tip Top, Dipi overheard a conversation at a nearby table about *the scandal at the Writers' Union and the provocation at the poet's banquet* . . . and somebody suggested that they write to Ernesto Sabato to ask him if his letter of recommendation to Julio Bayce was authentic!

## Saturday

A cocktail in Carrasco. I can't stand this comfortable bourgeoisie with its *aire acondicionado,* electric heating, two bathrooms for the servants, and a view of the ocean.

Michelangelo's David is lending luster to the town hall. A sudden, moving invasion of the Renaissance—a feeling, some sort of shortcut, of the countless delights contained in style in general, and in this style in particular, so happily rediscovered after so many centuries! A conversation with Asnito (Dipa) on the subject of the Renaissance—the Baroque— Cézanne—concrete art. I am amazed at the fluency with which this young nestling swims in today's complicated eddies.

A letter from a certain writer.

*"A few days ago I finished reading* Pornografia. Kultura's *announcement of it, done with your permission I am sure, speaks of the metaphysical substance of this book. . . . Until now, it seemed to me that I have always managed to decipher the hidden meanings beneath the surface of your works, but in* Pornografia, *for the first time, I was incapable of getting at*

*its hidden sense. That is why I am allowing myself to turn directly to you for help, with a plea for an indication of where I am to seek the metaphysical content of* Pornografia.*"*

But of course! This letter comes at a good time. It allows me to remember once again who I am and what my position on the spiritual-artistic map is.

I answer:

*"I had nothing to do with composing the announcement in* Kultura, *but I will most gladly tell you what, according to me, are* Pornografia's *ties to metaphysics.*

*"Let us try to express it another way: man, as we know, strives for the Absolute, for Completeness. For absolute truth, God, complete maturity, etc. To embrace everything, to fully realize the process of his development—such is the imperative.*

*"Thus, in* Pornografia *(in keeping with my old habit, because* Ferdydurke *is also saturated with this) another, probably more hidden and less legitimate, aim of man is revealed, his need for the Incomplete . . . Imperfection . . . Inferiority . . . Youth. . . .*

*"One of the key scenes of the work is the one in the church where under the pressure of Frederick's consciousness the Mass, together with God-the-Absolute, collapses. Then out of the darkness and emptiness of the cosmos comes a new divinity, earthly, sensual, underage, made up of two underdeveloped beings creating a closed world—because they attract one another.*

*"Another key scene is the deliberations preceding Siemian's murder— the Adults are not in a state to commit murder because they know all too well what it is, what weight it has, and they must do it with the hands of minors. This murder must, therefore, be cast into a sphere of lightness, irresponsibility—only there does it become possible.*

*"I am not just writing about this now, these ideas permeate all my work. And in the* Diary *I mention, for instance, that 'Youth . . . appeared to me as the only, highest, and absolute value of life. . . . That "value," however, had one characteristic, probably devised by the devil himself, that, being youth, it was always something beneath value.'*

*"These last words ('beneath value') explain why, in spite of the sharp conflict of life-consciousness in me, I did not end up in any of the modern existentialisms. The authenticity and inauthenticity of life are equally precious to me—my antinomy is Value on the one hand and Not-Quite-Value on the other . . . Dissatisfaction . . . Underdevelopment. . . . This is, I*

*think, the most important thing in me, the most personal and individual. A lack of seriousness is just as important to man as seriousness. If a philosopher says that 'Man wants to be God,' then I would add: 'Man wants to be young.'*

"And according to me, the various periods of human age are one of the tools of this dialectic Completion-Incompletion, Value-Nonvalue. That is why I attribute a significant and dramatic role to the introductory age — youth. And that is why my world is degraded: it is like grabbing the Spirit by the scruff of the neck and immersing it in lightness, in inferiority. . . .

"Of course, in Pornografia I am not so much seeking philosophical theses as desiring to extract the artistic and psychological possibilities of the subject. I am looking for 'beauties' appropriate to the conflict. Is Pornografia metaphysical? Metaphysics means beyond-physics, beyond-corporeality, and my intention was to get at certain antinomies of the soul through the body.

"This work is probably very difficult, although it has the appearance of an ordinary 'novel' and even a pretty indecent one at that. . . . I am impatiently awaiting its appearance in French, German, and Italian — these editions are slowly in the making — I hope that I will find more readers, like you, seeking its meaning on foreign soil."

# Sunday

Malvin, the beach beyond Carrasco, an oceanic revelation, the sudden salt, greenness of the waves, astonishment, admiration, regret — the wreckage behind me of an enormous river, its annihilation in splashing, salty, green infinity, whose whisper expresses nothing.

Perhaps I am more yoked to the nation than it seems? Again this suspicion. And if *Pornografia* is an attempt to revive Polish eroticism?

An attempt to recover an eroticism more appropriate to our fate and our history of recent years, which consists of rape, slavery, humiliation, dog fights, a descent into the dark extremes of the consciousness and the body? And perhaps *Pornografia* is a modern Polish, erotic, national poem?

A rather unexpected and strange idea — it never occurred to me while I was writing it. Only now. I do not write for the nation or with the nation or from the nation. I write with myself, from myself. But isn't my thicket joined in secret passage with the thicket of the nation?

I, an American, I, an Argentinean, walking the coast of the Atlantic . . . I am still a Pole . . . yes . . . but just from my youth, childhood, from the awful forces which formed me then, pregnant with what was to follow. . . . There, beyond Malvin, the proud insolence of land conjured up by the setting sun, like the most noble philosophy and the most splendid poetry. Downward! Downward! Degradation! I am my own degradation! How mercilessly man has to cast himself from the peaks — foul his own nobility — violate his own truth — destroy his own dignity — for his individual spirit to undergo slavery once again and submit to the herd, to the species. . . .

1961

# XIX

## Monday

A very peculiar book, I have never read anything like it, exciting in a strange way, Gaëtan Picon's *Panorama des idées contemporaines*. In Polish translation, Picon's work is called *A Panorama of Modern Thought* and has been published by Libella in Paris.

It has been a long time since I dove into a book with the enthusiasm I felt in reading these seven hundred pages, stuffed with the latest wisdom from recent decades. Philosophy and social science, art and religion, physics and mathematics, history and psychology, but also the history of philosophy and political problems and contemporary humanism . . . the volume encompasses various branches of science, not by giving a dry summary, however, but by presenting excerpts from the most representative works. This is the kind of anthology where the history of philosophy is reported by the selected texts of Dilthey, Lenin, Trotsky, Jaurès, Berdyayev, Spengler, Toynbee, Croce, Aron, Jaspers, and on quantum theory and associated problems by Broglie, Bohr, Einstein. One should not seek exhaustive discussion here — but rather an introduction to the style of today's science, its tone, temperament, "character" (because sometimes I have the impression that science is a person), and customs! It is as if you were listening to a meeting where first one then another sage expresses himself; what an opportunity to listen closely to their manner of speaking. . . .

## Wednesday

Buenos Aires. An interview with me in *Clarin* — Pat Leroy (Zdzisław Bau) conducted it. *Clarin* is the most popular daily in Argentina; the two-page interview with a huge photograph of me and a drawing by Quilomboflora — will surely cause a stir. I said (among other things) that "not being a premier Shorthorn bull, I could not aspire to fame in Buenos Aires."

# Thursday

And what if Cassandra appeared to Socrates in a dream with this prophecy: —*O mortal ones! O human race! It would be better for you not to reach the distant future, which will be diligent, scrupulous, forced, slick, shallow, miserable. . . . Let women cease bearing children —for everything will be born to you inside out, greatness will give birth to pettiness, power to weakness, and your stupidity will be born of reason. Oh, better that women should strangle their newborn! . . . because you will have functionaries for leaders and heroes, and decent little souls will be your Titans. You will be deprived of beauty, passion, and delight . . . a cold, tired, and barren time awaits you. And all of this will be perpetrated upon you by your Wisdom, which will break away from you and become impossible to comprehend as well as rapacious. And you will not even be able to cry because your misfortune will happen beyond you!*

Is this blasphemy against the Almighty Lord? Against today's creator? (I am speaking of science, of course.) Who would dare! Even I am prostrated before the youngest of Creative Forces—and I humble myself, hosanna; the above prophecy hails the triumph of almighty Minerva over her enemy, man. Let us take a closer look at these people of the future, these people of science—and today there is no lack of them, they are spreading fast. One thing is repulsive in this scientist: his smiling impotence, his genial helplessness. He is similar to a pipe that funnels food but does not digest it, so that knowledge never becomes personal in him; he is simply a tool, an instrument from head to foot. One talks to this kind of professor the way one would to a fish out of water; each of them dies if taken out of his special area—this is shameful, one should burn with embarrassment! Modest? In their place, I would also be modest, why not? Nothing they do enters the bloodstream. Accursed blind chickens who happen upon a kernel! Blind masons laying brick upon brick, ignorant of what they are building! They are workers. They are coworkers. If one says A, the other says B, and the third C, and so the prevailing opinion is formed: each is a function of each, each uses the other, all are always servants—sucked dry by the vampire of the intellect, pushed down by the more and more inaccessible Thought rising above them.

Even in my youth people laughed at the professor, an abstract old granddad, chasing his hat. Today no one laughs anymore, we are beginning to shrink, curl up, we begin to feel a little strange when we see how this kindly band of specialists tries to get at our hides, rearrange our genes, creep into our dreams, transform our cosmos, stick a needle into our central nervous system, feel our most intimate inner organs, which should not be touched! This brazen and vile unceremoniousness, this nasty thing that is beginning to happen to us does not horrify us enough—but shortly we will begin to howl, we will see how this friend and benefactress, Science, as it is more and more unleashed, becomes a bull that takes us on its horns, an element more volatile than anything we have had to deal with up to now. The growing light will be transformed into darkness and we will find ourselves in a new night, the worst one yet.

Professors love their wives. They are good fathers. Their attachment to the hearth is cozy and begs for forgiveness, since they know well that they never feel at home in their homes. They speak no language. A scientist betrays ordinary human speech for scientific language, but he does not wield this either—the tongue wields him, not the other way around. Formulas form themselves in this closed Land of Abracadabra. As long as a mechanistic interpretation of phenomena held up, things weren't too bad—but today when the mechanism no longer satisfies and we reach for a "whole" that does not lend itself to division into parts, when functionalism, finalism, and various coordinates fascinate scientific thought, the statements of biology or psychology are sphinxlike, headlong, no better than physical, mathematical, or philosophical statements.

Picon's anthology, mentioned above, is an excellent demonstration of the scientific style in various guises, in a thousand variations; here one sees how this language is created and what it does with these people. One sees clearly how expression becomes convulsive and goes crazy from the desire to grasp what is ungraspable. This is quite a circus. And how could the language of a rationalized international wisdom that is constantly growing from generation to generation and turning against the very nature of the individual mind in order to do it violence be otherwise? The pressure to utter the inexpressible becomes so overwhelming in the final phases of the development of science that its statements become related to philosophy. Translating the texts selected by Picon must have been pure torture; the translator must do ugly things with words here, it is unavoidable.

The hideous strangeness of knowledge . . . it is like an alien body introduced into the mind, it always obstructs. One bears this kind of thinking like a weight, in the sweat of one's brow; science often acts like poison: the weaker the mind, the fewer antidotes it finds and the more easily it succumbs. Take a look at the majority of students. Where, for instance, does their lack of joy come from? Is their fatigue merely a consequence of excessive work? Weren't their reactions poisoned by the habit of false precision, an exaggerated objectivity, did this not cast their judgments into uncertainty, fear? Let us see how the cult of logic kills understanding of the personality, how principles replace an inborn self-assurance and the certainty of one's own *convictions,* how theories extirpate grace and beauty . . . this is where the new type of student comes from ("Hey, pal, are you passing?"), a decent, upright, useful, but wan being . . . with a lunar pallor drained of all brilliance and heat, reflecting only that awful, incomprehensible light. Perhaps still alive but only as a weakened, twisted form of life.

Is this the introduction to a race of pigmies with swollen heads and white lab coats?

## Friday

Degeneration awaits us so we should brace ourselves for it today. I do not deny that someday science may lead us to paradise. Until that day, however, we are threatened by a series of operations, deforming, almost surgical interventions (which is what happens to patients who are subjected to only three introductory operations in a series of twelve that are supposed to improve their faces).

The transformation of the conditions of our lives, as well as of our psycho-physical structure, with the help of technology, will knock us out of our groove and unsettle us.

## Friday

Science muddles.
Science reduces.
Science disfigures.
Science warps.

Will scientism replace art? Oh, I am not at all afraid of losing admirers!

I do not fear that "future generations will not read novels," etc. It is probably a complete misunderstanding to conceive of serious art in categories of production, market, readers, supply and demand—what does this have to do with anything?—art is not the fabrication of stories for readers but a spiritual cohabitation, something so tense and so separate from science, even contradictory to it, that there can be no competition between them. If someone fine, dignified, prolific, brilliant (this is how one ought to speak of artists, this is the language art demands) is born in the future, if someone unique and unrepeatable is born, a Bach, a Rembrandt, then he will *win* people over, *charm* and *seduce* them. . . .

As long as superior and inferior people exist, a superior man, expressing himself in art, will be attractive . . . and nothing will weaken his existence.

You talk about engineers, technocrats, and other functionaries' indifference to art? Was a dialogue between an artist and a cog on a wheel ever possible? Yet everyday I realize how eager for the glow of artistry is a person who has been drawn into a rut yet has maintained enough humanity to feel that his back is being broken.

When a student of the sciences sits down at my table to look at me condescendingly (as I "shoot the breeze"), to scorn me (because this is "putting people on"), to yawn (because "one cannot prove this with an experiment"), I don't try to convince him. I wait until a wave of weariness and satiety overtakes him. For it is true that in science there is less putting people on, less claptrap, and less of the "personal dirt" that infests art—ambitions, striving for effect, posing, affectation, rhetoric—but it is also true that science gives these guarantees only because it functions in a very limited territory—and this laboratory "certainty" becomes odious and humiliating to a nature not entirely mediocre.

Average intelligence loves blinders, which facilitate an even trot; but a brisker and livelier intelligence desires uncertainty, risk, a play of more deceptive and elusive forces, where one lives . . . where one can preserve flight, pride, joke, confession, rapture, play, struggle.

A moment arrives when theory becomes a personal enemy; one desires man, one desires him, however he may be, vague, untruthful, unascertainable . . . just to see humanity and touch it again.

## Sunday

Publishing books at a distance of ten thousand kilometers ruins the nerves!

*Ferdydurke* appeared in Germany without commentary to explain briefly "what it is about"—thus some critics and readers did not know where to begin. I immediately wrote to the English publisher to have him add a brief explanation to the preface.

All for naught! The English *Ferdydurke* also appeared without the few sentences it needed so badly.

Let it appear, as it wants, I have to leave it all to God's mercy and shut my eyes. Let it happen by itself!

# Tuesday

When will we take the offensive?

Will we, artists, finally be able to attack the man of science in the name of a more radiant humanity? To attack—from what position? With what means? Are we in a position to attack at all? In past decades art has acted badly—it allowed itself to be appealed to, it almost fell to its knees, it received everything greedily from the hand of its enemy, it lacked pride and even an ordinary instinct for self-preservation. The results?

Painting overrun by abstraction and other concepts of form—all inspired by science—there is in this art a greater and greater diminishing of individuality, superiority, talent, the work is more and more "democratic" and "objective."

Music corrupted by theory, technique, followed by a breakdown of the personality and the violent shrinking of composers so that soon no one will know what to call these dwarfs.

And belles lettres, whose beauty kills itself more each year and which has become evil and brutal, almost rabid—or nauseous—or dry and stiff—analytical, sociological, phenomenological, laborious, boring, and off the mark.

What sort of attack can this kind of art dream of if it cannot even defend itself and is already half-conquered? Theories could not have achieved this if the artist had not personally—again I return to this key word—suffered a breakdown and had not allowed his separateness to be weakened.

The individual is a nut so impossible to crack that no theoretic tooth will be able to manage it. And so nothing will be able to justify your defeat, bumblers!

# Thursday

A letter from Maria Dąbrowska—so typical that I wonder if I should discuss it in the diary.

I decided to write the preface to the French edition of *Pornografia* myself.

Quequen.

Santiago Achaval, Juan Santamarina, Paco Virasoro, and Pepe Uriburu—wealthy young people from the oligarchy. How many brothers and sisters do they have? Paco has the least — a mere six. Forty-plus siblings altogether for the four of them.

Niaki Zuberbuhler has eighty first cousins. Rural reform is being carried out in bed.

The false erudition of the literati is also the result of their being depraved by science. How easy it is to arm oneself with a few encyclopedias and shine with quotations, everyone does that, from columnists to Nobel laureates! And what's more, it was always this way. But we live in an era that is unmasking us — why doesn't someone speak openly about the misery of quotations?

A taboo subject! Anything but this! It might turn out that the staunchest seekers of truth and strivers for ruthless honesty pretend to be more educated than they are. What a lack of dignity. . . .

## Saturday

I expect that in years to come art will have to shake off science and turn against it — this clash will take place sooner or later. Then there will be an open battle, with each side completely aware of its cause.

Meanwhile we have lots of camouflage, ruses, betrayal; even a fifth column is not lacking. The fifth column in art's territory is existentialism and phenomenology.

It might appear that existentialism wants to help art — but this very strange courtesan, who betrays everything with everything, can only compromise the person who socializes with her. This neither fish nor fowl cannot aspire to form at all — what then can it have in common with art?

Yet it is so tantalizing! It is so full of promises! In it dwells a concentrated and incorruptible (it seems) striving for the concrete, for the personality. . . . So what if this antiabstraction cannot sustain itself in any kind of philosophical thinking in which a conceptual schema is inevitable. In fact, existentialism becomes a trap: this antirational pork fat is supposed to entice the gullible into just one more conceptual cage.

Each spiritual stance creates its own style. But existentialism, conceived of nothing but contradictions and incapable of reconciling them à la Hegel (because dialectics fails here), does not lead to just any style but to one of the worst styles, obscurely precise, abstractly concrete, subjectively objective, to empty talk that splits its seams. One would swear upon seeing these thinkers that they want to dance sitting down — that is how pedantic and volatile existentialism is.

I prefer phenomenology; it is purer from the standpoint of form. One could even nurture the hope that it is a means of purging the waste of scientism; well, well, isn't this a return to a natural, direct thinking, immaculately virgin? Put science outside the pale! That's what we need to do!

Existentialism is a mirage! A ruse! If it can't stand science, then it is like a daughter who cannot stand her natural mother—Cartesian, conceived in a scientific spirit, passionless, cold, like ice—and her cadaver coldness is of no use to us at all.

# Monday

Bondy, the editor of *Preuves,* appeared in Buenos Aires preceded by a ringing of bells in the press. After reading these articles I was certain that at the airport there would be a group of dignitaries with the French ambassador at their head and that Bondy would be torn to pieces, at least like Barrault; I decided, therefore, to behave discreetly and did not appear at the hotel—which, having in mind the category of guest, could only be the Plaza or Alvear—until the following day.

Meanwhile, when I returned home that day, Frau Schultze told me that a certain man had been asking for me and that he had left his name and address. I read: François Bondy, City Hotel. I go to the City, a few blocks from me. We greet each other cordially. I explain why I did not appear sooner, that I did not want to take his time.

—Why? I had breakfast at Victoria Ocampo's but now I am free. Let's talk!

We go to the café and gab, gab. Evening. Once more I cautiously fish for mention of dinner at the ambassador's, the Academy of Literature, the Jockey Club. . . . No, speaking frankly, he has nothing to do and doesn't know where to go. I had been invited to Zosia Chądzyńska's house for supper that evening and not thinking much about it, I took him along. Zosia, a worldly person, did not betray surprise when he appeared behind me. I said: —Bondy! They greet each other as if everything were normal. The architect Zamecznik is visiting from Poland, I call the Lubomirskis and ask them to come over, we organize a small supper (very modest, as always at Zosia's, but the French bubbles like champagne . . . ), yet something unsaid hangs in the air.

On our departure the ladies wink at me: —Confess, who did you bring? Who is this? A poet? Italian, or what? Where'd you get him?

They thought I was putting them on! This important editor, whom it is difficult to imagine without four phones and three secretaries, is very much the poet. He is a poet so much that sometimes we, poets, harbor the suspicion that his indolence, his expression of a lost child, greedy eyes, the strange capacity for just appearing (instead of walking in normally), are to lure us and use us coldly to his own purposes. But I cheer myself that politicians are inclined to do the reverse, to nurture the fear that Bondy's cold organizational talents are to dupe them and to catch them in nets of poetry. Bondy probably (I know him very little) is one of those people whose strength lies in his *absence;* he is always removed from what he is doing, keeping at least one foot somewhere else, his wisdom is the wisdom of a calf that suckles two mothers.

## Tuesday

How should one mobilize against science? From what positions should one strike? To find a point of support in order to rouse contempt from its positions, the possibility of contempt. . . . And this terrifying perspective of a greater and greater division into *Homo sapiens* and . . . and . . . and into what? Into something that will reveal itself in a future art.

# XX

## Friday

In Fragata.

I asked them: — What should an ordinary man do when he meets a learned man? And when a scientist surrounds him with his concentrated knowledge — his *besserwisser?* How should he go about defending himself?

They did not know. I explained to them that the most appropriate counterargument would be a blow with foot or fist to the very person of the specialist. And I added that this is called in my terminology "paring a person down to size," or "reducing someone to a person." At any rate, it drives one straight out of theory. . . .

And I asked, could you, O artist, deliver a punch or kick to the professor? An indecent question. Yes, but a crucial one.

You are perhaps of the opinion that art and science ought to run forward together, passing the torch from hand to hand, like in a marathon? Leave this running to the athletes. The future looks unkind and even pitiless. Cooperation between art and science in the name of progress would be refreshing but a poet should know that the professor will strangle him in that tender embrace. Science is a rogue. Let us not believe in the humanity of science, for man does not steer it, it rides him! If you are interested in how the scientific "humanity of man" will look in the future, take a look at a few doctors. Their "goodness," their "humanity"? Yes, but what sort of humanity? A bit strange, isn't it? Yes, good but not really good, human but inhuman . . . what a guardian angel, dry and cold as a devil, an angel-technocrat. The hospital doesn't ruin his breakfast. Infernal coldness and *unbelievable indifference.*

*Unbelievable* — I emphasize this because all of the changes in our nature influenced by science bear the mark of the fantastic, as if they happened outside the normal course of development. We are at the threshold of a bizarre humanity. Reason will perform surgery on us that is unpredictable. It must go forward all the time, its syllogisms never retreat — they do not return to where they began.

It might perhaps appear to someone of rosy disposition that if science tears us away from our humanity, it is only to return us to it . . . that someday the degeneration dealt by reason will lead back to human nature . . . to a nobler, healthier man . . . and that at the end of this painful road we will find each other.

No! We will never recover anything again! We will never return to anything! In giving ourselves up to reason, we must bid farewell to ourselves for all eternity—it never turns back the clock! The man of the future, a creation of science, will be radically different, incomprehensible, unrelated to us. This is why scientific development means death. . . . One dies just as one is . . . for the sake of some stranger. Man, led by science, throws himself away—in his present form—once and for all. Don't you understand? By this I simply mean that if the man of the future has a second head growing out of his butt, they will find this kind of thing neither funny nor repulsive.

And art? What does it have to say about this, the art that is so in love with today's human form, so cuddled up to our person? There is nothing more personal, private, unique, or our own than art—the Brandenburg Concertos, the portrait of Karl V, *Les fleurs du mal,* if they have become common property it is only because the unique and unrepeatable character of the creator was imprinted upon them, like a seal claiming that it belongs to me, this is my work, this is I!

If, therefore, as I have said, nothing plants you as firmly in your personality as a fist or a kick—when, O art, will you stop being docile and begin to punch?

# Monday

I am not a brute. I am not looking for a street fight. Nor am I ranting, scaring, exaggerating in demagogic flight—no, I am not exaggerating—I have always sought strength in moderation.

I am not losing sight of the fact that science (even though it is inhuman) is our hope, that (even though it warps) it also saves us from a thousand warpings, that, even though it is a cruel mother, it is also a caring one. That this curse of ours is also our blessing.

I am talking art into kicking—smack!—but not so that the professor feels kicked but for the artist to feel that he is the one doing the kicking. I am not seeking to crush science, but to restore art to its own life, in full counterdistinction. Let the poodle ingratiating itself on its hind legs finally bite someone! After listening to a "modern" concert, after attending an art exhibit, after reading today's books, I get faint with this weakness, as if I were facing capitulation and mystification at the same time. One simply does not know who is speaking: a poet — or an "educated, cultivated, well-oriented and well-informed man"? The artist whose voice seemed divine not long ago today creates as if he were faking it. And he creates like a pupil. Like a specialist. Like a scholar. Enough of this outrage!

## Tuesday

Whack 'em in the stomach! Sock 'em in the jaw!

## Wednesday

Straight in the kisser . . .

## Thursday

Pow! Give it to 'em with all your might!

## Friday

Get ahold of yourself, rhetoric of hooligans!
But, artists, what else is left?
Yesterday in the bar. With a certain sociologist, or psychoanalyst.
I sat before him, like before a bureaucrat's window — on the other side of which someone is engaged in accounting, adding, cataloging, a whole process inaccessible to me yet defining. I felt as if I were in the hands of a surgeon or despot. I expounded to him on my homegrown convictions — but what were my individual convictions compared with his, which have debrained three hundred thousand minds in a thousand years, which are a mountain made of submissive and functional heads.

*Nec Hercules contra plures!*

But when I kicked him in the shins, he cried out! Oh, how liberating the shriek of a scholar is!

# Saturday

Punch 'im in the snout!

# Sunday

Speaking seriously, though, artists, you must strike. Well, perhaps not with a fist, because you might encounter stout men among them.

But it would be really wonderful if they felt our hostility. Then they would understand that not everyone judges them according to their usefulness and the goods they deliver. I will tell you what happened to my provider. This functionary was very pleased with himself, his function as a deliverer of baked goods was socially positive, everybody respected him; he felt, therefore, that he could allow himself a bow-legged figure, shallow mug, dull look, general mediocrity and drabness, in conjunction with indecision and an ample dose of the fragmentary.

I had to strike hard, therefore, once, twice, and draw blood, so that he would feel that *who you are* is more important than *what you do*.

Science is allowed to chase profit. Art must guard the human form!

# Tuesday

That communism is scientific in theory—that these two worlds, science and communism, are closely related—that, therefore, science has a communizing tendency—why this is as clear as day! Not long ago I was explaining to Professor Teranów (in Quequen) that if the young people at the universities usually like red it is not the work of agitators but the result of their scientific culture. They honor and profess knowledge; communism appears to them in the aureole of scientism.

Authentic kinship with the preeminent spirit of science is revolution's trump card in the game for the conquest of the world. If they reach their goal, it will be on this wave of science, which crashes over everything. Strange, on the other hand, is the behavior of art in the cold war—how could it not notice that its place is on the opposite side of the barricade? This is really quite amazing—art has so much anticommunism in its blood—occasionally I catch myself in the act of thinking that even though I might yield occasionally to my strong sympathies for some of their achievements there, behind the curtain, as an artist I must be an anticommunist, or, in other words, that I could be a communist only by resigning from that portion of my humanity which expresses itself in art.

Of course! If art is "the most personal thing," if it is "the most private possession one can imagine," if art is the personality, the "I" . . . Try, you adherents of combines and collective farms, to tell Chopin that the Sonata in B Minor is not his. Or that he is not the Sonata in B Minor and in the wildest, most ruthless fashion. Oh, I can imagine the dancing clown of artism seducing, loving, going crazy, thirsty for superiority and all the luxuries and not allowing itself to be ruled, apprehended, described—I can imagine this little, incomprehensible, but arrogant imp under the aegis of your regulation, fulfilling cozily and usefully its prescribed functions. How amusing this is: the madness of art, its conflagration, against the background of a stable, reasoned morality and all of this "socialization."

It eluded Marx that art is and will always remain his implacable enemy, whatever the circumstances, independent of the system of production that feeds it. Did he know art too little? And did he, like all those who do not know enough about it, not appreciate its elementary, explosive character? He felt that it is, or can be—civilized, normal, positive. He did not understand that it is an outlet, an explosion. And that from it one finds exactly what Marxism is incapable of fathoming. Communism's romance with art, which continues to this day and has borne such grotesquely miserable fruit, should be credited to the humble loyalty of the holy doctors and acolytes of the red church.

On the other hand—haven't the funds expended on the maintenance of "artistic production" and cultural tenderness to the artist been paid back lavishly? As mismatched as this couple was, it managed to create the appearance of a common front for decades. They said to art: — You must accompany us. In the name of progress! Morality! Humanitarianism! Justice! They lacked no arguments. They inundated art with arguments.

And today's artist, who has lost his instinct, is especially sensitive to arguments. This is what has been happening to him since the time when, intimidated by science, he drowned his temperament in intellect and began to smell the flowers not with his nose but with his soul. What should one demand from the naive but noble-minded scruples of those "working on themselves," perfecting themselves, analyzing, constructing their morality, trembling in the face of their responsibilities, suffering for all of humanity, those researchers, teachers, leaders, judges, inspectors, engineers of souls, finally martyrs, sometimes even saints — but not dancers, singers. . . . Art fried up in laboratories . . . but what should one demand from these fried eggs, what can this omelet possibly resist?

I am not thinking of political warfare. . . . Away with politics, art! Be yourself, pure and simple! Watch your nature, nothing more.

# Thursday

—How am I supposed to believe you when you make art a champion of the personality? You say that this "is the most personal expression of man," that art is "I"? Yet how many times have you wailed that man can never express himself fully? Your own words are: "to be a man means never to be oneself"—for the form in which we manifest ourselves is formed between us and other people, it is imposed on us. . . . You even claimed that we are "created" by others, from the outside. . . . And art? And the artist? How can you say that "Chopin is the Sonata in B Minor" if you have concluded that the work creates itself to a great degree with its own logic and is limited by its own exigencies? How can you accuse scientists of being warped by science, when, according to you, art warps its people in the very same way, creating itself beyond the artist, imposing a form on him? . . .

—Allow me. I do not deny that art is "extrahuman" or, more accurately, "interhuman." But an artist is different from the scientist in that he wants to be himself. . . . And haven't I already written in this diary that this "I want to be me" is the whole secret of personality, this will, this desire, defines our attitude toward deformation and results in the fact that deformation begins to hurt. And even if external forces crush me like a wax figurine, I will remain myself as long as I agonize over it, protest against it. Our authentic form is contained in the protest against deformation.

—And you claim that this protest is alien to scholars?

—Yes of course! They—objective—always ready to dissolve in their matter-of-fact truth . . . no, they are not called to experience disharmony between man and form! If they concern themselves with this at all, they do it scientifically—that is, without suffering—that is, without experience. . . .

—You think, therefore, that this pain, this experience, can be felt only by the artist?

—Oh, no! This is the daily torment of every man; but perhaps it is more concentrated in those who devote themselves with greater passion to expressing themselves. . . .

\*    \*    \*

And notice that the invasion of science promises art the most beautiful career.

We will one day recognize art as our sole friend and champion; it will even become our only identification card.

Yes! Just think! Upon waking one morning you may notice that, as a consequence of biophysiological methods applied to you, another head has grown out of your rear during the night. Terrified, you will become disoriented and no longer know which of these heads is your real one— what will remain except to cry out in terror, rebellion, protest, despair . . . that you protest!

This cry will then find its poet . . . and will declare that you are still the same being you were yesterday.

As for me, I expect the future scientific world to confirm what *Ferdydurke* proclaims about a distance to form and about not identifying with it. Tomorrow's art, the art of deformed people, will rise under this sign. . . .

They will consciously create their form (their physical form, too). But they will not identify with it.

## Saturday

I wouldn't give three cents that Scriabin got to the (altered) quartet chord in Prometheus independently of Liszt. And then—how should one trace the subsequent path of this chord in Debussy, Mahler, Dukas, and Richard Strauss?

And as for the quartet-sextet chord, does the fifth, I ask, being its base, really "play" emotionally—is this not convention upheld by the cadences of classic concerts (perhaps with a more codal theme)?

Hm, hmmm . . .

## Sunday

The unexpected visit of Siegrist, who is currently staying in New York and has spent the past two years at Yale and Cambridge. He came with J. C. Gomez. He seemed somewhat lukewarm to me, the flame that had warmed him in La Troya's time has gone out in this splendid man. As is his custom, he began drawing figures on paper that I hospitably slipped to him.

Both claim (but this seems to be mainly Siegrist's opinion) that the recent slowing down of the tempo in physics must be attributed not so much to the exhaustion of philosophical possibilities in the area of chief, inseminating contradictions of the type continuity-noncontinuity, macro-micro cosmos, wave and corpuscular interpretation, gravitational and electromagnetic fields, etc., as to the fact that physics has fallen prey to a system of interpretation shaped in the intellectual exchanges of scholars. They are thinking of the polemics between Bohr-Einstein, Heisenberg-Bohr, all the opinions exchanged about the Compton effect, the coexistence of such minds as Broglie, Planck, Schrödinger, that entire "dialogue," which, in their opinion, delineated the issues and their centers imperceptibly, gradually, but prematurely and arbitrarily, creating the necessity of moving along a certain line. This happened of itself, as a result of their desire for precision.—These are the sad consequences of too much talk—noticed Gomez.—They said a little too much. . . .

When I allowed myself to draw attention to the rare scrupulosity of the majority of these scholars in controlling their system of interpretation and delineating its role and cognitive limits, when I gave Einstein as an example, I noticed that Siegrist was writing something down on paper. He was writing out the word "MACH" in capital letters.

And he added:
—Stocks are dropping.

## Monday

I ate a tasty fish.

## Monday

The riddle of "light" in Mozart. Gide is quite right when he says that the drama in Mozart's music, illuminated by intelligence, spirit, stops being dramatic. The kind of splendor found in the first allegro of the *Jupiter* Symphony is the crowning glory of this internal process. Radiance conquers and reigns supreme. But in him, as in Leonardo da Vinci, I see an element of perversity, a kind of illegal retreating from life—Mozart's and Leonardo's smile (especially in his sketches) have this same characteristic, it is as if they wanted a forbidden amusement, as if they wanted to play and delight even in that which is forbidden, even in that which gives pain . . . a delicate but roguish game, sly, an archintelligent sensuality . . . but even the very juxtaposition "intelligent sensuality" is sinful. . . . Is the ascending and descending scale in *Don Giovanni* not a strange joke which pokes fun at hell? The high registers of Mozart sometimes assail me like something forbidden, like sin.

The reverse of Mozart would be Chopin—for here the affirmation of weakness, delicacy, executed with rare determination and stubbornness, results in strength and the capacity to look at life without flinching. He "insists so much on what is his," he wants to be who he is so absolutely that this makes him really exist—makes him unrelenting and, as a phenomenon, invincible. Thus, in self-confirmation, Chopin's despairing, lost, morbid romanticism, subjected to the forces of the world like a reed to wind, transforms itself into a severe classicism, into discipline, into mastery of matter, into the will to rule. How moving and sublime his heroism is when seen this way, and how declamatory, rhetorical, and paltry when one looks at it from a "patriotic" perspective. "I will cling most strongly to what is weakest in me"—his work seems to shout.

## Wednesday

Veal cutlet. Pineapple. Drab day.
*Come clean, "Gombrowicz!" There are at least nine of you and you have written a masterpiece unawares. . . .*\* I would like someone to translate this sentence for me, I feel a summons in it, but what could it be? . . . Who is calling me? And why don't I know English? Today I die unknown. Who is calling me?

## Friday

An exchange of letters with Adam Czerniawski and indirectly with Czaykowski, on the occasion of the appearance of the English edition of *Ferdydurke,* as well as the discussion about *Wiadomości* and *Kultura* in *Kontynenty,* leads me to wonder whether I should write in greater

---

\*Italicized phrase in English in original.

detail about this group of young émigré writers, so vehement in their Polish start on London soil. This would not cost me much and might come in handy to them. . . .

Scarcely do I dream this idea when I back out of it convulsively. I am flushed out by my revulsion to the collective character of literature. Oh dear, groups! Unions! Debuts! "Writers," "young writers," "old writers," "the young generation," "new values!" . . . It is enough for me to notice someone in literature and begin reading him for him to stop being a "writer" and to become Pasek, Chesterton, *tout court*. I see nothing in art except names.

If a spark of spiritual alliance did flare up between one of these young people and me, that someone would become . . . merely himself . . . not a literatus or a young person or a beginning writer in exile. But sparks do not fly so easily. It is easier to establish contact with young people in Poland, not here with these already one-quarter Englishmen, half-choked by the muzzle of their acquired English culture. Their Englishness stifles, inhibits, their Polishness. Their Polishness does not allow their Englishness to be grafted onto them. Their task is uncommonly difficult, almost breakneck: to join the two spheres in such a way as to generate a little electricity and loosen their tongues. (It would come easier to them if they wrote in English, like Conrad, like Pietrkiewicz, then their deepest Polish exoticism would intoxicate them).

Peculiar this shrub rising in our émigré garden—and on such inhospitable soil. If I were a gardener I would water it conscientiously day and night because oddities sometimes become valuable. Except that I am not a gardener.

# Friday

What did Śmieja say about me in the discussion in defense of my diary? "His brutality, egocentrism, and arrogance toward writers of lesser stature may be distressing. . . ."

But no! He misinterprets me! With me there are no "writers of lesser stature." This again is a collective viewpoint. It is true that I sometimes demolish, with gusto, in jest, by attacking, writers, but only those who prance around in their epaulets. I have never really taken part in a single duel while clad in my stripes and epaulets; I have never written a single word dressed in anything but my birthday suit.

# Saturday

Now people are accusing me of mystification. Not long ago a woman charged up to me in the Polish Center: — You mystify! It is never clear whether you are being serious, paradoxical, or just bluffing.

—A nitwit—I answered—fears nothing more than being turned into one. This fear never leaves him: they are putting me on! But listen, nitwit, what good will it do you to know whether I am "sincere" or "insincere"? What does this have to do with whether or not my thoughts are right? I can utter a soaring truth "insincerely" and say the stupidest thing "sincerely." Learn to judge the thought independently of who says it or how.

Sure, mystification is advisable for a writer. Let him muddle the waters around himself a bit so that no one knows who he is—a clown perhaps? Scoffer? Wise man? Cheat? Discoverer? Blusterer? Guide? Or perhaps he is all of these at once? Enough of this blissful sleep in the womb of mutual trust. Be vigilant, spirit!

Be prepared!

And so long, nitwits!

# XXI

## Wednesday

An enticing little morning, an idling little springtime, dust motes dancing in the streaks and streams of sunlight—oooh, ahhhh, I am happy to pull on my trousers with the thought that I am going for a walk, a little walk, I'll relax, I walk to the door—the bell, Irmgard goes to open the door and in a minute in walks Simon.

So I say: —*Hola,* what are you doing here at this early hour? Have a seat, *companiero!* To which he replies: —How are you?—and he sits down—sits down—sits down somewhat too easily perhaps, too quickly, or perhaps because he sits down in the nearest chair—enough that he immediately alienates me with his terrifying absence.

I say something again—he to me—but this conversation is and is not—as for him, it looks as if "he had forgotten to take himself along." It was as if . . . yes, as if he were not there. But what do I know, after all. . . . I smile and keep talking when suddenly his upper lip quivers, in a bad way, in a bad, bad way.

He looks.

Explains.

A vat.

A vat full of boiling water.

His daughter.

A vat filled with boiling water spills on his daught . . .

So, I see . . . and "it has been going on for hours in the hospital and is still not over" and he "doesn't know what to do with himself" and he "is of absolutely no use," so he came. And he apologizes for intruding at such an early hour. —No problem! Of course, certainly . . . But I go silent, he goes silent and we sit, if I can express it this way, nose to nose. Face to face. Alone. Hand to hand. Foot to foot. Knee to knee. Face to face. Until this stupid identity begins to irritate me in the room and I think, how is it that he repeats me, that I repeat him, face to face—all of a sudden the scalding of the child scalds me until I hiss— and then I see that even though we are so similar, there is no use sitting here and it is better simply not to sit at all but to leave, leave, leave,

exit, any kind of exit; distance, removal, become urgent, burning! . . .
And I say: —Shall we take a walk? He gets up immediately and we
leave; first I and he behind me with that daughter of his.

Zephyr.

We go out and the fact that we go out is just right. So we go. I
immediately turn right, although I could go left—streets, houses,
sidewalks, movement, hubub, ringing, honking, look—someone is hop-
ping into a tram, someone is bending over, someone is biting into a
chocolate bar, someone is buying something from a vendor—we feel
better immediately at the sight of this hive with hands, feet, ears, like
us, but alien, as if it were innocent. . . . And what relief! . . . because
even though that evil thing is lodged in us, there on the street corner
people call out to one another! They greet each other from afar!

I choose the most crowded streets to lose myself in the throng and
disappear—and I gamble that this is a race with time, that his daughter
cannot keep dying endlessly, it has to end somehow, and then Simon
will leave me alone. I haven't the least idea what is going on in him, a
conflagration or frost—he walks next to me. Sun. I see a fruit vendor
on the corner, he is weighing apples and somehow I like it that he
knows nothing and is weighing a kilo of apples, talking to a customer
. . . his ignorance appeals to me so much that I think that I, too, will
buy some apples and will at least relax for a moment with this man,
rest, somewhere at his place, far away. . . . —A kilo?—said the fruit
vendor.—Right away. Everyone is buying them because they are as
sweet as pears.

Suddenly I blurt out: —A terrible thing has happened to this man,
he has a four-year-old daughter and she is dying.

I bite my tongue . . . why?! It is out! Never mind. He weighs the
apples. I am humbled in this silence and empty, like an eraser rubbing
away everything. How awful—says the fruit vendor—such a misfortune!

When I hear this, it grows in me, unwinds, jumps and howls all in
one second, bursting all boundaries . . . I shout:

—Take these apples away! Take them!

Lightening bolt. I move forward, blindly, like a man possessed!
Behind me Simon with his little daughter, like a man possessed! And
again we are alone, he and I, I and he, but this time the secret is out,
the war declared, trumpets and drums, the march is beginning!

And at exactly this moment, note, a dog barks (I do not see him,
I merely hear his barking).

Trams! Buses! Swarm of passersby! The street is unrolling itself
like a carpet, I walk on, after me him, and after him, his daughter! We
walk in my outburst, in my outburst to the fruit vendor, which revealed,

betrayed, and announced . . . and it no longer helps us to be immersing ourselves in the throng, my cry follows us and behind it that horror . . . and with it something like an animal, why has an animal joined in? An animal? I am thinking of the dog's barking. Well, a dog not a tiger . . . at any rate this barking joins my outburst, my outburst, I remember it now, it rings out together with the barking of the dog and as a result my outburst changes a little into some kind of animal, well, it is enough that the animal is, that it has already joined in, dog or no dog. An animal. We walk. He walks. I walk. Out of a cornucopia come houses, windows, streets, street corners, signs, displays, and the human swarm, in which we are immersing ourselves more and more quickly, in order to lose ourselves . . . what will I do? Where are we going? What should we do? . . . but we go down Florida Street, where the crowds are greatest, and we tear through, push, rub shoulders. Until we stop because a passing omnibus blocks our way and an elderly gentleman asks Simon, very politely:

—Pardon me . . . Which way to Corrientes?

Simon looks at him and does not answer.

Then a little taken aback, the man turns to me with his question. And I look at him—and don't answer. NO. I agree, it is nothing too unusual, he probably thinks he has come upon foreigners who do not know the language . . . nevertheless, you must understand, this is a NO and a shove into nothingness . . . as if a knife were cutting it away. This is a REFUSAL, a dark, black, remote refusal in the bright sun. And we move ahead, like madmen, and then the shriek of a parrot reaches us, who knows from where, maybe from a passing taxi, this shriek joins to my earlier outburst and renews the earlier barking of the dog . . . and the Animal again makes itself heard and suddenly tears into our lack of an answer! Nothing. I still do not know what is in him, in Simon, although I am the same as he, and alone with him! Nor does he know about me. But bound by our outburst and by our lack of an answer, isolated and marked like criminals, we quicken our pace to get lost in the crowd, when the end loomed before me—the end, I say, which makes me feel queasy. . . .

Namely, Florida is ending. Before us the square—the Plaza San Martin—as if on a platter.

Return to Florida? But no . . . because we walk in a hurry, as if we were going somewhere and this would reveal that our movement is a lie!

Enter the square? Except that there are almost no people there. What are we to do in that square—the two of us, alone!

Too late for second thoughts. We are walking through the very center of the square—it is cool, quiet, fresh, and the wind blows over us from afar. The sudden distance practically knocks our feet out from under us. The square is sublime, overlooking the port and river, it hovers like a balcony, and there, in the distance, in the black and blue combinations of water, fog, and white sky, floats the cringing or straight smoke from ships immobile on the river, and this immobility of ships on the immobile river together with the stone skeleton of the port, sharp with the spines of buildings—from here, from the mountain—smells of stagnation and backwardness. We slow our pace. Stillness. Emptiness. Peace. Our gallop has exhausted itself, broken down in the immobility—and we stop. Suddenly our walk has completely exhausted itself.

What?

Face-to-face, but I have no idea what he is doing with himself in there—perhaps something, perhaps nothing—I have no idea. We stand, he a little to the side, and we stand, and there, in the distance, some sort of immobile gloom is forming and growing between the glassy water and the watery heaven of steam, fog, clouds of smoke, in the stillness of ships imperceptibly moving, in the lifeless outline of port fortifications. Silence, silence, when a piece of paper rustles at our feet, moved by the wind. I look at my companion out of the corner of my eye—he is holding the paper down with the tip of his shoe and his eyes are riveted to the ground. The paper rustles again. I glue my eyes to the paper, he glues his eyes to the paper.

Again the paper rustles. Then he looks at me with furrowed brow, with a look so concentrated and penetrating that it seems he is preparing to say something most urgent, important, and conclusive, in the greatest haste . . . but he says nothing, the paper rustles, he holds the paper down with his foot and looks at me, and there far away it goes on, grows and floats. . . . I think, what will happen if the paper rustles again?

One-on-one. I prefer not to look at him and in not looking at him, I begin to wonder if I am in danger . . . will he . . . me? . . .

It is important for me to substantiate this thought, it is not at all fantastic, I would not want to be accused of lacking common sense. . . . Let us agree: a man subject to such pressure could explode, is it not true that he could explode? But the very explosion worries me less—the nature of the explosion, more. For, let us understand that I do not know what is going on inside him, and more may be going on . . . well, much more may be going on than custom anticipates and one could even ask if this tormented creature is still residing with both feet in our, human, world . . . and in general this story is risky and elusive beyond expression, yes, risky . . . but perhaps I would not be so disturbed if not for the paper, if not for the paper flapping under his foot, like something living, like an animal, you see, completely like a shout turned into an animal, the result being that the animal joins us again, but this time, how shall I say it, low, at the very bottom, because it is no longer from a dog, a parrot, but from a piece of paper, a lifeless thing, and there, low, the Animal with the child answers, the child-animal. . . . And I wrack my brains, wrack my brains, why is the child turning into an animal, but there is no helping it, one has to bear it—except, that I am relating to "man" with suspicion, to a man who stands in a void, next to me, a man for whom a dying child has become an animal and who carries this within himself. . . . I do not believe in the devil. Simon is a good person by nature, he wouldn't harm a fly. Except that . . . this time . . . There is no grace to be found anywhere. Not a penny's worth.

What then might he be capable of . . . if the paper rustles again? (This is all connected to the paper.) But the breeze has died down. I prefer not to look at him too much. The worst thing is that this kind of animal is an unknown to me, even up close, but the fact that it comes from the child, and is linked to a dog and a parrot and paper, does not inspire confidence. There on the outskirts smoke and streaks of fog. A child? An animal? What kind of animal? I should not, in any case, have taken a walk with him, this is really unprovidential and now I have to duck out, detach myself—before it becomes too late—and what are we doing here like this anyway, on this elevated square, alone, one-on-one, without anyone except for us. . . . I have to detach myself. But how should I detach myself? Quickly, quickly, because at any moment the paper might rustle . . . it is really silly that even though he is so similar to me, nose for nose, ear for ear, foot for foot, I haven't the least idea as to what he might do!

I calculate that if I leave suddenly, at least a moment will pass before he can move—during which I can reach the stairs and quickly run down the stairs alone. Except . . . how am I to leave so abruptly? . . . I go silent inside—and then under the influence of my silence that silence returns to me, the silence with which we received the gentleman who asked me about Corrientes; that silence of ours returns together with the deafness and blindness, and in this deafness and blindness, I break with him, I suddenly leave!

I am already on the stairs. I am running down. This escape is like a challenge! Because I am fleeing from something like an evil spirit! And he remains behind like an evil spirit! Suddenly a diabolical evil finds itself between us. I was hoping to come upon a station and lose myself in it—I run, I run inside, I dive into a crowd and finally I stand in line for the cashier, any kind of cashier, just to stand. —Where to?—asks the clerk at the window. —To Tigre—I say the first station that comes to mind, because it's all the same, the important thing is to get on a train, to get away. But I hear behind me: —To Tigre—And it is his voice.

This frightened me and I am not joking!

Actually there is nothing shocking about all this—the two of us step out for a walk, then the two of us buy a ticket for a suburban train . . . well, yes, except that I am running away . . . and he, in order to catch me, has to run after me and this running after me is pursuit. . . . At any rate, he attaches himself to me again. And this time I am no longer able to escape, the possibility of escape has already been exhausted. So we take our tickets and together, shoulder to shoulder, await our train in a great hall of glass and iron; we stand over a line of sleek tracks, where slowly the passengers gather—we wait for the train.

Which is not arriving. We wait. He says nothing. I don't know what is in him, what he is like now, where he is going, I know nothing—zero—about this face staring at the tracks—and, at the same time, in proportion to the arrival of people, our intimacy grows, our acquaintance forces us to stand next to one another, it creates a pair of us. Who is this creature standing next to me and what sort of animal has his child—which he has with him—become? My common sense, as healthy as it is, does not leave me for an instant in these obsessions of fear and about ten times I become furious at my fantasies and chimeras—but—but—once the facade of the ordinary shatters, the place we occupy in the cosmos becomes what it is in essence—something abysmally inconceivable and therefore containing the possibility of everything. After all, I would not even concern myself with this too much—if not for a certain drastic detail, if not for a certain reptile, concealing itself in the dark womb of being—if not for the Pain—yes, if the riddle did not cause pain!

Pain! Only this is important—the cruel eyes of Pain in this black well—pain hurts!—This merciless finger transforms everything it touches into reality—even fantasy becomes truth in contact with this real thing, pain. I wouldn't make anything of this if it didn't hurt; but I have already been informed about the pain of the child in the hospital, the terrible pain that hurts here, right next to me, in this man—and this horror is not a delusion, because it hurts!—and I am close, close . . . and maybe it is beginning to look at me . . . that animal of a burned child . . . I do what I can to conceal it from myself, or, too, myself from it, but the undeveloped thought about the child turned into an animal, a bad thought . . . Animal? What kind of animal? The barking of a dog, a parrot, rustling paper, ah, I weave my deaf, dumb, blind arabesques from anything at hand and they would be so harmless if it didn't hurt, it hurts, O the pain, the pain, it hurts!—except for the pain of a child confirming my fancies!

Meanwhile more people arrive, Sunday travelers with bags and in spite of everything their normal demeanor somehow soothes our unusualness—until a train rolls into the vastness of the iron-glass hall, pigeons in the vault—and together with others we board, he and I— and we are confined to an overflowing train car. Whistles. The train moves. In a moment it emerges into the sun, devouring the tracks that run out of the sides of the road with a rhythmic rocking. We ride the relaxing, fleeing space and I am already thinking about what I am supposed to do in this Tigre for which I am headed, when—Tigre? Tigre! Why Tigre?!

Why to Tigre, for what, to do what? . . . And why not to some other station? In the crush I can see practically nothing through the gaps created by chins, spines, collars, and necks, but I feel hijacked to Tigre . . . why to Tigre? . . . and I know that in the train there is not one person who is going the way I am going there with him, without reason, so completely blindly (and deafly) to Tigre . . . and with the same kind of baggage. I look, truly amazed, at their faces, so similar, it is possible that they may even look like us—and this fact becomes a springboard for a mad leap, that we are going to Tigre without reason, borne away by the train. Tigre? What is waiting for us in Tigre? The train stops, then moves. I feel something . . . nearby . . . some sort of machination, some sort of indistinct effort to overpower . . . me . . . thirst for conquest . . . of me.

This is indistinct. Murky, dark, quiet. He stands next to me, squeezed. This is not a distinct, possessive movement—nothing of the kind. I catch him in rather tiny almost preliminary doings—the movement of a hand, perhaps the shifting of weight from foot to foot, the shy, crowded movement of an elbow—perhaps this is natural in the discomfort, but I seem to see something, that it is not he who is moving, but something within him . . . something I fear desperately, a child turned into an animal, that animal of his, which is endowed with its own movement like the rustling paper and which possesses him. Again I feel in him the movement, something like the movement of a fetus in a mother's womb, and I feel the presence of an evil with fangs, claws, furiously evil. I cringe again, for the cry of that child, in the hospital, really is—so my delirium has real fangs!

Then I realize: Tigre—tiger! Which has not occurred to me until now. So we speed on to Tigre . . . and I would laugh to tears over this, if not for the child in the hospital making it come true!

Simon moves again!—or it moves in him—and I run to get away— but in the crush all I can do is move away from him spasmodically and thus, moving my entire body, I crawl onto another—soft—body. An enormous, warm obesity whose face I do not see, into whom, out of horror, I am falling, into a sweaty, awkward, vulvar softness, into a probably quiet, humble, decent obesity, hospitable if suffocating. Oh, what a cozy little corner this is! . . . in which I slowly domesticate myself, make myself at home . . . in the warmth of his shirt plays today's and yesterday's sweat, mingled with the scent of vanilla, in his pocket he has a notepad, on his lining a label with the name of the tailor SMART, the shirt is patched. It is quiet here and good, a hundred miles from that . . . burning . . . problem, that other thing is completely inconceivable, it is something completely different, a different country, respite and calm . . . at the other end of the world. Finally! I am resting. I am elated. And suddenly a terrible blow is dealt beneath me from beneath.

I say "beneath me from beneath" because this is neither simply "beneath me" nor simply "from beneath," just as if it were divided and doubled—do you understand?—and this was not really a blow, rather a grabbing; and this grabbing was not "executed," but was becoming like a threat on my periphery . . . and suddenly I understand that my moment of laxity has been taken advantage of in order practically to bite! I freeze. My head is stuck between his chest and jacket. I cannot pray. I cannot move. I cannot shout. No, I cannot shout, but a god-awful shout breaks out from all over and embraces everything, tumbles head-long into the heartrending Animal to the very bottom. And, with my head hidden, immobile, I wait for it to jump.

But then . . .

Something . . . something . . . something! What? Hm . . . Suddenly . . . something like a tickling on the back of the neck. Can't be. Perhaps someone has pulled out a handkerchief and is touching the back of my neck? No. Someone is tickling me. Deliberately, his fingers on the back of my neck. . . .

I wonder. What could this be? Who?

The fat man? Why? I take all the possible solutions into consideration: madman, homo, joker.

Simon? Has he gone mad? Even if he has gone crazy, he cannot reach my neck from where he is.

One of the people standing next to me? Maybe an acquaintance is letting me know he is here? Highly unlikely with my head stuck in the Fat Guy.

Meanwhile someone's fingers are dancing lightly down the back of my neck.

I wonder—who? What? I puzzle and puzzle.

I wrack and wrack my brains, what sort of joke is this—but I have no illusions for I know that the lack of connection between the tickling and the Animal is precisely the guarantee of their diabolical *affiliations,* their plotting, their pact—and I wait for the Tickling to get chummy with It, with the Animal, before it sinks, like a knife, into the unknown, inconceivable, still unuttered scream.